W. A Wash, I. G. W Steedman

Camp, Field And Prison Life

Containing Sketches of Service in the South; etc.

W. A Wash, I. G. W Steedman

Camp, Field And Prison Life
Containing Sketches of Service in the South; etc.

ISBN/EAN: 9783744754149

Printed in Europe, USA, Canada, Australia, Japan

Cover: Foto ©ninafisch / pixelio.de

More available books at **www.hansebooks.com**

CAMP,

FIELD AND PRISON LIFE;

CONTAINING

SKETCHES OF SERVICE IN THE SOUTH, AND THE
EXPERIENCE, INCIDENTS AND OBSERVATIONS
CONNECTED WITH ALMOST TWO YEARS'
IMPRISONMENT at JOHNSON'S ISLAND,
OHIO, WHERE 3,000 CONFEDERATE
OFFICERS WERE CONFINED.

BY

W. A. WASH, Capt., C. S. A.

WITH AN

INTRODUCTION BY GEN. L. M. LEWIS,

AND A

MEDICAL HISTORY OF JOHNSON'S ISLAND

BY COL. I. G. W. STEEDMAN, M. D.

SAINT LOUIS:
SOUTHWESTERN BOOK AND PUBLISHING CO.,
510 AND 512 WASHINGTON AVENUE.
1870.

Entered according to Act of Congress, in the year 1870, by

W. A. WASH,

in the Clerk's Office of the District Court of the United States for the District of Missouri.

PREFACE.

Perhaps there are those who will conclude that the contents of this book are intended as an offset to the alleged inhumanity to Federal soldiers in Southern prisons. Not so; it deals as little as possible with the cruelties of war. Were I so disposed, I might now go back and drag up a thousand northern prison horrors to place beside the most revolting pen pictures of Andersonville; but who would profit or be made happier thereby? Indeed, would it not be calculated rather to open afresh wounds now partially healed, and to revive unpleasant memories that we would fain obliterate.

No doubt some will be deceived as to the anticipated contents of the book, for they will expect to see their own prison exploits jotted down, especially if they were somewhat notorious. Such will please remember that it would be utterly impossible to give more than a tithe of what actually occured, in a single volume like this. Besides, my notes of prison life were not originally taken with a view to publication. I expected some abler pen than mine would portray to the world our life during captivity, but as no other has seen fit to write our prison history, I have thought that my meagre sketches might be acceptable to my comrades and the friends who so earnestly sympathized with us while shut up on that little island.

Had I intended to publish my manuscript, I would have taken much fuller notes and preserved many items and facts which would have added greatly to the interest of the book. But the opportunity is now lost forever, since, in the great flow of events then daily transpiring, it was impossible to keep them all in the mind. What I have written will serve as an outline, to be filled up by each particular individual according to his experience.

The introductory of Gen. Lewis will be recognized and eagerly perused by many hundreds who were on Johnson's Island, for the tone and style are characteristic, and perhaps no one in prison was better known. The hearts of some will swell with continued gratitude as they think again of him who ministered to their spiritual welfare, and persuaded them to forsake their evil ways; and many a masonic brother will go back in memory and bless him for his zealous labors in their behalf, when sick and destitute in an enemy's prison.

A careful reading of what he has written will greatly assist the reader in correctly appreciating the book. Though I am quite sure that some Southerners will condemn the spirit of the work as being too nearly loyal, I hope it will meet the approbation of the mass, and I feel that it will be calculated, in many cases, to form bonds of friendship where hearts are now callous. If so, I have added a mite to the welfare and happiness of mankind, and am satisfied. AUTHOR.

St. Louis, March, 1870.

INTRODUCTION.

Having read the manuscript of this volume, and having been an eye-witness of the scenes which the author relates, I take great pleasure in commending it to the public generally, but particularly to those who were unfortunate participants in the horrors of the long imprisonment at Johnson's Island.

Time can never erase from the memory of any one of the latter class the prominent scenes of prison life in which he may have participated; yet, to many, the minor details, the humorous, the painful, the cruel, the oppressive experiences must have been lost in the immemorial past through the friction of every day life if the diligent hand of Capt. Wash had not embalmed them as they transpired.

To those who witnessed what is here related this volume will prove a source of great satisfaction and amusement. The materials from which this book has been collated were jotted down just as the scenes transpired, for the daily journal of the author recalls almost the entire period from June, 1863, to the close of the war.

To an outsider, who never had the misfortune to be locked up for safe keeping in modern bastiles, or to be guarded, not by angels, but by relentless brutes, who, afraid of the battle field, volunteered to guard prisoners, because all the shooting could be on one side, a peep inside is furnished and a slight glimpse of what we experienced. To us, the former prisoners, the old, gloomy past will be re-enacted, and faces, long since grown dim on the canvass of memory, will be retouched into their former freshness. We will stand again within those plank walls, see familiar forms, hear the laugh of the merry and the complaint of the sad-hearted—in fact, live over again the strangely mingled life of which it is a sketch. Who can not even yet recall the varied emotions experienced by the incarcerated patriot as he listened to the tale of defeat, greedily related and largely embellished? Who can fail to remember how keen the anguish realized as we heard of the want, suffering and ruin of the land we loved better than life?

Who can know, save those who were there, how the heart sunk when grim despair, like the head of Medusa, chilled the soul into stone at the contemplation of our home and loved ones given to merciless aliens and strangers, and we unable to raise an arm to save those precious treasures?

Prison life as seen from the author's stand-point and from mine were vastly different. His was exceptional, mine was the common lot of a vast majority of the three thousand Confederate officers on Johnson's Island.

He was more fortunate than many in being so close to family and dear friends who had influence with those in authority. To him came many a box laden with turkeys, chickens, hams and sweetmeats, obtained through an arrangement with the man Scovill, who is mentioned in these pages as prison provost. But to thousands, who were total strangers in an enemy's country, far removed from the sunny land of their birth, who were unskilled in wire-working, and dependent solely on the rations issued by their keepers, there was but little fun and less poetry in those sad years. The class to which the author belonged could hear almost daily from home and friends, thus affording relief from the fears which long months of silence begat in the minds of many who were less fortunate. There were hundreds of our miserable associates, who, captured in midsummer, with the light and insufficient clothing furnished by a hard pressed and closely blockaded government, suffered untold misery amidst the rigors of the winter of '63 and '64.

No one of all the vast number confined there at that time can have forgotten the intense cold of that inclement island, located in the open plane of Lake Erie and bordering on the shores of Canada. Insufficient clothing, shelter, food and medicine sent scores of victims to the grave. As success crowned the armies of the North their severity toward the prisoners increased, and, as the prospect lessened, to many, of getting a chance at rebels on the open and honestly contested field of battle, an itching desire grew to kill the unarmed and defenseless.

The avaricious officer who issued rations shared with

the contractor and grew rich upon the bread and beef denied to starving rebels.

For a short time we were guarded by soldiers who had earned the name of veterans—the buck-tails of Pennsylvania and others—who, under the gallant leadership of such men as Long, Sedgwick, Hancock, Meade and others, grappled, in dreadful carnage, with the grand old army of Northern Virginia, led by such men as Lee, Jackson, Johnston, Longstreet, Hill, Early, &c., names forever immortal in the memory of man. These knew how to treat the brave, whose misfortune it was to be prisoners. Those gallant and chivalrous men did their duty as guards, but showed to us, and that too in broad contrast to the Hoffman Battalion, how the brave can be generous. On both sides, doubtless, the *stay at homes* and the *shirks*, who were prison guards, knew how to be cruel to a degree that curses them forever. It is to be hoped that their names are not remembered, so that no record shall stand in time against them.

This book will furnish valuable material to the future historian, who will pen the more complete accounts of those "stirring times." It will be but the beginning of a series which will show up the hitherto silent side of "Prison Life during the War."

If we would have a just verdict from the grand juries of coming generations, to whom will be submitted the conduct of both parties to the late war, it is necessary that, not only a cursory view of Johnson's Island prison be had, but that a minute detail of it, as also of those miserable pens, Alton Penitentiary, Camp Douglas,

Camp Chase, Rock Island and Elmira, be placed by the side of the exaggerations about Libby, Belle Isle, Tyler and Andersonville.

The resources of each section must be fully canvassed and a dispassionate portrayal be given of the spirit that characterized both governments in their dealings with the unarmed and defenseless. If the North has nothing to lose by such an investigation, certainly the South has everything to gain.

The style of the author of this volume is purposely homely and peculiar, intended fully to revive the fading memories of which it is a description. If fastidious taste shall be disposed to term it "vulgar" and out of place, let it be known that the writer intended not only to recount the transactions and experiences of army and prison life, but to carry the reader back to the very times themselves by using the peculiar *patois*, if I may so call it, of the soldier.

Captain Wash has rendered, to his old associates at least, a service which must be highly appreciated by them. It will serve not only to give pleasure and instruction, but to recall to the minds of many readers much which they had otherwise finally forgotten, thus securing, if each will take pains to note down his reminiscences, a full and complete account of our imprisonment.

I most heartily commend this book to those who have a personal interest in its narrations. Many a one will delight to con its pages, from the relative connection they sustained to the sufferers.

To some it will bring many a merry laugh, to others the tears of yet unconsoled sorrow for the dear dead ones who still sleep on that inhospitable coast.

May God bless the survivors and grant to the bereaved that consolation which comes alone from the God of all comfort. L. M. LEWIS.

Arcadia, Mo., March, 1870.

CONTENTS.

CHAPTER I.

At Vicksburg, in April, 1863—March to the Front; Clothing and Papers Lost: Thrilling Incidents; Country, Climate, Seasons and People of Mississippi; Out among the Farmers; Army Movements Brisk; Conflict with Iron-clads; Almost an Execution; Enemy's Intentions Evident; Fiddle & Fun; More Iron-clads; May Campaign Opens; Bowen at Port Hudson; Outpost Duty; Musquitos *versus* Rebels; Steal a March on the Boys; Gunboats *versus* Water Batteries; Dinner with a Contraband; Stonewall Jackson Dead, &c.

CHAPTER II.

Reflections; Pleasant Jaunt; Commissary Supplies; Preparing to Evacuate; Big Black Bridge; Edward's Depot; Battle of Baker's Creek; All important Document too Late; Fight at Big Black; Surrender; Dinner with a Federal Officer; Why Defeated; Blue Coats and Gray Commingle; Vandalism; A Fancy Shoulder Strapper and I; Edward's Depot again; Patent Cooking; Confiscation; Big Black once more; Noble Women; "Chickasaw" Battle Field; Yazoo Landing; Young's Point, La.; The Contrabands; Northward Bound; Scenery on the Mississippi; Napoleon, Ark.; Elliott's Marine Brigade; Dead Prisoner Consigned to the Waves, &c.

CHAPTER III.

Memphis; Gov. and Adj't. Gen. of Iowa; Pleasant Meeting; Fort Pillow; Island No. 10; Monotonous Scenery; All about Cairo; Gen. Buford, U. S. A.; Passenger Cars for Rebel Officers; A Gymnastic Feat Dixieward; Natives flock in to see Johnny Rebs; The Ladies and Copperheads; Terre Haute; Muss with a Dirty Dutchman: Indianapolis Then and Now; Our Reception; Soldier's Home; Visitors and Incidents; Railroad Metropolis; Passage through Ohio; Sandusky City; Our Home in the Distance; Strange Feelings.

CHAPTER IV.

Over the Bay; Sail Crafts; Head Quarters; Funds or no Funds; The Place and the Garrison; Sandusky; Exterior Survey; In Prison; Thoughts; First Thing Done; Who We Found There; Rebels shot and Others under Sentence; Vallandigham; First Sunday in Prison; Preaching; Dress Parade; What Next? My Watch in Pawn; Sutler; Washing Day; Ring Making; Prisoners Arrive; Still They Come; Touching Incident; Lt. Read Dead; Galvanized Rebels; Exchange; Baltimore Merchants; Lee, Bragg, and the Southwest; Loyal Inconsistency; Meade, the 7th Commander; Difference in Northern and Southern Armies; Money from Home; Fourth of July; Divine Service; Gen. Archer and others from Gettysburg; My Ring Disaster; Sky Rockets and Cannon; John Morgan's Raid, &c.

CHAPTER V.

My first box from home; Cannonading Across the Lake; Foaming white Caps; Peculiarities of Prison Life; The Morgan Boys; Gunboat Michigan; Ironclad Prowess Defunct; Lee and Meade; Rebellion Most Dead (?); Siege of Vicksburg; Woman's Worth; Alabama Officers in Luck; Olden Times Made New; Foreign Intervention; Grand Proposition to the South; Four Hundred Veterans from Lee's Army; Thoughts and Talk of Escape; Smuggling Letters; Sutlers' Department; Our Mess Reinforced by Twenty Dollars; Northern Press; Death in Prison; Hospital Scenes; Morgan Raiders Arrive; Crittenden, Dead; John Morgan in Federal Clutches; His Achievements; One Hundred and Sixty Rebellonians from Port Hudson; Prison Scenes; Retrospective Look, &c.

CHAPTER VI.

Gloomy Prospect; Cartel Broken; Bone of Contention; Prison Scene; Off for the Penitentiary; Siege of Charleston; Mobile; True Friendship; One Hundred Gallant Sons from the Old Dominion; Eccentric Minister; Domestic Matters; Going Home; Conscripts; Hidden Fire; Our Possible Destiny; Contrast between the Naval Fleets; Why the Disparity in our Favor; Kentucky Election; Despotism; Inhuman Federal Officers; Changeable Weather; Yancey is Dead; Ourselves and our Friends; Soldier's Life; Two Years from Home; Then and Now; Fast Day; Pay Day; Capt. Law; New Pump; Lt. Kirby Smith; Northern Extract; Two Suits of Gray from Louisville; Manners and Customs in Prison; Celebrated Characters; Youngblood, Brantly, &c.; Prison Scenes and Prison Ways; Daily Routine; Captives from Helena; Col. Johnson's Jewels; Alton Prison; Sunning Day; Going after Straw; Bathing in the Lake; Skirmish with the Pump, &c.

CHAPTER VII.

Excursion Party; Preaching; Col. Lewis; Who are in the Penitentiary at Alleghany City, Pa.; Profession Life in our Midst; Lt. Minor and his Drinkables; No More Boots; Laid Away; Rebels Arrive; Mr. Lincoln's Intention; Sutler Enlarging; Washing Day; The Rebel that didn't go out in a Slop Barrel; The Loyal Folks want us back in the Union, and Why; Political Parties; Brantly and Universalism; Prayer Meeting; The Sisters of Lt. Brand; The Alabama; My Way of Cooking; Town Ball; Prison Scenes; My Facilities for Writing; Fashions Among Us; Hard-shell Sermon; Old Pap; Reflections; Theoretical *versus* Practical Knowledge of Persons and Things; What our Ministers Pray For; Retrospect; Mental Rehearsal; Chain of Memories; Our Prospects; Panorama of War; What the North Thinks and what the South Thinks, &c.

CONTENTS. XIII

CHAPTER VIII.

Almost Two Years since the Last Chapter was Written; Why the Original Manuscript was Written; My Present Quarters; Why in Jail; Long Chain of Events; Grave Charge; Before a Magistrate; Article in Jonesboro paper headed "Arrest of the notorious Capt. Wash;" Renegades; The Sequel Not Yet; Kindly Cared For; Bad State of Affairs; A Look Around Me; Thoughts of 1864; Memorable Cold Day; Four Confederates off for Canada; The Result; Death of Col. Cluke, of Kentucky; Blockade of Ice; Express Matter; Dead House; Plot Nipped in the Bud; Five Hundred Prisoners Ordered for Exchange; Act of Federal Kindness; Sutler Closed Out; Our Fuel; Exit Rebels; Re-enter Rebels; Papers Suppressed from Prison; Rebel Kicked out of Prison; Removal and Escape; Sermon by Col. Lewis; Death of Capt. Barnes; The Masons, a word in their behalf; My Bunk Mate Takes the Small Pox; Inspection by U. S. A. Surgeon; Prison Guard Increased at Night; Col. Pierson's Prison Report from Organization up to Date; Grand Snow Battle; Gen. M. Jeff. Thompson Captured; My French; Judge Breare; The Owner of our Island; Heavy Dixie Mail; Its Contents, &c.

CHAPTER IX.

Fourth of July, 1865; My Enemies and I; Celebration; No Secesh; Poor Beef; Major Scoville; Jas. B. Clay Dead; Death of a Choctaw Captain; Dr. Foster and the Bitters; Sharp Practice; Stir in Prison, Four Hundred Sent Off; A Joke on Some Who Stayed; Southern League; Col. D. Howard Smith on Parole; Lt. Alexander takes the Oath; Mountains of Ice; Blockade Described; Two Ladies in Prison; Rings and Autograph Albums; Confederate Captain Disgraced; Gen. Shaler; A Night in the Hospital; 22d February; Brantley's Rat, my share; Col. Lyle a Rebel, a Yankee and a Rebel Again; Revival; Promenading; Puerile Order; Arkansas Travelers; Conversion of Prisoners; Federal Chaplain; Short Rations; New Furniture; Lamp Broken Over Sutler's Head, and Why; Starchy Federal Popped in the Back and 'Don't Like It; A Good Old Capt. Praying in the Hospital; Col. Printup's Box; Nothing Lost by Kindness; Delicious Pudding; Escaped and Captured; Money Makes the Mare Go; Crowd at Sutler Shop; Kentucky and Baltimore Ladies, &c.

CHAPTER X.

Sub-Sutlers; April Fool's Day; Good Joke on Maj. Stewart, of Ark.; Dancing School; New Occupations; Southern Thanksgiving Day; "Asa Hartz;" Ladies from Kentucky; Galvanized Rebels; Camp Morton; Warm Times in Northern Congress; Not Captured on the Battle Field; Rebellonians; Prison Strategy; Dr. Woodbridge, U. S. A.; Dixie Mail; Rugged Lake; French Letter; Fun; Tunnels; Ditch; Lt. Williams, U. S. A.; Torchlight Procession; Dr. Brantley and Co. Trying to Bribe Sentinel; How the Dr. got his Title; Gen. Shaler in Rebel Prison; Muster and Inspection; Gen. J. E. B. Stuart killed; Fish, Butter and Eggs; Prisoners from Johnson's Army; Hawthorne and Giddings dead; Attempt to Scale the Wall; Tunnels; Quarters Searched; Result, &c.

CHAPTER XI.

June 1st, 1864; Our French; Lt. Tobey; Long Letters Forbidden; Underground Railroads; Col. Hill Excites Rebel Indignity; No more Coffee, Sugar or Candles; Box from Mrs. Lillard; Morgan Turns up Again; Grant

Changing his Base; Vallandigham back in Ohio; Swimming in the Lake; Five Daily Papers in Our Room; Gen. Polk Killed; Gold 226 to 235; Gen. Archer sent off; Secesh Arrive; Capt Jonas on Parole, and Why; Seven Surgeons Sent South; My Schoolmate; Lt. H. M. Baldwin, U. S. A.; Geo. M. Steever, the Youngest of our Class; Southern Gentry Aim to Scratch out; Disagreeable Roommate; Sentinel shoots a Ditch instead of a Rebel; July 4th; The Alabama Sunk; Box from Home; Thoughts; Prison Wall Moved Back; Talk About Rebelling; Prison Gardens; The Oath After Dark; A Dutchman's Order; Fifty Dollars from Home; Gen. Trimble; Circulating Library; Lt. Brown; Col. Boynton, U. S. A.; Chair Factory; Two Prisoners Wounded by Sentinel; A Dark Hour; Programme of Concert Given by Rebellonians, &c.

CHAPTER XII.

August—Arrival of Prisoners; Maj. Dick Person; A Dozen Surgeons Sent South; Bold and Successful Attempt to Escape by Lt. Murphy; Rebels in Blue Follow Out Sand Wagon; Value of Worn-out Blue Pants; Eleven Southerners Ride out on Two Wagons; Adjutant Newman as a Yankee; Lt. Seleceman Trapped; Loyal Troops Skirmishing for Seceshers; Seventeen Captured First Haul; Guard at the Gate; Prayer Meeting; "Fresh Fish;" Col. Baxter, C. S. A., as a Major U. S. A.; Cruel Order from Commissary General; Fuel Added to the Fire; Three Southern Gents Crawl Down a Slop Ditch; Lt. Dudley; How Lt. Clark and I confiscated numerous Plank and what we did with it; Our Study finished and described; French and Spanish; Cheating the Yankees; Ugliness Sometimes a Virtue; Rebel Hung; Ratastrophe Described; Col. Fite, President of the "Rat Club;" Exciting Era; Heavy Slam: Our Modus Operandi; Raid on Hospital Woodpile; Col. Lewis Gone; Escaped and Caught; The Washing Business; Capt. Furnish and Lt. Maris in a Muss over a Rat; Sequel, &c.

CHAPTER XIII.

"Pro Bono Publico" McClellan Nominated; We Indifferent; Golden Rule; Memorable Occasion; Graphic Description of a Tornado; Prison Scenes; Rich Jokes; Nothing but the Lord's Prayer; Thompson's Christmas Turkey; All About It; A Rich Affair; Short Rations; Fight in Prison; Privileges of Our Cook; Pleasant Surprise; How a Rebel Got to Canada; Col. Printup in Luck; About the Prison Officers; How and Why We Played Possum; Lt. Wilson, who will Appear on the Stage Again; Generals Removed from Our Prison; Studying Spanish in our Studio; Our Room in Luck; Gens. Marmaduke and Cabell Arrive; A Good Soldier Dead; What Breckinridge Did for Gillem; Reign of Terror in Kentucky; Cotton; Gen. Beall; Col. Fite Promoted; Sherman's March to the Sea, &c.

CHAPTER XIV.

Hot Weather in Jail; My Relative Situation; I Think Much but Say Little; Dec. 1st, 1864; Battle at Franklin, Tenn.; Southern Chivalry Scratch Out; End of Block 1; Death of Col Matlock, of Arkansas; How We Profited by Somebody being Three Sheets in the Wind; Memorable Occasion; Outbreak; Lieut. Boles Killed; Gen. Beall's Circular; Our Share of the Mobile Cotton; Port Holes in the Wall and Forts on the Island; Inspection of Blankets, and How We Juggled; Thief in Prison; Two Hundred and Eighty of Hood's Officers Arrive; Colonel Printup Dines with a Federal Major; Colonel Mike Woods; Fish in the Dab; Rebels Apply to Work on Forts; Gold 216; My Spanish Grammar Finished; Prospects; Good-bye 1864; All About Wilson's Chicken, &c.

CHAPTER XV.

1865; General Remarks; Why Prison Life was not Unhappy for Me; Grant Authorized to Exchange; Federal Policy; its Cruelty, its Results; Exchange Begins; Feelings in Prison; Two Hundred Rebel Officers Shipped; Scenes and Thoughts; Still They Go; Modus Operandi; My Time Comes; How I Felt; On the Outside; Passage over the Bay; On the Ice, and Incidents; Across Ohio; "No Use Grieving over Spilt Milk"; Mansfield, Ohio; Pittsburg; Through the Alleghanies; Our Finances; Happy Family; Juniata Valley; Old Friend in the Shape of a Bridge; Mufflintown, Pa.; Harrisburg; Pies and Pretty Girls at York, Pa.; Anti-Triumphal March through Baltimore; The Dear Ladies; Beast-like Federal Officer; At the Wharf; Down Chesapeake Bay; Historic Scenes; City Point; Up the James; Our Steamship; My Adventures among the Sailors; Twenty Dollars for Breakfast; Our Federal Escort; Scenes on Shipboard; Pleasant Parting; Harrison's Landing; Confederate Flag of Truce Boat; Colonel Mulford a Generous Foe; Unfurling of a Hidden Flag; Passage over Historic Space; Arrival at the Confederate Capital, &c.

CHAPTER XVI.

Disappointed, and Why; Spottswood Hotel; Colonel Leathers; On Parole Furlough; Wages Paid and Balance Due Me; Richmond Theater; Libby Prison; How I Felt Toward the Inmates; Confederate Capital; President Davis and General Lee; All Sober; Adieu to Richmond; Burksville; Pleasing Incident; Round the Jolly Camp Fire; Bound West; Unexpected Meeting; Lynchburg Excited, and Why; An Order from the War Department, and how it was Evaded; Wytheville; Our Luck at Glade Springs; Wicked Bedfellow; Abingdon; Bristol; General Vaughan and Others; Off for Carter's Depot; Johnson's Depot; A Circuit of Three Thousand Miles Complete, &c.

CHAPTER XVII.

The Future Looks Brighter; Pleasant Associations in Jonesboro; March in Retreat; Parting to Meet no More; Up the Holston; Miss Kate Worley; Bound for Old Virginia; Why not in the Army; Blue Spring; Dry Creek Gap; Incidents; We Part; Rev. David Sullins and Major John Sanders; Work in the Garden and Make Chicken Coops; Happy Times; Fishing for Trout; Pleasant Meeting; Lead Mines; Religious Community; Good Joke on Myself; Confederate Armies Surrendered and President Lincoln Killed; Sad Farewell; Washington Springs; Why I Laid Over; War Incident; Marriage at a Strange Hour; Blountville Then and Now; Jonesboro Again; In the Midst of Unknown Dangers; Fiendish Spirit; Jail Life Incidents; Good Friends all Round; Dr. Bill Sketer Smith; My Uncle Arrives; Our First Greeting; Colonel Brown, U. S. A.; Dr. Joe Clark and Sergeant Garber; The Dear Women; Almost a Good Time; The Bright Side of Prison Life; I'm Almost Free.

CONCLUSION.

Leaving Jail; Dark Ride; Bull's Gap; Old Friends; Was the Meeting Accidental; No; Why Preconcerted; What about the Bail; Gross Outrage; Barking up the Wrong Tree; Homeward Bound; Safe Arrival; The Country Along the Route; Meager Sketch; All Lost; Not Sorry; No Peace Yet; My Hopes Realized; Reflections; Verdict of the Reader; Conclusion.

CAMP, FIELD AND PRISON LIFE.

CHAPTER I.

Johnson's Island, near Sandusky, Ohio, }
July 10, 1863.

From the 1st of October last I have kept a minute diary of our camps, travels and the incidents connected therewith, from time to time writing them down in a somewhat connected narrative, in a journal I had prepared for that purpose. In October, 1862, we — that is, Vaughn's Tennessee Brigade — were camped near the western border of Virginia; in April following we were in the vicinity of Vicksburg, Miss., having traveled diagonally through Tennessee, Georgia, Alabama and Mississippi, tarrying a while at Knoxville, Montgomery, Mobile, Jackson and Grenada.

No one except a soldier knows how many incidents crowd into a 1,200 mile military trip through the South. Often, while at Vicksburg, I derived great pleasure from going back and reading over the occurrences that took place before we left

Tennessee, and I could imagine how much greater the pleasure would be in the great future, when all this strife is only in song and story, to rehearse the scenes and deeds of a wonderful era. I had my journal written up to within the month of April, and the tale consumed some fifty pages, descriptive of matters and things in general along our route, and about the cities in which we stopped.

"Martial circumstances" and increased activity in "war business" caused me to cease my scribbling, and leave my all, except war implements and a single blanket, to go and try the stern realities of the field, where I was soon to see the foe. As was too often the case, ne'er more did we return to that camp. Many sacrificed their heart's blood at the altar of liberty, and a host of others are, with myself, serving out a martyrdom, for their country's sake, in a Northern prison.

My journal, account books, clothing, many highly prized letters and tokens from friends, all are, perhaps, now smouldering in the ruins and waste about Vicksburg. That was the third time I had lost all my clothing, and the second my journal, precious at least to me, by the vicissitudes of war. And, though what I am now penning may meet the same fate ere the year is past and gone, still, to fill up vacant hours and to renew the scenes through which we have so lately passed, and for the curiosity of hereafter looking back on prison life as it passed, I will persevere.

I will go back to a thrilling occurrence near to the time at which my other journal ceased. About the middle of March our regiment changed the locality of its camp, very much improving our situation and comforts. Our camp was in an elliptical shaped hollow, containing some six acres, and surrounded on all sides, except one, by hills, towering above the stately poplars in the midst of our camp. The crest of one of the lofty hills that engirdled our secluded home was lined with brazen batteries and strong intrenchments, our camp being just outside of the outer line of defense of Vicksburg. We had very respectable shanties for both officers and men, and a good spring within the limits of our camp.

Everything was passing off in the usual manner of camp life, till the night of March 28th, when we were shocked by a sudden and terrible calamity. The day had been calm and serene, and there was nothing in the heavens or on the earth portending to human vision the coming sad spectacle. About ten o'clock at night the wind commenced blowing a steady gale, and black clouds loomed up. For an hour it seemed that we were only going to have a thunder gust, but the storm increased and the winds howled among the thick foliage of the tall trees. Not one in our camp dreamed of danger, till the limbs commenced crashing, and the huge poplars were being torn up by their roots in the very center of our camp.

All was flurry and consternation. Men rushed wildly from their cabins in their night clothes, seeking eagerly a place of safety. In many cases the cabins were crushed into atoms before the men had fairly escaped. A tent occupied by my brother and five others was torn into shreds in a moment after their exit. Six men were killed outright in one tent, and ten others injured in various parts of the regiment. 'Twas the most pitiable sight man ever beheld, to see six stalwart men lying side by side, mangled and bruised, in death. We buried them side by side on a neighboring hill. Never did a conflagration or tornado leave a more desolate and gloomy scene than was presented by our once beautiful camp. It required several days to clear up our camping ground so as to make it even passable.

About the 1st of February orders were issued from headquarters for officers to be sent home on recruiting service. I sent R. A. Anderson, my orderly sergeant, as being most suitable, because of energy and perseverance. On the 29th of March he returned with twelve men and no less than thirty boxes of provisions, and some clothing and a host of letters for the boys. Never was there more joy over the return of a stray child than then.

The provisions were prized more highly than gold, for our rations had for some time been slim, both in quality and quantity, and, besides, they were from the loved ones at home. That night at roll call the boys raised a lively yell, which they had not done before for weeks. The letters were anxiously perused and treasured away in the hearts and knapsacks of the fortunate recipients. Though I held no claims on any one for favors, I too was not forgotten. Mrs. Gray sent me a nice box of eatables, old Mrs. Winniford and Mrs. Bouldin each a ham, and I got no less than fourteen letters on every imaginable subject. The reasonable ones I answered and complied with their wishes, the rest I consigned to the flames. It may be well to say here that I was a Kentuckian, serving with Tennessee troops. Before the war I had never known a member of my company or regiment, nor a citizen of the region from which they came—East Tennessee.

Before taking up the incidents of April, I will go back and say a word of the country, climate, seasons and people. Those who live far away from Mississippi, and only know of it from history and the appearance and stories of those who live there, will find themselves deceived when they visit that boasted land. True, there is much good soil, much wealth, intelligence and patriotism amongst her people, but there are many qualities wanting to make it suit the tastes of those who live further North.

The great difference in temperature in the day and at night, the days being quite sultry and the nights most always chilly, is anything but pleasant or healthy to one used to a more uniform clime. The changes of temperature are very sudden, one day being melting hot, the next wintry and disagreeable. The seasons are very much more forward there than at my Kentucky home. About the middle of February the first signs of spring begin to appear, and by the middle of March the whole forest is in a full garb of green, and the ladies have nearly all their garden stuff planted. Roses and peach trees bloom in February, and by the 1st of March many of the farmers have finished planting their corn. Strange to say, but few of them have yet learned how to rightly cultivate corn; they prepare the ground badly, and put in too much for their force, which is not the secret of success.

For a month succeeding the middle of February I was in the country, recovering from a threatened attack of fever. I visited various planters, and had an opportunity of getting into the minutiæ of their social, agricultural and commercial relations. I saw a great many things that grated upon my ideas of right and wrong. I boarded with Capt. Wall, who was generous-hearted and did all he could for my comfort; but the old lady was too particular, penurious and curious. Their daughter, a young grass widow, was kind and obliging, but, like her mamma, the almighty dollar clung too close to her affections. They were well off, and had a good library, to which and the parlor I had free access, so I passed the time off very agreeably.

While there I formed the acquaintance of several quite pleasant ladies, and, as they belonged rather to the aristocracy, I took especial pleasure in letting them know, in a manner not calculated to give offense, my opinions of that class of humanity. They generally agreed with me, but sometimes we gave each other sharp cuts. I have met with some as kind and worthy people in Mississippi as anywhere in my travels. One can not now get a fair representation of what the State is, for most all the truly gallant and patriotic men are long since in the service of their country. As a general thing, only speculators and those without conscience or self-respect remain at home. They respect the soldier and will aid him only so long as his money lasts.

Come, April showers, April flowers, and April with thy verdant garb, and let us, ere smiling May is upon us, record the mighty events that were wrapped up in thy bosom. A seeming cessation of activity, and apparent stillness between two armies confronting each other, is often indicative of strategical moves, and such was the case before Vicksburg during the first days of April. The enemy's fleet had measurably moved out of sight; no gunboats attempted the passage of our batteries, and their motions fairly indicated that they were about to strike anchor and be off for Memphis.

During the 10th and 11th of April the enemy were making moves which we could not exactly comprehend, and evidently not intended for our good. Many of their transports steamed up the river. Some few, accompanied by iron clads, were reconnoitering in the Yazoo river, and some troops were moving back into Louisiana. Our Generals had a sharp eye on it all, and orders were issued that we must be ready to go at a moment's warning. At two o'clock on the night of the 14th we were aroused from slumber and ordered to cook four days' rations immediately. At daylight everything was ready, and our little tricks packed up to go whithersoever ordered. All day long did we, in suspense, await orders to move. Next morning there came an order to keep two days' cooked rations on hand, and await further orders.

The Federal move was soon explained, for on

the night of the 16th, just at twelve o'clock, the booming of the signal gun on the river told us the gunboats were coming. In ten minutes our regiment was in line, and we posted away to the scene, for it was predicted that the enemy might attempt to land troops under the cover of their gunboats. By the time we reached the theater of action, one mile off, the incessant peals of from forty to fifty heavy siege guns at our water batteries shook the earth, and made the air reverberate for miles around. Eleven boats started to run the gauntlet; two were sunk in front of the city, many of their crews going under, and one was disabled but floated beyond the range of our batteries. They hurled broadsides of shot and shell into the city as they passed, doing no damage except killing six mules. That was the most successful of the several attempts General Grant made to pass our fortress.

Some time in March, a soldier belonging to the 61st Tennessee regiment, who attempted to desert and go to the enemy, was caught, and sentenced by a general court-martial to be shot April 17th, in the presence of our brigade. On that day, at ten o'clock, we were ordered to repair to the place of execution, but on the way were met by a courier, saying the day of execution was postponed, by order of General Pemberton. The 6th of March we had witnessed the execution of two men for mutiny. They met their fate like martyrs, and said it was just.

I believe it was the 20th of April that one of my sergeants, who had been to the country to get some clothes washed, brought me a beautiful bouquet, which he said was handed him by an unknown lady. It was culled with taste and exquisitely arranged, but I dreamed not of the source till I drew a slip of gilt-edged paper from the mass, and found, "Compliments of Miss C. to Captain W." I had seen her but once; 'twas a freak of woman's nature.

Just before daylight of the 23d, six more of the Federal fleet, five transports and one iron-clad, attempted to pass the "Rubicon." The transports were partially protected by cotton and hay bales, but the searching and galling fire of our batteries sunk one, the "Henry Clay," and the rest were so riddled that they had to lay up several days at a landing below the city. The gunboat is, perhaps, yet quietly reposing in the bed of the Mississippi in front of Vicksburg. There were no longer reasons for doubt as to the intentions of the enemy. From the hights around Vicksburg we could see wagon trains moving down the river on the Louisiana side, and the camps of the foe, so long in our view, were disappearing. The transports were being run down to get them over the river below Vicksburg.

I was, on the 24th April, appointed by General Vaughn on a board of survey to examine army clothing, to be issued to the troops. Most of the pants were of goods manufactured at Lexington, Ky., and brought out by General E. Kirby Smith in the fall of 1862. The last day of April General Vaughn had an order issued that neither soldier nor officer should leave camp without written authority from his headquarters. That same evening one of my friends had been a short distance in the country to see his sweetheart, and she told him that Lieut. Billy R. and Jim B. would be there that night to play the violin, and requested that he and I should be present. We studied and calculated between the good to be done by obeying the order and the pleasure to be derived from going. The fiddle out-balanced, so, as the shades of night came o'er us, we took a stroll in the opposite direction, but landed at Mr. C.'s. Presently the boys came, but no fiddle. We fixed up and sent for a violin, pretending that it was to play in another part of the camp. In the meantime, Miss Mollie and Miss Henrietta happened in. We at first hinted and at last plainly asserted to the old folks that music was of no account without dancing, and after a little coaxing all round, they succumbed. The silvery rays of the full moon, which was then just in the zenith, made the night beautiful. We danced beneath an arbor in front of the house, and were having a most splendiferous time, till the exit of April and the incoming of May reminded us that it was time to be away. We crept stealthily into camp, and were up next morning at break of day, no one suspecting that we had been absent, nor did the secret ever leak far out. So you see a soldier may sometimes, if he will, have as fine times as anybody. But I have got ahead of the hounds. At broken intervals all through the day of the 28th heavy firing could be heard in the direction of Grand Gulf, thirty miles down the river. That night three gunboats attempted the passage of our frowning batteries, and one of them was badly used up.

The next day the enemy, with a half-dozen iron-clads and some twenty transports, loaded with troops, ascended the Yazoo river, landed a portion of the troops, and commenced shelling Snyder's Bluff. We suspected it to be merely a *ruse* to draw our troops from other quarters, and our predictions proved correct, for that night they re-embarked, went back to their old landing at Young's Point, and struck out through Louisiana for Port Gibson. The gunboats stayed and bombarded Snyder's Bluff heavily all the succeeding day. Some days previous, the bulk both of the Federal army and ours had left, and were marching toward Port Gibson, on either side of the river.

May 1st.—On this day began the series of battles which ended the 17th, resulting so disastrously to our arms. General Bowen met the enemy, who had crossed below Port Gibson, and were marching on it. He repulsed and kept them back a whole day, but as his force was small, and General Grant's whole army was coming against him, he deemed it prudent to spike the unmanageable guns and evacuate the place, which he did on the morning of May 2d. There was a sharp loss on each side. We lost General Tracy, of Alabama, and General Bowen's chief of artillery. Anderson's Virginia battery, having eight pieces, and the best equipped I ever saw, lost fifty six horses, six guns and thirty-seven men. The two remaining guns were lost at Champion Hills, and but few men were left.

My company was detailed on the night of May 1st to go on outpost guard, in the intrenchments at the bend of the river above Vicksburg. This had been a nightly duty for our brigade ever since the Yankee fleet made its appearance in the latter part of January. Rain or shine, hot or cold, some of us had to lie in the ditches every night, so that it had become commonplace. This night was warm and pleasant, and it was quite as agreeable there as in camp. We placed our guns in proper place in case of an alarm, listened to and chatted awhile about the booming cannon at Port Gibson, then spread our blankets and laid us down for a good night's sleep.

At the hour of midnight we were aroused from our slumbers by the heavy tread of troops crossing a bridge not far from us. They passed directly by us, going, as we supposed, to Port Gibson, and the boys were in high spirits; they had heard the rattle of musketry before. It was General Moore's brigade, which had just come from the Yazoo and Deer Creek country. The next evening we had to go on picket duty, in front of Chickasaw Bayou. Though no enemy was visible in that direction, we thought it best to guard against any emergency. Our picket line was over a mile long, and it was no fun posting and instructing sentinels. The days were then getting hot enough to kill a fat man, and at night the mosquitoes were far more terrible than anticipated Yankee shells and bullets.

Just now there was a grand move in our whole army. All the troops that had been stationed around Snyder's Bluff had orders to go below that evening. At dusk the column commenced passing our post, and for three long hours they filed by, three brigades and several smaller detachments going. The artillery, which can move faster than infantry, struck camp before day, and away they went lumbering down the valley. The 3d Maryland battery was camped near our picket post, and left at sunrise. We began to feel kinder ticklish, for we knew not of any brigade save our own that was left to defend Vicksburg. At the same time, we felt honored by being trusted with so important a duty.

Everything was now on a war footing. All along our picket line there was a war going on all night between the boys and the mosquitoes, and next morning many of them reported no sleep but many oaths. Some blessed the critters, and some the Yankee nation. Now, the great waters, which had for several months submerged the whole Chickasaw battle-field, had subsided into their proper channel, and were yet fast sinking, to the great discomfiture of the pillaging iron-clads.

I worried out the night with the biters, saw all in proper shape next morning, which was the Sabbath, and as the beams of old "Sol" were getting well nigh perpendicular, I concluded to steal a march on the fellows, and go to the shade for a few hours, though contrary to a strict line of duty. I sauntered leisurely away, no one noticing my course, and when I had got half a mile and on higher ground, it was cooler, and I was tempted to go further. On and on I went, through a rather rugged and constantly ascending country, till I suddenly came to a nice little cottage, more than a mile from my post. Knowing that there was a charming somebody there, and that I might get a good dinner, I accidentally happened in, to blow a few minutes. Minutes stretched into quarters, and quarters into two hours, when in came a contraband, who, with a pleasing countenance, announced, "Dinna's ready." A pleasant chat, a glorious dinner, and then I hasted back to my post, many not knowing I had been absent. So the world moves.

On being relieved from picket and going back to camp, we found orders to cook four days' rations. Times looked squally, and we went right at it, and in a very few hours were ready for the fray. We had scarcely got to bed when the booming of cannon said something was wrong on the river. Notwithstanding we had been constantly on duty three days and nights, we had to get up quickly and go double-quick thence. As we hurried on we could hear the steam rapidly escaping from a Federal craft. When we gained the top of the hill overlooking the scene of action, the object was in the range of our heaviest and hottest batteries. In a few minutes smoke and flame burst forth from the craft, the batteries ceased firing, and she burned to the water's edge in front of the city. Twenty-three out of the crew of twenty-five were captured, some of them being badly scalded.

It proved to be a tug-boat, laden with medical stores, with a barge on either side protected by cotton bales, and the two said to contain 50,000 rations.

That was our last experience with night visitors on the water. They "smelt a mice," and came no more.

The morning of the 4th came, and no indications of an immediate move. A week previous, Capts. Blair, Gammon and myself had made arrangements with an old negro woman, in the suburbs of Vicksburg, to prepare for us on this day a good dinner—an important desideratum to a soldier. We got the semi-approbation of Colonel Crawford, and went to comply with our promise, not forgetting to prepare for a notification if the regiment should move. The good old Auntie fixed up the best dinner I ever ate in Mississippi, having every variety of vegetables, meats and other things, and a splendid dessert. It only cost us $3.00 each; at the Washington Hotel, the best in the city, dinner cost $2.00, and was not much better than we got in camp.

On our way back to camp we visited the public cemetery, and saw many nice marble tombs and beautiful, shaded walks. One portion of the cemetery was assigned for soldiers' graves. Six noble youths of my company are entombed there. I wrote all the consoling and encouraging words

I could to the parents of each. Some one has appropriately said that, "when this strife ceases, the proudest monument that could be raised would be to the unrecorded dead."

On the 5th of May glorious news came to us from two quarters. The lightning's flash said that General Lee had defeated and driven the enemy back across the Rappahannock at Chancellorsville. A few hours later it said that General Forrest had captured a whole command, 1,600 cavalry, near Rome, Georgia. They were making a Morgan raid. The next two days were exceedingly cool and chilly, and we spent our time in drilling and otherwise preparing for a muss. Everything was as calm and quiet as though no armies were nigh. To add to the gloom caused by the weather, we got news that Stonewall Jackson was dead. History will record him as the mightiest hero of the field. His place can not be filled. The nation mourns his loss. He died of wounds received at Chancellorsville.

CHAPTER II.

Room No. 19, Block 4, Depot Prisoners of War,
Johnson's Island, Ohio, *July 18, 1863.*

As a soldier's bark tosses about on the uncertain ocean of life, though there is much monotonous routine of rough, hard duty, and not a few unexpected and ungenerous mishaps, still there is, now and then, an episode to make one forget it all, and feel that he is in an oasis in the midst of the desert. Dark clouds sometimes have silvery linings, and every picture has a bright side, if we will but search aright for it. Some fore-knowledge, experience and a free good will, have taught me to avail myself of every opportunity, yea, sometimes to make an opportunity, to seek out these bright and pleasant places, and full many an hour of bliss has it brought me.

About the 1st of May I sent one of my men, who had undergone a long spell of fever, and was again threatened, to the country, where he could get more tender treatment than in camp or hospital. A week later, by permission of the Colonel, I chartered Dr. Ernest's horse and rode out to see him, at the hospitable mansion of Capt. Edwards, the best old farmer in all the country about. Some four or five other convalescents from our regiment were there. Mrs. E. cared for them as kindly as if they had been her own, and the boys loved her for it. She told me there had been no less than thirty-seven sick men in her house since the troops had been stationed there. I found my man so much recuperated as to be able for camp in a few days. I partook of a good dinner, said adieu, and started in a hurry for our camp, four miles distant.

Not far off my route was the residence of Dr. Cook, with whose family I was intimately acquainted. I thought it very probable that we would move soon, so I easily persuaded myself to halt and say farewell. I am not sure that I would have ever known the Doctor but from the fact that he had three accomplished and interesting daughters. It was my first visit for a month, and they seemed glad to see me. First I greeted the madam, and soon there came tripping in the ones I most desired to see, fresh as morning roses and full of life. The eldest, Miss Lucy, was thoroughly educated, being well versed in several languages, quite good looking, brilliant, witty and sarcastic, the very kind of a "sawyer" I sometimes like to strike against. Misses Potia and Mary Vic, though not quite so brilliant, were amiable and interesting, and the hours glided by till, the first thing I knew, the sun was gilding the tree tops. I called for and heard a few choice pieces on the piano, by Miss Lucy, accompanied by Miss Potia's vocal melody. Then, taking several bouquets for their friends in camp, I lingered on the portals as I bade adieu, perhaps forever. Striking a lope, I reached camp at dusk, delivered the mementoes and messages, and followed on after my company, which had just gone on duty at the breastworks on the river bank. That's the last piano I've heard, the last parlor I've entered and the last refined society I have been in up to date.

Our brigade commissary got a supply of flour and sugar on the 11th of May. I procured for my mess, consisting of myself, three Lieutenants and our cook, eighty pounds of sugar at 12 1-2 cents, and sixty pounds of flour at 20 cents, which was our allowance. With what other little stock we had on hand, we thought ourselves in good fix for awhile. But the sequel was, we lost it all.

That evening, Lieut. J. T. Earnest and myself borrowed a metal skiff and took a ride on the bosom of the great Father of Waters. We started to go over to the Louisiana shore, but being warned by a sentinel that we might be fired on by the water batteries, we thought it discretion to desist.

Just at dusk, Mrs. Hinson, a poor, good woman, who lived near our camp, and whose husband was in the service, sent for one of my Lieutenants and myself to sit up with the corpse of one of her children. We could not refuse to go, and were glad to give rest and comfort to a distressed mother. The morning of May 12th was the last one that ever dawned on us in our camp, that had become so home-like to us. For several days past matters had been so quiet that we had ceased to be in suspense, and, instead of active, restless, field duty, were enjoying customary camp life.

At two o'clock, P. M., orders came from General Vaughn to cook three days' rations. So often had similar orders come that it startled us not, and we went leisurely to work, not dreaming that we would leave before next day, if then. At four o'clock another order said everything must be ready to move at six o'clock, taking nothing except what we had on our backs, one blanket, war equipments, and a single cooking utensil to the mess. This time we were actually going to leave, and the prognostications were, for very active service. Everything was now astir, hurrying up the beef and cakes, and fixing up duds to leave in the care of the sick, of whom there were almost a hundred. As the appointed hour drew nigh the hurry increased.

At half-past five the long roll beat for all to arms, and though many of the men had not finished cooking, there was no longer time to tarry.

Officers were busy seeing who were and who were not able to go, and leaving instructions for the sick. I had to leave fifteen of my men who were not able to travel; never a word have I heard from them since. Precisely at six all were in line, and with various feelings and expressions we bade adieu to our romantic home in the hollow.

We were met at the main road by the other regiments of our brigade, the 61st and 62d Tennessee, commanded by Colonels Pitts and Rowan. Ours being the senior regiment, took the advance, and the column moved on through a stifling dust, we knew not whither bound. At ten o'clock in the night we turned aside from the road and struck camp in a woodland near Mount Albion Church. We built huge log fires, and chatted around them for awhile, then wrapped up in our blankets and laid down to sleep and rest our weary limbs. All was soon hushed and still, till three next morning, when the long roll aroused us. In fifteen minutes all were up and ready to move again. Just as streaks of light began peeping from the East we entered the main road at Dr. Newman's; following that to its intersection with the Jackson and Vicksburg Railroad, we left it, taking along the latter in the direction of Jackson. We now knew our first point of destination, which was Big Black Bridge, ten miles away. We halted at eight o'clock, partook of a frugal but refreshing snack, then plodded on, reaching the bridge near noon. We passed over to the east side and took quarters in the intrenchments just vacated by troops ordered forward.

There was a general move to the front. Two brigades were then leaving, and during the evening General Stephenson's division passed. From the dense clouds we knew the storm must be brewing, and that the clash of arms might soon be heard and seen. Already had the advance pickets on each side been fighting, and the enemy had been making a reconnoisance to within ten miles of that very place.

That day I first saw General Pemberton, who, accompanied by his staff and General Tom. Taylor, of Kentucky, was going to the front.

Now, a word about our afterward unfortunate position. The country all around is low and level. A line of intrenchments something over a mile in length had been cut in a zigzag, circular shape, crossing the railroad, and terminating at the river above and below. Nature afforded no favorable elevations, but those earthworks were certainly in favor of the holders. The whole bottom was one vast corn-field, containing perhaps 300 acres. Several gin houses and sheds were partially filled with cotton bales, and several hundred bales had been used in constructing batteries and defenses for ammunition and the wounded. As an inevitable result, much of the corn, which was about a foot high, was trodden down by the soldiery in the construction of the works. We learned on the 14th that the Federals had taken Jackson with little or no resistance. The cause of the weak defense we never learned.

That morning, seeing that everything was right, I started out on a foraging expedition, and after a smart tramp found a lady who sold me two pounds of butter at $1.00 per pound, cheap enough; and she gave me a gallon of milk, for which we usually paid $1.00. I engaged more for next day, and while I was sitting in the piazza resting and admiring the beautiful flowers, shrubbery and evergreens in the yard, a rain storm came on and poured for an hour. It abated and I started for camp, but got soaked to the skin. I found the boys standing wrapped in their blankets, and taking the pelting rain like wet turkeys, the greatest care of each being his gun. All our ditches were filled to the brim, and had the Yanks come then, it would have been face to face. When it cleared off that evening we drained and bailed off most of the water. That night the cold, wet ground was our pillow. Next morning we heard desultory firing some distance off, in the supposed direction of the enemy. Many thought the battle had begun, but it proved to be General Buford's brigade firing off their wet guns. We spent the forenoon in cleaning and fixing up our contraptions for a Yankee hunt.

In the afternoon of May 15th we were quietly basking in the sunshine about the intrenchments, expecting to fight there if the enemy came. But how vain the expectations of man. At three o'clock orders came for our regiment to be ready to move in ten minutes. All rushed to arms, for some one whispered that the foe were not far in the distance. Right soon we were on the march to Edwards' Depot, five miles east, where we arrived at sunset, and camped in an old field hard by. We found an immense wagon train just moving toward Clinton and Jackson. Our whole army had been concentrating there for several days, and had only a few hours before moved forward. That night my company and that of Captain Hale were ordered on picket duty. We took position on the main Raymond road, keeping a small outpost some half mile in advance, and still two miles farther out was a cavalry picket. We were suspecting a dash of the enemy's cavalry that night, but they came not.

Various were the rumors in regard to the movements of our adversaries, but the fact was that Grant, from Port Gibson, and Pemberton, from Vicksburg, had been marching almost parallel, their lines converging and coming in contact some four miles out from Edwards' Depot on the morning of 16th May. General Gregg's brigade had, a few days before, fought a Federal division at Raymond, but had to give way before superior numbers, after his noble Fort Donelson and Chickasaw Bayou boys had repulsed them gallantly for several hours.

From our picket post, on the morning of the 16th, we could plainly hear the opening of the contest at Champion Hill. First came the usual skirmish firing, sometimes in volleys, then a few cannon commenced blazing away, and as the sun neared the zenith, faster and hotter became the engagement. Up to near noon was spent in strategy and manœuvering, the lines of battle getting changed almost perpendicular to their original position. Then the work commenced in earnest. Now, for perhaps an hour, the artillery roars like thunder, deadening everything else; now it measurably ceases, and the din of small arms, as thick as hail pattering on the roof, can be heard for several miles along the line. Sometimes successive volleys belch forth, then again we hear the random, desultory firing. And now the brazen batteries open anew from a fresh place. For a while the deadly combat goes on, then all breaks off into silence. But again, like a smothered fire, the battle breaks forth at a new point in all its former fury, and we imagine that the enemy are being driven back, for the sound seems to get more distant; but it proved that the contending parties had got into a hollow, and there was a mighty slaughter on both sides. At one point our troops occupied the edge of a wood fronting a corn field. Twice did the enemy attempt to charge them, but each time with a sad result to the attacking party. Then a fresh storming party came in front and on the flank, and our men were routed and driven with heavy loss.

About two o'clock the wounded and stragglers commenced passing our post, going to the rear. The latter we halted and kept with us. Within an hour, several hundred men, wounded in every conceivable manner, passed by, about one half of them being shot in the hands and arms, as is usually the case in a battle. Stragglers were constantly reporting that our army was being whipped—that the enemy were too many in number. From the increased stream coming back, it began to seem too painfully true, for at four o'clock the whole road was lined with fragments of regiments and parts of batteries.

Half an hour later, General Pemberton came up to my post and asked why my company was not to the front. I told him we were on picket, and he said it was all right. To my inquiry as to the shape of the battle, he said: "We are whipped, but the enemy outnumbered us three to one." Though calm in conduct, he appeared greatly agitated in mind. While there a courier came up with a dispatch from General Joseph E. Johnston. He read it, studied a moment, gritted his teeth, and remarked to his staff: "Had General Johnston sent me this dispatch yesterday, this battle would not have been fought!" He handed the message to his Adjutant General, saying, " Here, preserve this, it may be of value to me some day." I afterward found out that the dispatch was an order to avoid a collision with the enemy, and unite his force with Johnston's in the vicinity of Clinton. And I then surmised that he wanted it preserved, believing that his conduct would undergo an investigation.

Now the whole army was in full retreat, several brigades tarrying on the battle-field to hold the enemy in check. General Tilghman, of Kentucky, lost his life late in the evening, while keeping the enemy back at a bridge on the left.

It looked like another stand was to be made at Edwards' Depot, for all the troops were stopped there; but near dusk the army resumed its march toward Big Black. As we left the Depot, car loads of provisions, ammunition and medical stores, as well as cotton houses all round, could be seen in flames, to keep them from the enemy. As our rear guard evacuated the place the Federals occupied it, sending grape and canister after the boys, but not pursuing further. Before ten o'clock Big Black was reached, and a portion of the army passed on in the direction of Vicksburg. The rest remained to give the enemy fight.

Our regiment was ordered to the extreme right, beyond the real line of defense. We took position behind the levee, and with a few spades soon had some rough earthworks constructed. After the excitement of the day, and the night march, we wrapped our martial cloaks about us at the hour of midnight, and slept soundly till day.

Perhaps four thousand men and twenty pieces of artillery were left to defend the place, and we felt sure the enemy would march on us next morning. That night, while intrenching, I said to our Colonel and several others that we would surely "go up right there," for there was no means of retreat, the river being directly in our rear and no crossing save near the bridge, and that was frail and inadequate. I was sure that an army at least four-fold of our number was coming against us, and, with such a position as we had, it was preposterous to think of holding out for more than a few hours. However, nothing daunted, we made the best preparation we could to receive them.

At seven o'clock next morning our pickets began a brisk fire with their cavalry advance. In one hour more their infantry and artillery came up, and soon an artillery duel commenced, lasting a half hour. Then there was a silence while the guns of the foemen were being put in better places and in closer proximity. Then again they opened, and shot and shell rained for awhile, but doing no serious damage. The whistling rifled cannon balls that split open the trees in our rear made some of the boys open their eyes, but most of them were perfectly calm. Some hours were occupied by the enemy in getting their various infantry columns into position.

They encompassed our whole line, and in many places dense columns could be seen advancing. On our left a thick forest was within a half mile of our line, and here it was that the enemy made their first demonstration. First the sharpshooters tried their hands; then several brigades of infantry, like brave Spartans, came out into the open ground; but the Southern boys soon made them hustle back to the cover of the timber. Next an advance was made upon our center, and a brisk fight, at long range, continued for perhaps an hour.

Soon a column was seen filing to the right of our line, and we were fully expecting a brush there. The tide of battle ebbed and flowed till near eleven o'clock, when the enemy finding, through a deserter, a flaw in our works, made a bold and successful charge through the unguarded space, about the center of our left wing. In overwhelming numbers they were now upon our flank and rear, so that our men had no earthly show of resistance: they must run, surrender, or be shot down. The commanding officer, seeing the situation, gave immediate orders for evacuation; but the Federals could reach the only crossing of Big Black river as soon as we possibly could.

My regiment, being on the extreme right, was not aware of the situation for some minutes; then, after a short consultation by the regimental officers, we thought it best to attempt an escape down the river; accordingly we made tracks in that direction, but had gone only a little way when we saw ourselves hemmed in, and the blue-coats swarming from the brush half a mile in our front. Colonel Crawford had made his escape, so Lieut.-Colonel Gregg consulted with the officers, and it was conceded by all that there was no alternative but to surrender. We formed the regiment in line, threw down our arms and accoutrements, and Colonel Gregg rode out to meet the enemy, who were rushing on with wild huzzas. I and many others shed tears for a few moments; then I summoned up my manhood, and counseled my boys not to be dejected or cowed, but as valorous as ever, for we had tried to do our whole duty, and were guiltless.

We surrendered to General Burbridge, of Kentucky. Some few of the Northern soldiery were inclined to be insolent, but seeing the spirit of our boys, the officers had us treated justly. I found several Federal Kentucky regiments, and many men I had known in days before. An hour after I was captured I took dinner with Colonel George Monroe, of Frankfort, Kentucky, and got the first genuine coffee and good old ham I had seen in many a day. Need I say it made me feel delicious all over, and that I can not forget the kindness of that Federal officer?

In his regiment I met a Dutchman who was once our bootmaker at the Kentucky Military Institute. Approaching me with a broad, genial grin on his countenance, he said in his broken twang, "I knows you, but can't tell who you are; I used to make you boots." I told him I was glad to meet him, but sorry to find him in such bad company. "No," said he, "it is you what be in bad company." One of my schoolmates of two years before was on the staff of Gen. Smith, who was against us. The casualties in the Union army far exceeded our own. In their last grand charge they lost several field officers and several hundred men.

To any one familiar with military matters, it was evident that weak generalship was the cause of our terrible disaster. Many cried out that General Pemberton had "sold us," but the impression was far from universal. At Baker's Creek he allowed the enemy to out manœuver

4

him and flank our troops, and crush out our brigades in detail—so say those who participated. The defenses at Big Black were badly planned, and wise generalship would have dictated a means of escape in case of emergency. But we are too prone to condemn a commander when he meets with defeat. When the matter is sifted I think it will be found that General P. had a willing mind, but was deficient in the martial talent necessary to manœuver an army in the field.

Now comes a new era in our existence as soldiers. We are no longer strong armed and brave hearted boys, ready and willing to rush on into the ranks of the foe at the bidding of those we loved to obey and follow. True, we still possess the same physical qualities and the same hearts, but they are powerless now. We are prisoners of war, subject to the will and mandates of those into whose hands we have fallen. I must say that, so far, we have generally been treated with the courtesy due a prisoner.

But I left us in the hands of the exulting Yanks on the verge of the Big Black. We were formed in two lines and marched along the line of our deserted intrenchments to a shady woodland half a mile off.

Big Black bridge, a splendid structure, was now in flames, and a sharp cannonade was going on between our men over the river and the Yankees, who were trying to cross. Had the engagement lasted a half hour longer, a whole division of troops and twelve rifled cannon would have come against our single regiment. We were going to try them a whack, though they would have overpowered us after we had slayed perhaps a hundred or so of them. Our nerves were all braced for the expected onset, and the boys would have battled valiantly.

It was now the 17th day of May, and the sun was blazing hot, so the shade to which we were escorted was quite pleasant. Stragglers were being picked up in all directions, and our captive band soon amounted to 2,500, the whole number captured. A guard line was formed, and we were allowed loose range over several acres of ground. The Yankee boys soon mixed all among us, and were anxious to know why we rebels were fighting so ardently against "the best government the world ever saw." Some would argue the subject matter like philosophers, others would get mad and fly off. There was an entire freedom of intercourse, and the Federal officers came in, too, and, when they could distinguish them from the privates, talked with our "big officers" about things in general.

They were exceedingly jubilant, for their telegraph said Richmond had fallen, and they said they were going to take Vicksburg next day like a flash, which they didn't, neither had the Confederate Capital gone under. Altogether, it was a semi-interesting occasion, and that vast general admixture of gray jackets and blue coats was a fit subject for the graphic pencil of an artist.

While the time was thus passing, the rear of the Union army, wagon trains, cavalry scouts, plunderers and contrabands were constantly arriving. They had the best equipped wagon train I ever saw, nearly all six horse or mule teams, splendid stock, and all in excellent condition. It was a wonderful sight to behold the three heavy siege guns, drawn by sixteen oxen each. They were fifteen feet long and otherwise in proportion. I had not dreamed that such ponderous things could be transported through the country from Port Gibson.

For half a mile around us the woodland was thick with Yankees, Confeds, stock, wagons and colored folks. The loyal troops, who had been living on half rations for some time, were taking a hasty snack. Though most of us had eaten nothing since the day before, not a bite did we get. The house of a planter near by, and who had fled when the battle came on, was splendidly furnished with costly things, and contained a large, choice library. The whole premises were sacked by the Northern soldiery, and that too right under the eyes of several Generals who had made headquarters in the house. It was within our guard line.

All the afternoon the enemy were engaged in tearing down several barns and making pontoon bridges across Big Black river, and just before nightfall the bulk of their army passed over and on to take Vicksburg next day. We remained on the ground that night, being promised something to eat next morning. Several times we were got into line and counted, and after being numbered the last time, the officers were relieved of their swords and pistols. Some had thrown theirs away rather than surrender them.

My revolver had already been taken by an impudent puppy of a staff officer. Without orders and with a haughty air he ordered me to give it to him. I told him I had been thus ordered several times, but had refused, and did still refuse, to give it up unless ordered by a competent authority. A Major-General was standing near by. I approached him and asked if I must deliver it over. He said "yes," and I did so. The pompous, contemptible manner of the being with shoulder straps on who demanded it deeply aroused my indignation, and I had a burning desire to tell the chap what I thought of him.

At two P. M., 18th May, the officer in charge of us said he would take us to Edwards' Depot, where he could get some rations for us. Our escort were the 23d Iowa and the 54th Indiana. Upon getting to the Depot we found Gen. Hovey's division of the army there, and all along the road we noticed Federal soldiery occupying the farm houses. The citizens were generally gone, and their homes were being made desolate.

The darkies were congregated about in groups, congratulating each other upon their supposed freedom. Many of them were ludicrously dressed in all the good clothing of their masters and mistresses. Poor creatures, did they only know of the degradation to which they are drifting.

We were marched out a half mile to an old field where there was an abundance of water, and there we pitched camp again. It was now sundown, and from long fasting our appetites were whittled down to a keen point, but the commandant said we should have rations before we slept. Many of the boys had not tasted food for two days; now and then a generous Fed. would share his mite with a hungry Reb. At ten o'clock beef, sugar and meal came, but no salt, and nothing to cook in. So, many again wrapped up in the arms of Morpheus, and dreamed of good things to eat, just out of their reach.

It was in this wise that I got my supper: My orderly sergeant skinned some bark from a green tree in which to make up the dough, which he wrapped up in writing paper, and wetting the paper, covered it up with embers. The bread cooked without burning the paper, and of a truth never did bread taste more sweet and palatable. Many were the ways in which our rations were served up on that occasion. Indeed is necessity the mother of invention.

Perhaps it may be no honor to tell of light-fingered tricks, but I'll risk the condemnation and tell what Captain Blair and myself did. At ten o'clock at night a huge pile of beef, bacon and meal, guarded by Yanks, was surrounded by a thousand rebels, all anxious as children round a Christmas tree. That commissary stuff was to be divided among the whole camp, Federal and Confederate, and would make the individual ration rather slim. While the commissary sergeants were busy dealing out rations to the representatives of various companies and detachments, Blair managed to get his clutches on a bacon ham, and my fingers tightened on a hundred pound sack of meal, and in triumph did we march to where our boys were camped, and the presumption is that we had full rations next day. The meat and meal had been captured from our army, and it surely should be no offense to take back our own. At any rate, I did not then feel, nor have I ever since felt, any compunctions of conscience over the matter.

At three o'clock May 19th we took the back

track, arriving at Big Black just at dusk. We crossed the river on a pontoon bridge, and camped in a corn field on the river bluff. That night Col. Gates and his adjutant, Frank Clewell, of the 2d Missouri cavalry, escaped. Next morning we got beef and meal for breakfast. I managed to get out of the guard line and "borrow" a little coffee and bacon in the Yankee camps, and while out I managed to "draw" a coffee pot, which accompanied us to prison. Almost before we had time to cook our lean rations orders came to move.

Before eight o'clock we were traveling toward Vicksburg. We passed many beautiful mansions, and everywhere the ladies came out to give us a look of profound sympathy. Some, whose hopes and fortitude had almost sunk, shed tears; others, with stronger and braver hearts, waved their white 'kerchiefs and audibly blessed us, wishing us a speedy return to battle for Southern rights. We gave them cheers, told them all would yet be well, and some whose feelings were more tender could not restrain the tear drops that flowed in sympathy for these noble women of the South.

At noon we halted for water and rest directly in rear of Vicksburg, and but a few hundred yards from the Federal line of investment. A brisk cannonade was then going on from either side. We stopped in sight of the residence of Dr. Cook, where I had spent so many pleasant hours. He had taken his family and gone into Vicksburg among the besieged. His house was now a hospital, and his yard, orchard and fields a dense wagon yard. Mrs. Lake's residence, near by, was also being used as a hospital; all was gone to rack.

After an hour's rest we marched on, going close by our old camp ground, and taking in the direction of Snyder's Bluff. After traversing some three miles, we turned abruptly to the left, and descending the rugged hills that overlook that memorable spot, we passed directly over the battle ground of Chickasaw Bayou, which proved so disastrous to the Federals about the close of the old year, four hundred having been captured and at least a thousand killed and wounded, on an area of not over four acres. Very many of our boys along knew all about the matter from experience, and some of our Federal escort had a slight idea of the place, the 54th Indiana having lost over two hundred men there.

It was at this point that we commenced meeting wagons laden with army stores for the troops besieging Vicksburg. They came over a corduroy road from Lake's Landing, on the Yazoo river, where still other boats were then landing. Snyder's Bluff, which had withstood many a pelt from the Yankee iron-clads, was now evacuated, and several gunboats were already dispatched to

Yazoo City, in hopes of capturing two splendid gunboats being built there. But the bird was flown; the torch had done its work. The supply train that we passed numbered a hundred wagons, and we met a brigade going to Vicksburg, they said, but we assured them they would get no admittance.

We arrived at the Yazoo about dark, having traveled over twenty miles since eight o'clock, most of the time through a stifling dust. We found a dozen transports and a host of soldiers, citizens and boatmen, all full of joy, for they thought one-half of Pemberton's army was there. Within an hour's time we got plentiful rations, but had no way of cooking, and besides that, most of us were too weary to think of anything but rest and sleep. All night long, at regular intervals, the enemy's mortar boats were throwing shell into the city.

During the forenoon of May 21st, we managed to get our appetites satiated and our bodies well saturated, for a beating rain poured on us for an hour, and we had the opportunity of taking a refreshing bath in a bayou close by. All day long a heavy bombardment was going on at Vicksburg, by both gun and mortar boats, being occasionally relieved by volleys of infantry. So many and so great had been our misfortunes that many of us were almost willing to concede that

Vicksburg must succumb in a few days, but hope and faith in the future still buoyed us up.

Late that evening we took passage on some transports bound for Young's Point, Louisiana. My regiment chartered the steamer "Chancellor" for the occasion. At dusk we went out of the Yazoo onto the broad Mississippi, and at eight o'clock rounded to at Young's Point, and remained aboard over night. We could plainly see the mortar boats shelling Vicksburg, which was in full view of our position. We could only distinguish the light of the fuse in the bomb, which would go up and up for several thousand feet, then down, down, down into the devoted city, but not more than one-half of them exploded, and the damage was slight. They threw shells a distance of two and a half miles, and it was a beautiful sight to behold those seeming streaks of light traverse the midnight darkness in pleasing curves.

From our camps around Vicksburg we had seen the Federal fleet anchored at Young's Point since Christmas day of 1862, but had never dreamed of being there in that capacity; though the boys often joked each other about going to "Camp Chase" and other Northern prisons. At nine o'clock May 22d, we for the first time set foot on Louisiana soil, and camped where the phalanx of Yankee tents had been arrayed all winter and spring.

Often had we heard of the great mortality among the Federal soldiers stationed there, and now saw ample cause for it all. There was a low, flat country behind the levee, both swampy and filthy. All along the edge of the levee were thick groups of graves, with here and there a rough slab to mark the last resting place of some poor, deluded fellow, who thought he was fighting for the preservation of the government in its purity, instead of for the subjugation of the rights and institutions of the Southern people.

Here the rebel officers were separated from the privates, our camps being a quarter of a mile apart, and it was with difficulty that we procured the privilege of going to see our sick men. We had to go a half mile to the river to get water and wood to cook our rations. But three could go at once, and were invariably escorted by a chap wearing a blue coat and sporting a musket and a "six-shooter."

The whole number of prisoners now collected from various quarters was about 3,500, some 170 of them being officers. The sun was almost insufferably hot, and we made shades with brush, and with our blankets stretched on poles.

May 23d was a dull, monotonous day, except when relieved by the artillery duels going on around the city. It seems that at two o'clock the gunboats were to make a combined and stubborn attempt to silence our river batteries. It was reported that in the onset one iron-clad went to "Davy Jones' locker;" anyway, men came from that direction dripping wet, and the firing died away.

The next day was Sunday, and everybody but us put on good clothes, and went sauntering about to see what they could find. We were excusable, for we had none to put on. Quite a number of Federal officers who had not yet seen the "monkey show" came loitering around our guard line, prying into the general physiognomy of the boys and old men that were fighting against "the best government the sun ever shone on."

Our boys would meet them at the guard line and discuss the matter freely—concessions were sometimes mutually made, but I never knew of any one being convinced or converted. We struck them heavy on the nigger question, giving freely our opinion of those who were willing to equalize themselves with the sweet-scented sons and daughters of Africa. They would most always "whip the devil round the stump," and deny many patent facts. Many "up the river men" lurked about our camps, anxious to see what kind of stuff rebels were made of.

About noonday we beheld a stately column approaching from the direction of Richmond, La., and lo! when they came near unto us we perceived it to be composed of nearly three hundred contrabands, with their cubs and bundles of rags, hunting freedom.

Hundreds of them were already squatted about in squalid hovels and tents, with no means of subsistence, save the scraps they could pick up round the soldiers' camps. 'Twill be a dear-bought freedom to them, for the Northerners don't really love them, and won't take them into brotherhood. They only want to destroy the institution, thinking not and caring not what will become of the unfortunate wretches.

Though very many in the South believe, and more contend, that it is the desire and aim of the whole Northern army to free the slaves, it is a false imputation. The majority of the Northwestern men do not care to interfere with the institution where it now exists. But it is the policy of the administration, and the commanding officers must do the will of him at the helm of State. They say to the soldiery that it is a military necessity to weaken the strength of the rebels, pretending that it is all only for the restoration of the Union as it was.

The Democracy of the North seem to have just awakened into the light of the true issue. But it is now too late to avert the storm. Arms must decide the case.

On the morning of the 25th we were notified

that steamboats were coaling up to transport us up the river. Three days' rations were furnished to last us to Memphis, and we spent the forenoon in getting ready for a journey. At two o'clock we took up our beds and walked for the landing, accompanied by the 23d Wisconsin and 80th Ohio. Our fleet was made up of the following boats: the Crescent City, Ohio Belle, Gladiator, Omaha, the Gen. Robert Allen and a gunboat to keep off the guerrillas that infested the river. I was on board the Omaha, which had some 800 men. The gunboat mounted ten heavy guns, and one-half its crew were gallant boys all the way from Africa.

All this while the siege had been going on at Vicksburg, and the enemy during the past week had made several heavy concentrated charges, every time being driven back with frightful loss. Our faith in the invincibility of Vicksburg was growing stronger.

At four o'clock we steamed off, taking a last, lingering look at the gallant city as she faded in the distance, and leaving our blessings and best wishes with her noble defenders. We were glad to get away from the hearing of a contest in which we felt so deep an interest, but could not lend a helping hand.

Near dusk we passed Millikin's Bend, and in a little while a cannon shot whizzed over our heads, making us feel somewhat ticklish, thinking the ubiquitous rebels were firing into us from the shore. But it proved to be a signal from the iron-clad·for the boats to "haul to;" then they were ordered to get in line one after another, in which manner they traveled all night. I took sleeping quarters in the open air on top, it being too warm on the inside. As we glided along over the placid waters I watched the varied scenery, lit up by the pale moonbeams, till near the hour of midnight. Then I wrapped up in my blanket and knew no more till the sun was shining in my face next morning.

The natural scenery on the Mississippi is the most dull and monotonous imaginable. But few high, rugged, picturesque cliffs meet the view, and the conformation of the earth and the growth along the shore presents an unpleasing sameness. In many places, for miles, no habitation could be seen, and ofttimes when we did pass a plantation it was devastated and deserted. At three o'clock we passed the steamers Luminary and Ben Franklin, carrying subsistence to Vicksburg. They were convoyed by the rebel gunboat "General Bragg," a craft of novel construction but beautiful appearance, lost by the Confederates at Memphis in the spring of 1862.

At nine o'clock on the morning of the 27th we passed Napoleon, Arkansas, once a thrifty place, but now deserted; only a few forlorn looking women and children could be seen. 'Twas a true picture of the deserted village. Oh! the horrors of war. About noon we came up with Ellet's marine brigade, consisting of a fleet of thirteen boats, some new ones, but mostly old New Orleans packets, transformed and barricaded against rifle shots. The mission of said brigade is to patrol the river and keep off the partisan rangers in the service of "Dixie." They had cavalry, infantry and some small field pieces, and when attacked they aim to run their cavalry ashore, surround, and "gobble up" the daring Confederates.

They are a heavy expense to the government, but don't catch many of our boys. Their duty is to halt and inspect every craft going up or down the river. The presumption is they were glad to find so good a cargo of rebels on board our fleet. After an hour's consultation among the officers we passed on. Several men on our boat had been taken very ill, and that morning a poor fellow, belonging to the 49th Tennessee, died. He was put in a coffin and consigned to the deep, to know the turmoils of earth no more. We know not who was left to mourn at home, or whether friends ever knew of his fate.

As we passed on, the eye and the mind became weary in contemplating the prospect all around. But seldom did we notice a human being, and it was only here and there that a horse or cow could be seen grazing in a field. It seemed as if a great plague had come over the agricultural resources, for where was once beautiful corn and cotton, rank useless weeds were now growing.

At daylight May 28th we were in front of Helena, Arkansas, and, as at Napoleon, the people were most all gone, and it bore anything but a pleasing aspect. The post was well fortified, being surrounded by rugged hills. We noticed that the garrison was partly composed of colored troops. During the day we passed the ruins of several towns that had been burned by the soldiery. Toward night we could see increasing signs of habitation and prosperity along the shore, and when darkness came we were making ready to cast anchor in front of Memphis.

CHAPTER III.

"Uncle Sam's Confederate Hotel."
Lake Erie, *July 24, 1863.*

Arising quite early from my couch on the cabin floor of the "Omaha" on the morning of May 29th, I gained the highest elevation on the boat, and beheld a great city risen up before mine eyes since the daylight had left us. But, like Memphis of old, much of her former prowess and life was gone. Memphis is a large and well built city, and boasts many splendid, towering edifices. The Gayoso House is a magnificent structure and a model Southern hotel. The commercial interests of the city have been very heavy, it being the terminus of several railroads running through fertile and populous regions, and besides that being the central mart of an extensive trade on the Mississippi.

Like all cities that have undergone the devastating influences of the presence of an army, life and activity is, to a great degree, crushed in every department except military supplies. But from her geographical position, the facilities for transportation, and the intelligence and enterprising character of the surrounding community, trade must prosper there so soon as untrammeled by military guardianship.

Most all of our first day at Memphis was spent in coaling and taking aboard a supply of rations to last us to Cairo. We had now been cooped up on the waters for several days, and the inactivity and monotony was becoming quite irksome. We longed to set foot on dry land once again.

During the day the Governor and Adjutant-General of Iowa, with several other notables, visited our boat, as they said, to see what made us rebels hold out so obstinately against the "glorious Union." They were anxious to find out if we were not most willing to lay down our arms and come back to former allegiance. We inquired of them what inducements were offered, and if they expected to make us love them by stealing our negroes and making them equal with themselves, not us. We asked Mr. Adjutant-General if he was willing to fight beside a negro. No! but he was in for any possible means to subdue the rebellion. After an hour's gossip, in which I think they were not as successful as they anticipated, they took with a leaving.

In the afternoon our guard was changed, the old guard going back to Vicksburg, and the 43d

Ohio taking charge of us. They were rather Vallandighamish, were well raised and edu[cated] and had a fair conception of the consid[eration] due a prisoner of war.

That night we expected to weigh anchor and be off; but when the following morning dawned we found ourselves still in front of Memphis. We knew not the cause of the delay. Some twenty sick prisoners were taken ashore and sent to the Memphis hospital. Two men of my company were of the number. Poor fellows, I'm not sure that we will ever see them again. During the day one of the rebel Lieutenants played a Yankee trick on the Yankee nation. He exchanged his Confederate dress for citizen's garb, deliberately walked aboard of a little boat that came alongside, went ashore, and I reckon is now in Dixie land. Our craft was anchored midstream as a safeguard against escape, yet several fellows swam ashore and got away the first night we stopped at Memphis.

The monotony of the day was somewhat relieved, in my case, by finding two neighbor boys of my youth prisoners on the same boat with me. With Sam. Maguire and John Walker I had gone to school many a day, but from long absence they had been almost forgotten, till my eye fell on their familiar faces. The surprise was mutual, and the meeting a happy one. They had lately heard our old Kentucky home, and could tell me many things that had transpired during the long months that I had been cut off from communication with my people.

It was four o'clock P. M. when we raised steam and bade adieu to the great Western city. The gunboat no longer accompanied us, for the Confederates then seldom operated above Memphis. From Memphis to Cairo the trip was much more agreeable than below. We made better speed, and the atmosphere became cooler and seemed purer. The scenery was more varied, and there was a perceptible change in the soil for the better. Signs of habitation were more frequent, and many plantations were under cultivation.

Some time during the night of the 30th we passed Fort Pillow, and in the forenoon of the next day we passed the well-known Louisville and Cincinnati mail packet "Jacob Strader," with troops and sanitary stores for Vicksburg. The great difference between above and below Memphis is attributable to the horrors and ravages of war; the line of the river, on both sides, from Memphis to New Orleans being an active military theater.

It was about nine o'clock at night when we passed Island No. 10, a once well-known Confederate fortress, which was taken by an investment rather than by force of arms. The island contains some sixty acres, and is well fortified. A number

of troops were stationed there, and several gunboats were tied up along the shore. The commanding officer hailed our fleet, but finding that
our cargo consisted mainly of Southern boys going
up to board with Uncle Sam, and they not being
contraband, under the circumstances, we were
allowed to pursue our journey.

Before daylight of June 1st we passed Columbus, Kentucky, and at eight o'clock stood in front
of Cairo, having been six and a half days out
from Vicksburg, and traveled about six hundred
miles. I don't know of a single one who was not
fully satisfied with his boat ride, and willing to
go into bond never to go aboard of a steamboat
again, if it could be helped. We were sickened
out with too much of a good thing.

I had all my life entertained a curiosity and
anxiety to go down the river to New Orleans,
imagining that, besides the sumptuous entertainment on a first-class New Orleans packet, I would
find one almost continuous scene of magnificent
plantations, splendid mansions, elegant cities and
cosy villages, the whole being interspersed here
and there with romantic cliffs, quaint places and
picturesque shores. Though seen and enjoyed
under disadvantageous circumstances, I'm sure
the reality came far short of my conceptions.
Experience has taught me that this world, as seen
by the naked eye, is far from what it would appear

when magnified by the press and the representations of others. In all my travels by land and by water I have seldom found a place just what I anticipated. Sometimes our imaginary pictures of persons, places and things in the distance are made too dim, but too often we magnify them.

The first day of June we were anchored in the mouth of the Ohio river, before the city of Cairo, which was once noted for thieves, pickpockets, murderers, blacklegs and every other class of inhumanity, but is now more civilized and refined. Were it not for its low position, being subject to overflow in high water, Cairo would, ere this, have been a large city, being naturally a central point and a terminus of the great Illinois Central Railroad, and famous for its arrivals and departures of steamboats. A splendid levee has been constructed at great expense, which renders the city, to some extent, proof against high water. It is a larger and better looking place than I expected to see, and was full of life and business. It was a great shipping point for military stores. We saw several gunboats anchored in the stream and others building. I noticed about thirty pieces of heavy artillery lying at the wharf, not mounted. A large number of new government offices, shops and storehouses were visible all about. During the day a number of steamboats arrived from and departed for St. Louis, Louisville, Cincinnati and

Memphis. In fact, Cairo exhibited more of the activity of olden times than any place I had seen for a long time.

About noon General Buford, attended by Col. Spalding, of General Grant's staff, and who had charge of us prisoners, visited us. He was quite jovial, and talked freely and reasonably; said he loved us, and was going to compel us to come back into the good old Union. He had the manliness to acknowledge that he believed we were honestly deluded, and said he gloried in our spunk, but hoped we would soon be convinced of the error of our ways, and be willing to come back. After an hour's exchange of ideas, which differed widely, he left us in our glory and went his way rejoicing.

All day long trains had been making up to carry us we knew not exactly where. Late in the evening two trains got off loaded with privates. While laboring under a bright recollection of how the Federals treated property, private as well as public, in Mississippi, I "confiscated" a haversack, of which we stood in need. It contained a plate, knife, fork, cup, spoon and other little articles to be found in a soldier's toilet. I acted in retaliation for wrongs that I had suffered. It's mighty hard for a soldier to follow the Bible doctrine in that particular.

Between Memphis and Cairo I had written a long letter, portraying the acts and intentions of the Northern army, as seen and expressed before my eyes and hearing. I had the satisfaction of saying precisely what I thought and felt, and I managed to hire a boy to mail it at Cairo to a friend at home. That was the last time up to date that I fully expressed my sentiments, but, though necessarily silent, my feelings are unchanged.

June 2d.—In the forenoon transportation was ready for the balance of the prisoners. The officers were honored with passenger cars, but the privates were shipped as live stock. When we had proceeded some thirty miles out on the Illinois Central, our limited privileges were suddenly cut short by a rather disagreeable incident. A Lieutenant belonging to my regiment jumped from a car window while the train was running, and made his escape back to the "land of cotton." The train was immediately stopped and a vain search made for the daring, reckless traitor, who had no time to tarry, but was making tracks for "Dixie." Colonel Spalding came through the train giving us a lecture; said he had taken pains to make us comfortable and place us under as few restrictions as possible, trusting to our honor not to abuse the privilege, but that he must now double the guard and curtail our liberties. We were after that required to keep the car windows down, and two guards were placed at each door.

For some twenty miles from Cairo is a dense wilderness of small growth, and scarcely a house could be seen. Then we struck a better country, but it was lately cleared, and the houses were new and unpretentious, and their crops of wheat and corn, though late, looked well. As we got further into the interior, habitations became more frequent, and the villages along the road were numerous. In fact, it seems to be a favorite way for the people in that whole section to dwell in little towns. Presently we struck one of those broad and extended prairies so common in the Western country. Thousands of acres stretched out before the vision, with scarcely a hillock to disturb the uniform surface.

Sometimes I noticed hundreds of acres under one fence, the various farms and crops being only separated by a turning row. Then again I saw vast pastures inclosed with fences constructed with posts and only two rounds of plank, well up from the ground. In these beautiful fields were every description of stock, luxuriating midst the rank prairie, herd and other grasses. And now again we rolled along for miles, seeing neither houses, fences nor trees; nothing but great herds of horses and cattle roaming at large, being known only by each farmer's particular mark.

As we glided along by the various farm houses, the women and children would come rushing out to see the rebels, who were rapidly whirling on prisonward. The first town of any note that we came to was Duquoin, where a great multitude of all sorts had congregated to see the Vicksburg boys. To some of the prying and inquisitive the rebellonians would say, "Take a good look, gentlemen, the show is free," and sometimes a devilish chap would take off his hat and say, "Come up closer, and see my horns." Instead of finding us cowed, they would get ashamed of themselves and go away.

At three o'clock in the afternoon we found ourselves at Centralia, a railroad junction of some importance. It is a beautiful town, and has many signs of wealth and prosperity. Here whole troops of the fair sex flocked out to see us. Many waved their snow-white 'kerchiefs and had a smile on the countenance, seeming to mean "hurrah for Dixie." As we had to stop for an opposing passenger train, we had an opportunity to talk with many of the citizens, and found right smart of the "Copperhead" spirit prevalent.

All night long we rattled on over the Illinois prairies, and at daylight were at Terre Haute, Indiana, bound for Indianapolis. We were detained here several hours, and our field officers, some ten in number, were allowed to go up town for breakfast. Those of us who had greenbacks bought little things from the peddling boys.

Greenbacks were now all the go, Confederate money being worth from ten to twenty-five cents on the dollar, and but few buyers at that. On the way up from Vicksburg I exchanged thirty dollars at the rate of fifteen cents per dollar.

Terre Haute is a large and handsome place, and full of thrift. The folks here looked kinder crooked at the Southern boys, and were not much inclined to talk. Mine eyes have never before beheld so many women and children as are all through that country. In a few more years Uncle Abraham will have a young army to relieve the sick and weary.

The only man that I ever really wanted to harm in my life I found right here. The morning was sultry, and our car being crowded, it was almost suffocating when the train was not in motion. A sergeant came through the cars, and I asked permission to raise a window just a little, for fresh air, which he granted. In a few minutes a black Dutch soldier came along on the outside and yelled out to down with the window. At first I pretended not to hear him, hoping he would go on; but when I saw he was determined to be heard, I turned to him and said the sergeant had given me leave to keep it up. He said it made no difference, the window must come down. I lowered it, and he went on, and I raised it again. Presently he appeared a second time, and poured forth his broken gibberish. I began to expostulate and reason with him, when he lowered his gun, cocked it, and swore he would blow my brains out if I did not close the opening straightway. I had read somewhere, when a little boy, a fable, the moral of which was, "Discretion is often the better part of valor." The happy thought struck me, and I acted upon it immediately by closing down the window, for I did not know but what he would be fool enough to fire away. Who would like to be unjustly ordered by and compelled to obey such a creature? I can not better express my feelings toward him than to say they were such as most of us generally experience when we see a mean, venomous snake.

Leaving Terre Haute about the middle of the forenoon of June 3d, we glided on at a good speed through a fertile and thickly settled country, passing a number of neat towns and hamlets, and arrived at Indianapolis at two o'clock. I had been to Indianapolis before, but under different auspices. 'Twas the day after the battle of "Bull Run;" then I could laugh on the other side of my mouth.

Though many prisoners had been in Indianapolis, and one would have imagined they were no curiosity, the lawyers, the doctors, merchants, mechanics, women, children and contrabands all ran out to see us. They wanted to get one long, lingering peep at the "seceshers" who were trying so earnestly to break up the "glorious Union." The soldiers, too, left their barracks to do us homage. They were so very polite and kind-hearted as to come out in full uniform, with shining bayonets, to see us well cared for.

Inasmuch as we had left all our good clothes at Vicksburg, and had for several weeks lived in the rough, and without any change of clothing, we were truly a hard-looking party. No doubt the loyal lookers on imagined we loved fight better than dress, and thereby, in their own minds, accounted for why we usually whipped the Yankee boys so when we had a fair shake.

After some fixing around, an escort was formed and we were conducted, not to "Camp Morton," as was first intended, but to "The Soldier's Home," in the suburbs of the city. It was really the nicest and most agreeable soldier's quarters I ever saw. It is a camp of instruction on rather a large scale, and the several rows of neat cottages, with broad spreading oaks all about, and the nice graveled walks and ornamented grounds make it truly like a home. There are several wells of pure, cold, limestone water near by, and the buildings being neatly white-washed, looked quite inviting. We, the "secesh" officers, 170 in number, took lodgings in the spacious dining hall, which was clean and by far the best quarters we had occupied since Uncle Sam undertook to care for us.

At four o'clock long rows of tables were set, and we partook of a delicious repast, prepared for us by the garrison cooks. We relished it the more because for some weeks we had been living sorter on the wing. In the evening I wrote to my mother, informing her of my good luck in finding myself alive, and telling her of my future prospects.

That night we roosted on the floor, and the guard was so accommodating as to stay on the outside of the building, but they kept strict vigils over us while we slumbered.

We rose with the next day's sun, took a refreshing bath, and then a good warm breakfast. The difference between the temperature there and in our Southern home was quite perceivable. At an early hour curiosity seekers, those in search of old friends, newspaper correspondents and others, began flocking in to see us. By consent of the officer of the guard, but few were debarred the privilege of free intercourse. In one case a resident of the city found his brother in our midst; he did not seem to censure his course, but gave him money and clothing. A very interesting and affecting incident was the meeting of a young lady and her rebel brother. Some of our fellows found acquaintances who were renegades from the

South, and oh! but they were bitter against us. Many visited us merely for the curiosity of finding out what we really thought about the affair. When we told them in unvarnished terms, they could not exactly see it in that light, but what was to be done about it?

The morning after our arrival a dirty little sheet, the *Indianapolis Gazette*, spoke of us in terms that some people would call left-handed compliments, but, as the little boy did upon one occasion, we considered the source. It said, among other things, that we rebel officers were *most* as intelligent as the generality of their privates, and strongly intimated that, if we behaved ourselves, we were *nearly* as good as the flat-nosed sons of Ethiopia who are at the bottom of all this muss.

The capital of Indiana is a large, well-built and flourishing city, and is one of the most pleasant, comfortable looking places I was ever in. It is a great railroad metropolis, at least a dozen roads centering at that point. The grand union depot from whence all the trains start is a magnificent affair. Trains are arriving and going at every hour of the day and night, and one unacquainted or unused to traveling would be perplexed about what train to get on to go in the desired direction. Considering how patriotically the State had responded to every call for troops, we were astonished to find so many Southern sympathizers, elegantly denominated "Butternuts" by the Abolition faction.

The stubborn resistance to the draft shows the latent spirit that has been suppressed in the hearts of the people, not only of that State, but the whole North. The Democracy of the North now see and feel that of which we were convinced more than two years ago, that the fanatical demagogues in their section would take away our liberties and destroy our institutions, even at the price of the Constitution, which the Democracy have tried to maintain in its purity. But it is now too late for them to retire from the unholy alliance. They can only use their powers of persuasion and entreaty that the war be carried on as they thought it was begun, alone for the safety and perpetuation of the Union and Constitution; an appeal to arms, not words, must now settle the contest.

At eight o'clock, P. M., June 4th, we bade farewell to Indiana's capital, and on board a good passenger train on the Bellefontaine road we hied away for the lakes. A crowd were at the depot to see the last of the "Dixie lads." All night we ran on over a good, easy riding road, but could form very little idea of the towns or country along the route. We passed through Bellefontaine just as streaks of gray began to appear in the East, and at nine o'clock were at Tiffan, Ohio. Long rows of large, elegant storehouses, beautiful mansions, with tasteful surrounding embellishments, and towering, gilded steeples, were before us. The day before nine men had been arrested and sent to Johnson's Island for burning a church in the neighborhood because Abolition doctrines were preached from its pulpit.

Though we passed through some splendid and flourishing lands in Ohio, there was not that fresh, inviting look about it as in Illinois and Indiana. Most of the soil has a red, sandy look, and seems as though it were worn out. In some localities timber is large and plentiful, but I noticed much scrub timber.

The farms are mostly in good repair and well stocked, and all about the farm houses I noticed many conveniences not to be met with in the South.

About midday we came in sight of Sandusky bay, and in a very little while were running over a trestle work some distance in the water, and when we looked out at the car window it seemed as if we had taken wings and were flying over the bay. In due time we checked up in the populous and thriving city of Sandusky. As we neared the bay we could see our future prison home in the distance. It had a picturesque and pleasing appearance, and the star-spangled banner floated majestically over all.

It could but bring curious thoughts and strange, indescribable feelings to think of going on that lone isle in the lake, to be shut up from the world for we knew not how long.

CHAPTER IV.

Prison Home, Lake Erie,
Near Sandusky, Ohio, *July 26, 1863.*

'Twas about two in the afternoon of June 5th that we marched to the dock and took passage on a nice little steamer, the "Bonnie Boat," that constantly plies between the city and Johnson's Island, a distance of three miles. She glided like a swan through the pearly, placid water, and in twenty minutes we floated up against the island dock. But few of us had ever before been on a lake or seen a sail craft, of which dozens were now in sight, flitting about with the breeze, seeming to have no particular destination. Many of them were fishing smacks that rode at ease wherever the wind blew, trapping the finny tribe.

We disembarked, and, marching between two files of blue-jackets, were halted in front of Major Pierson's quarters, where the laddies were called up, one by one, and politely advised to turn over their funds for safe keeping. Many of the gray-jacket gentry did not relish the idea, as they thought themselves quite old enough to take care of their own chink, besides having a slight presentiment that there might be a Yankee trick in it I had prepared for the emergency by putting away $300 in Confederate scrip in my other pocket, not visible to the outer world. Like a man, I forked over forty odd dollars, and opened wide my purse to show them that I was acting honest, and not keeping any back.

Lieutenant Allen, of my company, had nearly $400, part his own, part belonging to members of our company, and the balance to Uncle Jeff, which, in the hurry of the moment, he had put in his day book, and aimed to secrete it in a pocket in his drawers, but he missed the hole, and when called up to "shell out," intending to give up some $20 he kept in his pocket book, the hidden treasure fell down his pants leg before the Yanks, and he picked it up and planked out all his cash.

Upon first sight, the island had quite a prepossessing appearance, being slightly sloped, having a nice sward of green grass, with here and there a stately shade tree. The cottages, offices and barracks were neat and clean, and, on the opposite side from where we landed, a beautiful forest made the whole look quite genial. The garrison consisted of "Hoffman's Battalion," which had been on duty there since the first existence of the institution. They were all dressed in the full uniform authorized by army regulations, and formed quite a contrast to soldiers in active service. But few of our party had ever before seen such splendid uniforms, and some of them concluded that they surely were a stuck-up, aristocratic set of fellows. It seemed to them not in good taste for a soldier to have gloves on. Our uniform being so mottled, and so little cared for save as it gave comfort, the dissimilarity was so much more striking.

Our fellows have now, however, got over their curious notions about Federal garb, and don't care how much they show off. We were forcibly impressed with the notion that fine dress and haughty demeanor don't constitute the soldier, and, though in parti-colored and seedy attire, we felt fully able to cope with the same number of those fine soldiers, who had never heard a cannon except at a jubilee or celebration.

Before entering the prison yard we'll take a view of the city and surrounding prospects. Sandusky is a place of smart merit and importance, being a port of entry for the lakes, and a system of railroads bringing it in close proximity to New York, Pittsburg, Cincinnati, Chicago, St. Louis and Canada. It is a brisk manufacturing place, quite a number of fine and commodious factories being in full blast, and her public edifices look quite as imposing as those of larger cities. From a communication with the citizens through the press and other channels, we have found out that they are deeply tainted with Black Republicanism. The water front of the city, stretching along for nearly a mile, is in plain view of our island home.

In surveying the high walls, the portals of which we were about to enter, and the surroundings, one could not be much elated with the idea or prospect of escape. I found out right away that the most pious and sensible course would be to resign myself to fate, and await the action of those in power, and I suited the action to the thought.

Now we for the first time entered the walls of a prison in the capacity of prisoners of war. Some of our party, who were surrendered at Fort Donelson, spent last summer here, and know the proper *modus operandi*. We could but feel somewhat unpleasant at the thought of being circumscribed by such narrow limits for an indefinite length of time, constantly guarded and watched by a chain of sentinels whose beat was on the outside, and near the top of a wall some twelve feet high. Then the thought that we were to be subject to the mandates of those who were our known enemies was not cheering. But I am glad to say that prison life — in so well selected, arranged and conducted a place as this — has been far more agreeable than I anticipated. But of course there is no patriotic soldier who would not rather be battling and suffering for his country than stay in an enemy's prison, though lounging in ease, opulence and security.

Very much like young fellows first going to college, we were smartly puzzled when we first entered, not knowing where to go or what to do. But a fellow who has been out soldiering some time learns to pitch in if he would do well. Learning that the first thing to be done was to get rooms, we split out for a choice. The squad I was in was to occupy Block 4. I got room No. 19, having only four beds in it, hoping to avoid taking in another man, as myself and three Lieutenants filled the beds. We did not have to increase our number, and our room proved one of the best in the block.

Our building contained eighty prisoners, divided into two messes, there being a dining and cook room for each, and a stove tolerably well supplied with vessels. Our cupboard ware consisted of tin plates, tin cups, knives, forks and spoons, and, though rustic in appearance, they served our purpose as fully as a lord's outfit. Our rations were the same as issued to the Federal soldiery, consisting of baker's bread, beef or bacon, coffee, sugar, rice, hominy, vinegar, soap and candles. My mess employed two regular cooks, at $15 per month each. Whatever extra articles we got from the sutler we cooked for ourselves, and, according to our notions, many a savory dish did we prepare.

Our second day of prison life was spent in forming new acquaintances, getting posted as to the laws and regulations, and learning the ropes of the institution. Most all the prisoners we found here, some fifty in number, were citizens suspected of sympathizing with the rebellion, Confederate soldiers held as suspected spies, guerrillas, and eight unfortunate partisans of the South who had been tried and condemned as spies. They were kept in a small building in one corner of the prison yard, with balls and chains on their ankles and handcuffs, and we were not allowed to go near them.

Two weeks previous to our arrival a couple of rebel captains were shot as spies, and two others were under sentence for execution the very day we got here, but for some reason they are yet permitted to live. Most of these men were condemned in conformity with the infamous Order No. 38, I believe, of General Burnside.

Several prominent and free-spoken newspapers in his Department were attempted to be suppressed in pursuance of the same order, but the mass, the advocates of the freedom of speech and the press, cried out against it, and were ready to vindicate those precious boons, by force if necessary. The papers continue to speak boldly of the unauthorized and impolitic doings of the Administration.

In accordance with the same vile order, Hon. C. L. Vallandigham, the champion of Democracy and the rights of the people in Ohio, was dragged from his home before a Military Commission for no offense against the military laws of the land, was found guilty of nothing the laws of his country did not allow, and sentenced to banishment from Northern soil. That is but a single item in the long catalogue of deep wrongs committed by those wielding power under a government where *once* the rights and the property of all were sacredly respected.

The men we found in prison had been incarcerated from three to ten months. Against many of them no special charge had ever been instituted, and over and again an investigation of their cases had been promised. Some had been sentenced to confinement during the war. Several citizens have lately been released upon giving heavy bond and security. Most of them were from Kentucky.

Our first Sunday in prison, June 7th, was rather a lonesome day, for, having no military duties to perform, nor anything to do or prepare for the morrow, many a one of us gave up the day to reflections concerning home, the happiness once experienced there, and the prospect of ever again greeting the loved ones and finding such a home as we once had. With little effort one can forget passing events and fall into a reverie to rehearse and pass before the vision of imagination the panorama of past life. As in a dream, the joys are sometimes almost real, but alas! something startles us from the reverie to find only fleeting phantoms where was once genuine life and happiness.

During the day I wrote a letter home, thereby recalling many pleasing incidents and associations, and almost feeling sad because I was doomed to spend days, weeks and months in an enemy's bastile, instead of the home circle, from whence the light of genuine, unfading happiness shines. But no sooner did I find myself temporizing in a desponding mood, than, by an effort, I dispelled all such thoughts from my mind, and resolved to have fortitude to bear up under whatever might be my fate.

The Feds. had preaching in the chapel "on the outside," many ladies coming over from the city of Sandusky, possibly more for the novelty than the benefit of the thing. We poor devils are sinners trespassing against Uncle Abe's laws, so we must work out our own salvation. Late in the afternoon the garrison battalion went on dress parade, fixed up in their gayest attire, including blacked boots, a rare sight down in Dixie. They went through the various appropriate evolutions in good style, and a splendid brass band added materially to the interest of the performance. Many of the fellows from the South land had never seen a dress parade in so gorgeous a style, and many a curious remark and ludicrous suggestion was made by said rebellonians.

People at home have but little idea what Sunday in camp is. No duty is dispensed with save drill—in fact, the recurrence of the day would often be forgotten but for somebody suggesting the propriety of putting on a clean shirt. However, when there are services, there is generally a good attendance and strict attention.

By Monday, our fourth day in limbo, we were pretty well up to the ways within that little world, and began to prepare for the siege. The first item of importance was to let all our friends know of our whereabouts and destitute condition generally, not forgetting to remind them that a little to wear, a little to eat and a little to spend would soothe our feelings monstrously. Many an old and long forgotten acquaintance was scraped up, generally for the supposed money value.

Up to date the secesh gentry have had all kinds of luck. Some got help with a free good will; some got it, the sender hoping to reap a rich reward hereafter. Others were proffered assistance if they would forswear themselves, and take the oath of allegiance to Uncle Sam's monarchy. Some of the rebels played Yankee on the pretended generous and patriotic donors, by professing to be of weak faith in the Southern cause, and rather forced into service by circumstances, intimating that they would leave the service soon as possible. It is easy to imagine their chagrin when the fellows would write back, acknowledging receipt of funds, and divulging that it was a trick for a purpose, saying that they proposed still to fight, bleed, and, if it needs be, die for the land of their nativity and love.

That day I put my watch, my only relic of home, in pawn with the sutler for some things we wanted, with the privilege of redeeming it so soon as I got money from home. I bought some butter and potatoes as a kind of pastry to our soldier fare. The sutler has an establishment inside the prison walls, and is allowed to sell us anything not contraband of war. At first his prices seemed marvelously low, compared with Vicksburg rates, but now we find he makes a large profit.

That day by ten o'clock the space all around the pump was lined with wash tubs, and many a one of the Southern chivalry, who in times not far away had not known what it was to wait on himself, might now have been seen with sleeves rolled up, and on his knees, washing his shirt, which he had not changed for a month. Some were naked to the waist, after pugilistic fashion, simply because they had no clean shirts to put on while they washed the dirty ones. Some were scalding their blankets, partly to get the dirt out and in part to slay the "gray-backs" obtained on the boats coming up the Mississippi.

Having some days previous made a requisition, and my appearance being a sufficient voucher that the articles were needed, I, on the 10th day of June, drew from Uncle Abraham's bounty a pair of pants, socks and drawers, bargaining to pay for them in board, as he keeps us cheap. In fact, he will have us stay with him whether or not, and he was so anxious to have us sojourn with him for a time that he actually furnished transportation gratis all the way from Vicksburg, almost a thousand miles.

Having undergone so many privations and severities, and being so long cooped up on a boat, I now began to feel the deleterious effects, nor was I by any means alone in being under the weather. My ailment seemed to be nothing more than general debility, a loss of appetite, attended with a languid feeling. The day after that was rainy and gloomy, such as are complete bores indoor, unless one has some employment. Making rings of gutta percha buttons was a favorite occupation with the prisoners to wear away the time. Those who had friends north of Dixie could send them specimens of their workmanship, some of which was really exquisitely nice. An ingenious fellow would take a gutta percha rule and some buttons, and a few bits of shell, silver or gold, and, with no implements but a knife and file, in a little while be able to show rings and other trinkets not to be scorned even in comparison with a jeweler's stock. He would cut the shell and precious metals into squares, diamonds, hearts, triangles and other shapes, which, neatly fitted and imbedded into the face of the polished black surface, added to the beauty of both by the contrast.

My room had almost been turned into a ring manufactory, our little shelf being piled full of rude, home-made tools and material, and my companions were filing and gouging away right earnestly, as though they were convicts, with a task before them. As I never had any mechanical genius, I contented myself with looking on and making suggestions. Some of the prisoners who had been there for a long time, and expected to remain till Gabriel sounds his trump, had managed to procure complete sets of tools, and made it pay by disposing of their trinkets at fair prices, the Yankee boys buying many of them as curiosities for their friends and sweethearts.

The next few days were clear and fine, and the only record I have of them is that I obtained some medicine from the post surgeon and formed the acquaintance of a rebel officer, a nephew of Gen. Breckenridge, who could tell me of many of my old friends about Maysville, Kentucky. In the afternoon of June 15th there arrived 150 prisoners from Camp Chase. They were privates, and were sent there for some special reason, as the prison was intended exclusively for officers. They were from various parts of our army, and had been captured some two, some ten months. As they filed past my quarters I got a glimpse of one that I took to be a neighbor boy of my youth. As soon as they got settled I made search and found that he was the same. He had joined Scott's Louisiana cavalry last fall, when Gen. E. Kirby Smith was in Kentucky, and losing his horse, was left behind, and evaded the enemy till a few weeks since, when they nabbed him up at home.

That was a memorable day with me, for I got a letter from my mother, the first one since I left her side, two years before, to try my fortunes in the South. Having been cut off from communication with home, I was totally ignorant of the state of affairs. The missive was full of interesting news, which I swallowed down like a sponge imbibes water, and the kind, sympathetic words of my mother made my heart swell and flutter with ecstatic joy, and my soul felt that it was good to be once more in communion with my best friend on earth. As I read the endearing maternal sentiments, briny tears coursed their way down my cheeks, and for a good while I was overcome with feelings that pen can not portray, and only those can appreciate who have been similarly situated.

The next day went off wearily to me, for I was indisposed, and that intensified my thoughts of the comforts and endearments of home. The day following the Federal corporal who came into my room to see if all was right brought me a lump of ice, for which I was very thankful, and which helped me very much. I relished the cold ice even more than my food, and for a week used no other water. During the day about sixty officers came in from the prison at Alton, Illinois. They, with a number of privates, had been started for exchange, but were stopped at Pittsburg and sent here, as we all supposed, on account of retaliatory measures. The bad faith with which both parties have kept the cartel agreed upon for exchange has caused many a gallant man to languish and die in prison. Thousands of soldiers are now suffering in prisons, who, at a word from those in power, could be honorably exchanged and serving their cause.

Little incidents are constantly occurring in military affairs which in civil times would be regarded as almost inhuman, but are now lightly passed over and forgotten, save by those smitten with the iron rod of despotism. It was the 19th day of June that the parents of a young Missouri officer came to see him, he having been absent from them for almost two years. After pleading and trying in vain to see him, they left with saddened and embittered hearts because of such uncalled for treatment. From Sandusky City they sent him some clothing and money, with their sympathies and blessings, then retraced their way to the old homestead, where one seat of that once happy family is vacant.

The same day a few more Southern gentry came in, and I received a message from a lady friend in the home land, it being of peculiar interest. because it led me anew over the paths and with the lasses of my youthful days.

It was about that date that we heard of the death of Lieutenant Read, of our regiment, who we had left sick at Indianapolis. He was taken to the Camp Morton hospital, and our men, all of whom had been taken to that prison, were with him for help and comfort in his last moments. He was a noble fellow, respected and beloved by all who knew him at home and in the army, and an affectionate family are left in East Tennessee to mourn his loss.

The 23d and 24th were dull, heavy days, nothing of any interest transpiring within our walls. I obtained permission from the post commandant to send home for clothing and money. For some ten days previous the armies of Generals Lee and Hooker had been very active. Hooker had changed his base to the front of Washington, and the people of Pennsylvania were alarmed for fear of an invasion, and not without cause, *and effect too.* The story of a disastrous defeat of the Federals at Port Hudson some weeks ago has just leaked out. It appears that a select storming party attempted to scale the redoubts, but had to give back with great slaughter.

Vicksburg, the proud monument of Southern valor, still stands, notwithstanding the satellites of General Grant proposed to eclipse its glory several weeks ago. There, too, have the Federals met with some of those terrible repulses which rash Generals, in their zeal for conquest and glory, have brought upon their soldiers, who know nothing but to obey those whose duty it is to command with prudence as well as courage. In this international struggle, thousands have fallen victims to the inconsiderate judgment of inefficient commanders.

General Joe. Johnston ain't far off from Vicksburg, and is watching with an eagle's eye an opportunity to take advantage of Grant, and give relief to the gallant army besieged therein. June 25th was a calm, pleasant day; scarcely a wave rippled the bosom of the lake that stretched out before and around us. The day was in every wise suitable for the excursion party that went out that morning in the "Island Queen," a nice little craft fitted up specially for excursions.

The Queen, with loyal pennons floating on the breeze, and a jolly crew and cargo, came alongside Mr. Johnson's Island to get a peep at the "Rebel Home," and the ladies waved their white 'kerchiefs as if to tantalize us, for they well knew we would liked to have been in their stead, with our sweethearts from Dixie by our side. Our only consolation was the thought that all things work together for the best, and that our day would come bye and bye.

The next day was consumed by the usual routine of prison life, and the ensuing one we were reinforced by eighty naughty fellows who couldn't see the thing in an abolition light. And at that identical date the arch rebel Robert E. Lee was threatening both Washington and Harrisburg, producing consternation North and gladness South. During the last days of June several Federal officers were going through our prison trying to enlist a company of Confederates for loyal service in the Rocky Mountains, being afraid to trust them anywhere else. They succeeded in gulling a few into the trap by means of a nicely woven and brightly painted story. Their gain was also ours, for in almost every case, their converts were men who had been driven into Southern service by public sentiment or the conscription act. For some days I had been fast convalescing from my weakness and debility, and now felt almost like a new man.

About a prison, as well as about a camp, there is always a "grape vine telegraph," operated by some unknown, mysterious agent, sometimes denominated "Madame Rumor." Every now and then, when there is no exciting news, and most all hands are moodily groping about, soliloquizing and theorizing upon the dim future, she makes known some startling and often thrilling event that has occurred or will take place.

This time, July 1st, a dispatch says that the Commissioners, Messrs. Ludlow and Ould, are busy fixing up a new cartel of exchange, for a general and speedy release of all parties in the hands of the enemy. So much did we desire such an action that the very whisper of a probability gave unction to our feelings and spirits, even though we had a hundred times been deceived by similar reports.

One pleasant feature of that day which I knew to be true, for I witnessed it, was the receipt of $25.00 from Baltimore by Lieutenant Allen, of my company I could readily appreciate how unctious it was, for I knew part of it would go for butter to go on our biscuits, and for various other little tricks to be shared by our little family of four.

The merchants of Baltimore have done a generous part by the Southern officers in confinement here, having sent fully $1,000 to the sons of those who were their patrons from the South in civil times.

General Bragg has just fallen back from Tullahoma—as we predict—because of having sent so many of his forces off to the support of Johnston, and finding himself unable to cope with the overwhelming force of General Rosecrans. Besides, he can find equally as strong a position between Chattanooga and Bridgeport, to attack which it will require months of preparation by "old Rosy," since he will be so much further from his base of supplies, and will require so much more force to guard his rear from the raids of our cavalry.

Perhaps by the time he is ready to give fight the urgent necessity for troops elsewhere will have ceased, and Bragg be able to draw his men back again. Anyhow, that's our consoling mode of reasoning.

It would seem from the Northern papers of the past few days that "Uncle Robert Lee" was everywhere, and the Feds. afraid to strike any one place, for fear he will turn up somewhere else, not to their advantage. General Ewell, with his ten thousand veterans left under his guardian care by the immortal "Stonewall Jackson," was threatening Harrisburg, which was guarded by thirty thousand militia, under General Couch. Longstreet, Hill, and some other Southern leaders, not unknown to fame, were in various quarters, and might at any time pounce upon Washington or Baltimore. Then the whereabouts and doings of Stuart's, Fitz Hugh Lee's and Jenkin's cavalry was full of mystery.

At the same time there was stirring news from the Mississippi, too; Kirby Smith and Price were reported not far from Vicksburg, threatening to cut off Grant's supplies. Some rebel force had almost completely wiped out the nigger regiments at Millikin's Bend, and General Dick Taylor was making somebody smell frost way down in Louisiana.

The 2d day of July we were allowed to go swimming in the lake. The water was clear and pleasant, and one hundred yards from the shore was not over waist deep, which made it delightful bathing. A guard was placed on the bank to watch us, and pop a fellow if he proved to be too expert a swimmer, and made off for the mainland.

That day the magnetic, not grape-vine, telegraph brought tidings that the 1st of July Meade and Lee had a fight, the contest being undecided at nightfall. The tone of the dispatches was anything but jubilant. General Meade was a new commander, and naturally the army had not implicit confidence in him, because so many of their prime commanders had, in the hour of greatest need, failed, and been laid in the shade. "Fighting Joe Hooker's" light has expired, and he is turned out to graze.

Just see the consistency in the acts of the Federal administration. Hooker ordered the evacuation of Harper's Ferry that he might concentrate and make his army more powerful. Major-General Halleck, the "Dictator," ordered General French not to respect that nor any other order of Hooker, but to *listen to him*. Hooker said if he was to command the army, he must dictate his own policy, and asked to be relieved, which was done.

The very first act of his successor, Gen. Meade, was to withdraw the troops from Harper's Ferry.

Meade is the *seventh* Major-General who has commanded the army of the Potomac, each having been relieved because he failed to out-manœuver and whip Robert E. Lee, acknowledged by Gen. Winfield Scott and the rest of the knowing ones to be the master military mind in America. Never in the annals of warfare has a nation who could boast of so many men with superior military educations failed so signally in producing one who could give satisfaction either to the administration or populace.

Nor is it to be wondered at when the facts in

the case are considered. At the beginning the people of the North conceived that the spirit of revolution could be crushed in three short months, and with 75,000 men. Being deceived in that, they began to count the facilities and materials each party had to raise, equip and subsist an army, and taking into consideration the disadvantages under which we would labor, because of our ports being blockaded, and we severed from intercourse with the outer world, their fertile but not considerate imaginations led them to believe that they had the power and the means to wipe out the rebellion so soon as an army could be organized. History and the deeds of our forefathers had not taught them by powerful examples that eight millions of people, armed in the holy cause of liberty, were not so easily quelled.

What a great relief it is for one who has not seen home or friends for many long months to be able to communicate therewith, and draw comfort and pleasure from their stores of hospitality and love. Such is my situation now. On the 3d of July I had just finished washing my clothes and scalding my blankets, when the mail brought me an affectionate letter from my mother, with $20.00 inclosed to ameliorate my physical wants. Only those who have been far away from friends and in need can appreciate the gratification produced by such a receipt. Concurrent circumstances almost made me forget my hard lot, and conclude that my situation was enviable. In the afternoon thirty prisoners were brought in from Nashville, who belonged to Bragg's army, and with some of whom I had served in the early part of the war.

Here is the substance of what I find in my memorandum for July 4th: "This morning, at early dawn, we were aroused from our slumbers by the sharp peals of cannon not far away. It put me in mind of the roar of our batteries on the river at Vicksburg. A couple of brass 6-pounders were firing in celebration of the 87th anniversary of American independence. Perchance, in a few more years, we of the South will commemorate some other day as our birthday as a free and independent nation. This day is calculated to bring to each of our memories many pleasing and some sad incidents and reflections. The life and hilarity of the citizens in this region remind us of the joyous times we've had in years gone by round about our own homes. In the inland regions picnics and the incident festivities seem to be all the go, while here on the lake shore excursions to the islands and elsewhere on the beautiful lake are the order of the day.

"At nine o'clock this morning the "Island Queen," with a full cargo of live and happy flesh, steamed out from Sandusky to spend the day at Kelly's Island around the convivial board and in dancing, and to-night she makes a grand moonlight trip. We in our island home are spending the day generally in talking and thinking rather than acting. Who is there that can contemplate this our national birthday without feelings akin to grief?

"When we think of the good old constitutional palladium, that grand, beautiful and powerful temple, under whose shadow we were born, and under whose guardian protection we have grown up from an infant republic to be the most able and prosperous nation on earth, and see that noble fabric perverted to unworthy purposes, dismembered, dishonored, it makes us feel unhappy. Although honor and all for which we live have compelled us to dissever the alliance with those who shared the boon equally with us, still we cling to its genuine, intrinsic principles, and are aiming to take them from a mass of corruption to an ark of safety in a goodly land, and we have staked our lives and our fortunes for their protection and perpetuity."

The 5th day of July was hot and sultry. To change the monotony of prison life, on Sunday we had preaching by a rebel minister. There was good attendance, strict attention, and all professed to be well paid in listening to the discourse, which was plain, unvarnished and to the point.

While so many thousands were dissipating and

taking life easy on the 4th of July, the two master armies of the continent, that had been fighting and manœuvering in Pennsylvania for several days, were struggling and dying in an intensely severe contest at Gettysburg. The loss in Federal general officers was the most startling ever known, no less than fourteen being killed, wounded or captured. A Wisconsin regiment which went into the fight on the 3d came out with but forty-six men and a single officer, him wounded. And while all this was going on, the ranks of General Lee were being sadly depleted. He made seven unsuccessful attempts to storm one position of the enemy. In the charges hundreds fell, and General Archer and nearly his whole brigade were captured, and the officers are now here.

The Sandusky *Register* of July 6th said General Lee was defeated and Longstreet killed, but they both yet defiantly ride the storm. The succeeding day a letter from home announced that there was a box of clothing on its way to me, and it made me feel good all-over, for my stock on hand was exceedingly slim, and besides they were not from my own dear home. The same day I bought some gutta percha buttons, preparatory to going into the ring manufacture, and at the same time I purchased a fifty pound sack of flour at $2.50.

We get tired of nothing but baker's bread, and a biscuit now and then is a luxury. Most of us imagine that we can fix up about as good biscuits as the ladies; anyway, they taste as well to a hungry fellow. I may as well here state that my ring business proved disastrous; I lost one button, spoiled a second, and made a botched job of the third, after which I became disgusted with the profession, and turned my remaining stock over to a more expert artisan.

Thirty odd officers of Bragg's army arrived at our house July 8th, and among them were several who had been captured at Perryville, Kentucky, in the fall of 1862, some minus a leg, some with an arm off, and several others on crutches. It seemed strange for the enemy to keep them so long, especially as they could do them no harm if released.

That day the report was that Vicksburg had fallen, and at night cannons fired, and the showers of sky rockets in Sandusky City looked beautiful from our little island home. We didn't put much stress on the news from Vicksburg, but next morning came a confirmation of the report, bearing on its face the shadow of plausibility. Various and curious were the speculations in all parts of the prison as to the veracity of the dispatch, and the probable consequences if it were true, and some were excited and anxious to bet that our noble city was yet standing.

At that date General Lee was at Williamsport,

massing his troops, either for a fracas or to evacuate Maryland, and the Yankees could not determine which. They reported his loss in the late engagements at 30,000, theirs at 12,000; one was too much, the other too little.

It would seem that the notorious and ubiquitous John Morgan made his entrance into Kentucky early in July, and captured the 20th Kentucky regiment of 400 men at Lebanon, where his brother, Lieutenant Tom. Morgan, was killed. Tommy was a former schoolmate of mine, and was a noble boy and gallant officer.

A telegram of the 9th said that Morgan's band had captured two transports below Louisville, and crossed over into Indiana. The people of Northern Kentucky were in an uproar, some praying that the Morgan men might come, others that they might never come, for horse-flesh generally took with a leaving wherever Morgan's boys went.

CHAPTER V.

Rebel's Retreat, off Sandusky, Ohio,
July 31, 1863.

While I was quietly revolving in my mind what should be the order of the day after I had eaten a hearty breakfast July 10th, I heard my name called, and went out, and with gladness met the express messenger with my box from home. The officer of the guard examined it, and finding no contraband, I, with triumphal look and feeling, bore the trophy off to my room, while many a poor fellow who had no friends up North to help him looked after me, thinking, "I wish it was I." My box contained many nice articles of apparel, and the pictures of my mother, sister and grandmother. Olden times and scenes were made fresh to my mind, and I almost involuntarily wished I were in the midst of those scenes again.

But such desires were only produced by the sympathetic impulses of the moment, for in reality I have no desire to go to my home as matters now stand. I could not feel that I was a freeman, nor could I, except for a short time, enjoy the company of those with whom in other days I loved to be. I have cast my lot and my all with a cause containing all the constituent elements that make life agreeable and home pleasant, nor till the fate of that cause is decided do I wish to return to my home.

About ten o'clock at night July 11th, we heard a heavy cannonading in an unknown quarter out across the lake. Some of us were conceited enough to imagine that some Confederates had slipped through, captured a vessel, and were making for Johnson's Island to give us a lift over into Canada. All over the prison fellows were scouting about, trying to learn what was up.

The Sandusky paper of next morning said it was a celebration at Toledo; it also announced that John Morgan was in Indiana with 7,000 cavalry. The news from Vicksburg was vague and unsatisfactory. They didn't know exactly what General Lee was doing, but the predominating impression was that he was manœuvering to bring on an engagement near Antietam, where a sanguinary battle had already been fought.

Morgan and his raiders turned up at Salem, Indiana, the very next day, captured 500 prisoners, burned the depot, and was gone. General Hobson seemed to be after him, with 4,500 men. Southern accounts say that Lee captured 40,000 and killed half as many during his Pennsylvania raid, an exaggeration almost equal to that of the Northern press. Extracts from Southern papers represent our prospects as never brighter. Momentous events have been and are transpiring on the arena of military action, and a few months may bring startling changes for better or worse.

By consulting my diary for July 13th, I find that it was damp and chilly, a stiff gale blowing nearly all the time, and heavy waves and foaming white caps lashing the shores of the lake. The little fishing barks all took down their sails and were hugging the shores. That evening Colonel Gregg, of my regiment, took supper with us, we having pie, biscuit and butter, extra items to soldier fare

A singularity in camp life is that, although soldiers are generally on fair terms, they comparatively seldom visit the quarters of each other, or extend invitations to take tea. It is just like in a great city. Often men camp for months within a few yards of each other without intermixing or knowing each other. As a common thing, a soldier's rations are no more than he can eat himself, and he don't care to call in help, nor is there often an inclination on the part of others, as they have just as good themselves.

The dispatches of that date said Morgan's raid was extending into Ohio, and General Hobson was still just a few hours in his rear, the probability being that he deemed it prudent to keep an amicable distance between columns. John Morgan's boys cared about as much for the militia as a horse does for a fly—they are annoying, but not dangerous. At one place in Indiana the Federals cut the road full of trees for fifteen miles to impede the progress of the raiders. Most probably while they were felling the timber Morgan was quietly going along some adjacent road. General Grierson's raid through Mississippi is thrown entirely in the shade by this daring attempt.

Gunboats have become so famous and so necessary to any marine enterprise, in the estimation of the Northern soldiery, that they even have a craft of that nature upon these waters. During the afternoon of the 15th the sloop of war "Michigan" came gliding into the port of Sandusky. We could not surmise the intent of her visit, unless it was to pacify us and let us know we were safe, and to warn Jack Morgan of the danger of trying to cross the lake as he had the Ohio.

There has been a time when the prowess of iron-clads was claimed by the Federals and acknowledged by us. After the battle of Shiloh, the gunboats at Pittsburg Landing sheltered the flying Federals and terrified our men, thereby causing a drawn battle when victory was in our grasp; and, for some time after, the iron-clads roamed the kings of the waters. But, before the year 1862 had died out, gunboats had dwindled down from elephantine proportions to almost pigmies in the estimation of the Southern soldiery.

General Wheeler astonished the Yankee nation by charging and taking a gunboat on the Cumberland river, with cavalry, and ofttimes since have the would-be monsters fallen a prey to the valiant, unflinching sons of the South.

The press says Lee has recrossed the Potomac, and the Federal populace are railing out against General Meade for not taking him in. But 'tis now too late, "the bird has flown," and the only remedy will be to lay brother Meade in the shade, and manufacture another great commander out of mediocre military talent. The New York *World* said: "If Lee succeeds in recrossing the Potomac, he will be the victorious party, but if Meade can succeed in capturing his army, he may be regarded as having got the best of the game." Now, if the *World* man spoke words of wisdom and truth, Uncle Robert E. wears the crown of success, and has driven to the rear many fine teams, horses, cattle, mules and precious stores.

And they say, too, the rebellion is nearly dead, when the rebel army can go hundreds of miles into their territory, and carry off rich spoils—staying several weeks to collect them. Though the Confederacy is so near played out, they have to steal our darkies, and by draft force their own people into the ranks to keep the naughty, bold Southern lads off of Northern soil.

For an instance of the rigors, cruelties and horrors of war, turn to the siege of Vicksburg. There, during a terrific bombardment of forty-seven days, several hundred women and children were shut up in those fiery walls, living in holes and caverns dug out in the steep banks, and subsisting on the roughest and most meager soldier fare. Several were wounded, and some even torn into fragments by the barbarous shells of the enemy. In a list of the former I noticed the name of Miss Lucy Rawlings, a highly accomplished lady, and an intimate acquaintance of mine.

History tells of dauntless and heroic courage exhibited by women in other days of trial and turmoil, and their sisters of now are not wanting in those traits. The valor and uncompromising firmness and fidelity of the women of this generation will shed a lustrous brightness over the pages of its history that is as yet unwritten except in the minds and the hearts of the people; and when the cessation of this strife allows us to return to the quiet, pleasant shades of home, we can more highly appreciate woman's worth, and will respect and love her more dearly than ever.

So many items concerning affairs inside the lines at Vicksburg, together with the official correspondence of Pemberton and Grant, are now filling the Northern papers, that most of us are willing to concede that both Vicksburg and Port Hudson are no longer ours. The one taken, the other is no longer of any consequence This is a great event in our struggle for independence.

For more than a year, by holding two far separate points on the Mississippi, we have held in check two mighty armies of the North, and cut off national commerce on the " Father of Waters." Now they have, by dint of perseverance and bulldog strength, succeeded in cutting in twain our infant nation, and partially succeeded in opening the track of the river, but never—till we are subdued—can they claim the Mississippi as wholly their own. Every cargo of flesh or stuff sent South will be at a hazard.

Our mail of July 16th brought a check and a letter donating $10.00 each to twelve Alabama officers. The gift was from a young lady in Dubuque, Iowa, who once lived in the South, and profoundly sympathized with us and our cause. The next several days was pleasant weather, and nothing new or strange passing in our midst. All that I had to relieve the tedium of the hours. except the little duties incident to keeping our room in order, was a sweet-scented, delicate *billet-doux*, a reminiscence of olden times about Clay Village. Ky. Full many scenes and incidents through which I had passed in days of yore were made vivid again, and I reveled once more with happy feelings 'midst those realms of elysian joy.

The cry of foreign intervention again resounds through the land, and the whole press is agitating the question, as to its probability, results and the manner of disposing of the elephant. Matters, and the relations of kingdoms and nations in Europe, have assumed such a shape that hostile acts on the part of any of them would not be very surprising. But we have had the soft chat of intervention in our behalf whispered in our ears so often that it has ceased to be a balm to our hopes and anticipations.

The time *was* when we would not have given up the Federal Government for the essence of all the rest on earth. The time *is* when we would gladly welcome an alliance with France, for therein we can see some hope for freedom, prosperity and happiness, while the gulf between us and the North seems so wide and so beset with everything uncongenial and unpropitious that the breach could never be healed.

The Federal Government look upon intervention as a not wholly improbable thing, they, as well as we, believing that interest, not love, would actuate other nations to interfere on our side. Uncle Abraham and his long-headed minions well know that they can't fight us and a foreign foe at the same time, and those who claim to have an inside view of matters say that they are now fixing up a proposition to the South to this effect: That Missouri be a free State; that the people of Maryland, Delaware and Kentucky decide by a vote as to slavery or no slavery; that the rest of the States hold their original status; that we be "high fellow well met" again, and pitch the Northern army into Canada, the Southern into Mexico, increase our territory, and win a fame that will astonish the world. It sounds nice, but it don't taste good, and we can't swallow it.

When the daylight of the 21st instant ushered out of darkness, we found that we had been reinforced by four hundred veterans from Lee's army. It was a splendid battalion, composed entirely of officers, from the rank of Brigadier-General down, General Archer in command. But now the General has been relieved of his sword, and Major Pierson is lord of us all. We work with our jaws and drill with our teeth; the Federal sentinels on the parapet have charge of the guns.

Never were a more gallant set of men, or men who had braved an enemy's galling fire oftener, marched into an enemy's prison house. They are a band of veterans worthy to be likened to the "Emperor's Guard." Among them I found Captain Horace Blanton, a schoolmate of mine at the Kentucky Military Institute just before the war. He could tell me of many old chums who were weathering the storm, and of some who had rendered up their lives in the cause of their native land of the South. They seemed not yet quite sure that Vicksburg was gone up, and expressed even less faith in some folks than we had, measuring theirs by an infinitely minute apparatus.

The last day's fight around Gettysburg was described as the most terrible in which they had ever engaged, and they were somewhat capable of judging of a fracas. Like Morgan's men, they were dreaded by the foe, and since their arrival the sentinels and officers have been more vigilant—all the guards now carrying, in addition to their usual accoutrements, a six-shooter, to make the secesh look sharp. Were there nothing more to check us than the garrison here and the walls that inclose us, we would make them look sharp and get to the rear.

The propriety of making a break is often discussed, and various are the ingenious schemes laid out. We all feel sure we could make impromptu ladders enough to scale the walls, and thrash out the garrison with the brickbats that make the platforms for our stoves. But then comes the insurmountable difficulty about getting off the island, for the main land is three miles distant. Some are so fool-hardy as to be willing to risk the chances for that; but long-headed ones won't bite, for when their calm judgment weighs the matter, the chances for defeat and disaster by far out-balance the other side.

The "Sandusky lying *Register*," as we call it, of the 22d, reported 1,500 of "Morgan's horse-thieves" as having been taken, which proved to be only too nearly true. The following day twenty-five prisoners taken at Perryville, Kentucky, the past year, and who had been held for months with paroles in their pockets, were sent off for exchange With them went a fellow whose "*nomme de guerre*" is "Buck," and who was sent from here to Vicksburg last fall to be exchanged, but refused; this time he was anxious to be off.

We wrote many letters to send through the lines to our friends, who, if so fortunate as to get them, will be quite happy to hear that we are in such a thriving condition. Some of the letters were examined and approved by the commanding officer; many were sealed and secreted in boot-linings, hat-crowns, coat-linings and other cute places. Necessity was the mother of many inventions at our house.

At that time the weather was splendid, being clear, cool and bracing, and it was a real luxury to get up early and snuff the pure breezes as they came wafting from the Canadian shores over the crystal bosom of beautiful, delightful Lake Erie. The other day a jolly fellow said: "If a body couldn't live easy, laugh and grow fat here he ought to die, for we have nothing to do but to eat, drink, sleep and be merry."

Our sutlers are driving quite a brisk trade just now. Twice each day they bring in a wagon load of vegetables, provisions and all kinds of stuff, and at night all is gone. The machine works in this wise: When money comes for a prisoner, it is retained at headquarters on the outside, and credited to him on the sutler's book. The sutler gives us checks to any amount desired, we at the same time giving him an order on the Post Commandant for an equivalent sum. The checks are taken at the sutler's store for the amount on their face, which ranges from five cents to one dollar. Such is our circulating medium in prison.

Our sutlers are quite obliging, especially when a fellow has a smart chance of funds to his credit. As we have no other source of procuring what we want, they charge us to the limit of their conscience, and in some cases it seems wonderfully elastic. Their little establishment is altogether a popular place, being crowded from morn till night; nor do the Southern boys care for expenses when they can raise the "all needful."

The mail of July 24th brought me a bundle of New York *Ledgers*, from my mother, and they fill up many vacant hours, to say nothing of the interesting and instructive matter in them. The next day Lieutenant Lotspeich received $20 00 from a relative in Missouri, and it made us all feel glad—I mean myself and the three Lieutenants of my company—for it is, in part, a family fund. We feel and act toward each other just as the members of an affectionate family would at home, which is the proper spirit to be exercised among soldiers, if they would live and toil together in harmony.

The day after that, the "lying Sandusky *Register*" *made us feel so bad* by saying: "Lee can't get to Richmond; Meade is about to take him in." The Federal press must have something new and exciting to make their papers sell and *to please the people*. One day they mourn and rave that General Lee has slipped through their clutches with so many rich spoils; the next, they get wild, and imagine, whether or not, that he must *not* get back, and tell us how he is trapped. Our papers down in Dixie have caught the contagion, and tell some whoppers, too

During the night of July 25th a man died in the prison hospital, and his funeral was preached next day in front of the building. Hundreds congregated around with solemn faces and sorrowing, sympathizing hearts. The effects produced upon a soldier by seeing his comrade fall on the battle-field in his country's behalf are not near so touching as under other circumstances; it may be because one necessarily nerves himself up to the point of being partially callous to the unpleasant things around him.

The field of strife is not the only place where the evils and horrors of war may be seen in aggravated forms. Go to the hospital, where those stricken by disease lie around by hundreds on their humble couches. You find them in every conceivable condition, from the emaciated but cheerful, prospering convalescent to the wild, haggard mortal whose coil of life is almost wound off. There is a picture worthy of grand admiration and profound sympathy—admiration for the heroic manner in which they bear up under affliction, all for their country's sake, and deep sympathy, for they have no mother, sister nor other dear friend to soothe the aching brow, and by a thousand little deeds of kindness ameliorate their sufferings. Reflections upon such a scene must move any heart, unless it be like adamant.

The morning of July 28th brought a host of Morgan's boys to our island home. Among them I found Colonels D. Howard, Smith, Basil Duke and Dick Morgan, as well as Captain Dawson, and Lieutenants Fenwick and Leathers, of my county, and many others that I knew. For some days previous we had regarded their capture as almost certain, for it is no exaggeration to say 20,000 Northern troops were on their trail. Notwithstanding the prevailing impression in the North that Morgan had 7,000 men, it is a fact that at no time did his force north of the Ohio exceed 2,500 cavalry. The Governor of Indiana, with his militia, General Burnside, with all his available troops, a greater portion of the cavalry from Kentucky, and a goodly number of transports and gunboats, all joined in the chase to surround and "gobble up" the notorious raiders.

About the time of the arrival of Morgan's men the vile secessionists thrashed out the loyal troops and took possession of Richmond, Kentucky, which has before been under rebel sway. The Federals retired in no very good order in the direction of Lexington, and that city was put under martial law. Groundless fears were entertained that Mr. Bragg might be on his way to the glorious Blue Grass region of Kentucky again.

The lightning fluid tells us that the War Department are preparing to build two more huge military prisons—one at Rock Island, Illinois, the other in Maryland. That is anything but ominous of a speedy exchange. Maybe the President is going to take the balance of our army by detail, then make us give bond, take the oath, go home and be better boys till next time.

The Hon. John J. Crittenden, of Frankfort, is

just dead. He has been a great and good man, and has wielded a mighty influence at home and in national affairs. Though patriotic, and though it grieved him to see the dissolution of the government that he had spent his life and energies in perpetuating, he did not approve of the policy assumed by the Administration.

And, sure enough, General John H. Morgan has been caught at last, and is now in the calaboose at Cincinnati. For nearly two years past he has been the most daring, most feared and most successful raider in our Western service. The sequel proves that this time he acted bravely, but not wisely. But the greatest and most tried military chieftains sometimes strike erring blows. Even Napoleon, whose army and whose military genius were regarded as almost invincible, fell while in the zenith of his glory.

Considering the size of his command, the achievements of General Morgan have eclipsed those of almost any other cavalry officer, North or South. He has been over more of the enemy's country in rear of their main armies, and has destroyed more public property and army transportation, railroad and otherwise, than any leader with the same force in the Confederate service. In the beginning of his career his achievements were looked upon as almost miraculous, and even the women and children doated on and loved to talk of John Morgan.

Last summer he was actually taken from the cars and detained over night at Marietta, Georgia, by a crowd of ladies, who, having learned that he was on the train, assembled to see and congratulate the gallant chieftain Alas! all things mortal must perish and pass away; but the deeds of men may be made imperishable, and, in the galaxy of brilliant, dashing heroes that entered the lists for Southern freedom, no name will be more conspicuous, or shine with more lustre, than that of John H. Morgan.

In the evening of July 28th, 160 officers from Port Hudson came in. They looked jaded, and showed evident signs of having seen hard service. The story of their endurance and suffering is enough to make the heart of the whole South beat with gratitude to and sympathy for them. For 48 days did they lie in the intrenchments, the scorching rays of a tropical sun coming down on them by day and the chilly dews by night. For a whole month they subsisted on mule meat, and, in order to make their corn last, had to grind it, cob and all. They manfully resisted the multiplied assaults of the enemy till they only had a single day's rations and ten rounds of ammunition left, and necessity, not the valor of the enemy, compelled them to give up.

The 29th day of July was a bright era in the history of my prison life. A nice box of provisions, anticipated for some days, made its welcome appearance that afternoon. It was a gift from my grandmother, who is ninety years old, and who, from my earliest childhood, has wanted no greater happiness than in ministering to my every want. The box contained one old ham, two cans each of butter, honey and blackberry jam, sausage, apples, maple sugar, cake, a pair of pants, shoes and daguerreotypes of my uncle and his daughter.

The same day I got, per express, $50.00 from my mother, which made my joy complete, and I felt like a thriving farmer who, having reaped the fruits of his labor, has plentiful stores of everything around him and feels at ease. Every day of my life I realize more fully the adage that "home is the dearest and best place on earth." The farther I roam and the more dependent I become upon, and the better acquainted with, the world, the more I learn to love home and its inmates.

On the 30th day of July Lieut. Chambers and Dick Taylor, of Anderson county, Kentucky, came in from Camp Morton, where they saw my brother, all right. I had supposed he was sent on exchange a month ago. Taylor, who is a private, exchanged name and place with an officer, and is now known here by the authorities as "Lieut. Hoggins." He tells me that, on the day of his capture, he was on his third horse since morning.

Our prison pen is now chock full of live rebels, and there is a constant hum, and busy scenes of many kinds, constantly going on. Some are blocking out rings, some filing shell, and some hammering out gold or silver for sets. Again, some are making fancy canes, some stools and shelves, while others are playing cards, checkers or chess. In another quarter not far away you may find one fellow making pies to sell, while another deals in lemonade, a third sells ice cream, and a fourth has cakes and beer to exchange for sutler's checks. Two tailors are kept all the time employed, and, to wind up with, we have a boot and shoe shop.

Then at the pump is another constant busy scene—for there, at almost any hour of the day, can be found from twenty to fifty men, with sleeves rolled up, going into a tub of clothes with as much grace as though they had been brought up at the calling.

Some 1,400 of us having to get water from the same pump, from daylight till dark there is a crowd at, and a stream to and from, that necessary institution.

And from eight A. M. to five P. M. four clerks are kept busy in the sutler's store. The first thing there is a rush for the morning papers, of which we soon eagerly devour the contents. In the next place, butter, onions, beans, cabbage and potatoes must be secured in time for dinner, provided a fellow has the checks. Then the day is consumed in selling wearing apparel and notions of all sorts. One team is almost constantly on the go, hauling in rations and wood. And the postoffice is a busy institution; at every hour in the day some one is inquiring for a letter. Some make a daily pilgrimage to the postoffice who don't get a letter to the month.

Our postal arrangement is in this shape: We write our letters and drop them, unsealed, into a box with our rebel postmaster. The Federal postmaster opens and examines all letters received for us, and about ten o'clock each day brings them into our office, and takes out the mail deposited there, to be inspected and forwarded, if not contraband. I have both written and received several contraband letters; in the one case it would come back marked "contraband;" in the other, the letter would be destroyed and the envelope sent in indorsed, "letter contraband."

After such a showing forth, the world must acknowledge that our "Confederate city" is more thriving than many a Federal city of greater age and pretensions. Confederate scrip is now worth only five cents on the dollar. As we came by Memphis we got double and quadruple that much.

The sporting gentry here buy up Confederate from needy fellows, and bet quite freely. Thousands often change hands at a single sitting.

On the last day of July I went swimming in the lake. The most important news of that day was that Morgan and the officers with him had been sent to the penitentiary at Columbus, Ohio, *to be treated according to the rules of that institution,* as a matter of retaliation.

A retrospective glance at the month that has just faded away and been blotted out from the book of time—but not from the memory of man or the record of history—will show some of the grandest achievements and the most persevering and valorous deeds of men that the history of modern warfare presents to view. Vicksburg, the great Confederate fortress and stronghold, upon which the interest and welfare, almost, of the two parties hung, and which astonished and won the admiration of the whole civilized world, has fallen. Port Hudson, a Gibraltar of lesser magnitude, but wearing none the less bright laurels, has had to succumb—not to the superior valor, but long protracted siege of the Federal arms. The army of Virginia and the army of the Potomac, each standing in front of the capital of its nation, have met in the clash of arms again and again, thousands falling on either side, and millions of property being destroyed. A division of rebel cavalry have traveled hundreds of miles to the rear of the Federal army, crossed the Ohio, and roamed the States of Indiana and Ohio, but they, too, have gone the way of Vicksburg and Port Hudson. The loyal forces have, with terrific earnestness, been bombarding the defenses at Charleston, but with no material result, and several not unimportant battles have occurred among the cavalry commands in various quarters.

Perhaps never since the prime days of this republic have so many and so thrilling and important events transpired in the same length of time. As to what will work out from it all is too deep and mysterious a problem for the ingenuity or penetration of the human mind. We must admit that the Federal arms have been more successful than ours, and that a seeming gloom is cast over the Confederate cause. But ofttimes the darkest hour is just before day; and, as the darkest days of our forefathers, in their struggle for the same cause that we are now vindicating was near the close of that struggle for freedom, maybe all is for the best, and that a brighter day is not far hidden in the future. God grant it!

CHAPTER VI.

At Home, Johnson's Island, Ohio,
August 5, 1863.

To-day two months have gone to that eternal bourne from whence nothing earthly returns, and still we are imposing on the hospitality of this institution, with every plausible indication that we will continue to sojourn here for an indefinite period. Though, about a year ago, commissioners from each government met and agreed upon a cartel of exchange that should be permanent, there is now as wide a split in the matter as between the governments themselves.

Negro equality, guerrillas, misunderstandings and faithlessness on the part of both belligerents have been the prime causes in the case, and to-day, because of that infidelity, not less than 75,000 soldiers are languishing and perishing in Northern and Southern prisons. Such are the horrors and injustice of war, because the men of great rank, but small caliber, who rule and determine the destinies of the people, are inadequate to the trust bestowed upon them. I can not see any probability that we will break up camp and emigrate South till both parties back down from the laws and affirmations made by each, and agree upon more equitable terms. The "American citizen of African descent" is the great bone of contention at present.

Here comes an instance of the barbarities inflicted because of the injudicious acts of "big (?) men:" We arose from our humble couches of straw on the morning of August 1st to find a chain of sentinels stretched along the whole front of our barracks, and a squad of soldiery at Block 12, besides the regular guard. I surmised the state of affairs in a moment, for Morgan's officers were in Block 12. It was soon found out that fifty of them, the highest in rank, were to be taken to the penitentiary at Columbus, Ohio, to be held as hostages for General Straight's men, captured at Rome, Georgia, while on a Southern raid.

Before sun up all the field officers and captains filed out at the small gate, and went submissively, but not without burning thoughts of the future, to serve out the will of the Federal dynasty. As to the right, propriety and necessity of retaliation, in some instances, there can be no doubt, but it seems unjust and cruel that innocent men should suffer in return for the evil doings of the wicked, especially when so many cases could be averted by the wise administration of superiors.

"The siege of Charleston is progressing finely," so says the Federal press, but still it seems that General Gilmore's forces had to retrogress the other day, being driven back on Morris Island with heavy loss. The Feds. have for a long time, with what they term "the best naval fleet in the world," and a host of land forces, been pegging away at that great Southern port, the cradle in which the rebellion was first rocked, and where its fire will be the last to die out, even if the city should fall or sink into ashes.

The telegraph says Mobile will soon become the theater of active military operations, for both armies of the West are tending to a focus at that point. It is not at all unreasonable to conclude that the next effort of the Northern army will be against that position, for, considering their geographical situation, and their great faith in being close to water and iron-clads, we would naturally suppose their inclinations would lead them thither. The wonder is that the place has not been attacked before this, for it is a point of importance to us, and its defenses are far inferior to those of Charleston.

Mobile has some manufacturing facilities for our army supplies, its harbor gives protection to blockade-runners, and it is on the main railroad channel from Mississippi east. But that would not be so deadly a blow, for there is a railroad just finished from Meridian, Mississippi, to Selma, Alabama, from whence there is communication by steamboat to Montgomery, striking again the main trunk of our railway. Even if we should have to give up Mobile, the loss here would be a gain there, for a garrison and many other troops would be thereby relieved to strengthen our armies in the field, and it would require a large fleet and heavy land force to hold it.

The value or the importance of true friends is seldom known or appreciated till one gets in a dependent situation, where, if he gets the luxuries or even comforts of life, they must be dealt out to him by other hands, and where the sympathies and kindly assurances of other hearts are necessary to strengthen and encourage his hopes and anticipations of a better time coming. What a balming solace it is for one to feel that he is not an outcast upon the world—that there are hearts beating in unison with his own—that there are those who would share his toils and sufferings, lighten his burdens, and scatter beauteous, fragrant roses in his every pathway.

I feel that I am thus blessed, for now, when in adversity, the same as when in prosperity, my friends are true to me. August the 2d I received a letter and picture from a cousin in Kentucky, to freshen the reminiscences of the past, give food for contemplation now, and, in future days, when I am in another region—maybe on the couch of affliction—to remind me that there are those in the native land who invoke the blessings of heaven and earth on me.

This afternoon about one hundred of General Lee's officers arrived. They are mostly cavalry officers, and gallant sons of the "Old Dominion State." They fill the void left by the *evacuation* of Morgan's men. This evening at four o'clock a minister, formerly of Stonewall Jackson's brigade, preached in front of our block. His sermon was full of good, sound logical reasoning, but he was altogether the most eccentric speaker I ever saw. His gestures of body were so passionately expressive as to give one a feeling of uneasines. Still he enchained a respectable audience for a full hour, and his peculiarities, with his good sense, will never fail to draw hearers.

August 3d.—This morning I purchased a sack of flour and a new bucket, and ice-water now inhabits our shanty. My old countymen, Chambers and Taylor, took supper with us this evening, and said we had several extra touches to cavalry fare.

General Herron's division of Grant's army is now on its way 'round the coast, "bound for

Mobile," but it's not known for certain when it will get there. There is no telling where Mr. Banks will go, since it took him so prodigiously long to go from Baton Rouge to Port Hudson, a distance of fifteen miles. But one thing is sure—most of his army are going home, their term of enlistment having expired. A dozen regiments have arrived at Cairo in the past few days, bound home—mostly Maine and New York troops

It appears that Father Abraham and his helpmates are having a hard time with the conscripts down East just now. The visible mobs in New York and other large cities have been suppressed, but, like Southern cities within the Federal lines, though mute and submissive, the fire is not out, but only lies slumbering till the weight of oppression is taken off. Certainly there would not have been such powerful and stubborn resistance to the draft had not those engaged in the rebellion against it believed it unjust. Force of arms can quell their resistance, but can it change their opinions? It will prove like the attempt to change the channel of the great river at Vicksburg.

A reaction has for some time been going on in the Federal nation, and the elements of resistance to the Administration—not the old Union in its purity—which are measurably in subjection, have, now and then, burst forth, only to be smothered again by brute force—not moral conviction.

A study of precedents in civil revolutions, and a survey of the results, portend that this nationality is forever gone; yea! that the two nations into which there is being made an attempt to divide it will not stand, but that other petty kingdoms will rise up, causing a diversity of opinion and interest, and a confusion, the end of which no man can see. If such should be our fate, God protect us from the avaricious intrigues and greediness of the nations that are now looking down upon us with eagle eye and wolfish rapacity. I will not suffer myself to believe that such is to be our destiny, but the teachings of history point to such a conclusion as not at all impossible.

To show the disparity in spirit and earnestness between the two sections, let us quote a semi-official record from a Northern paper: "We have nearly three hundred blockaders and war vessels of every description on the high seas. The Confederate naval fleet consists of but three vessels; yet they roam the seas with impunity, destroy trading vessels by the wholesale, and have captured and burned millions of treasure; still our armament allows them to go at large. Where is the fault?"

'Tis in this: The Southern navy feel that they

are engaged in a great and good cause, upon the issue of which they have staked their all—their very existence—and they pursue their calling with a zealous vim, thinking rather of the good to their country than the harm to themselves. Not so with the Federal navy. They are serving for pay—not principle; I mean the generality—not all. It is more pleasant, and not half so dangerous, to be drifted about on the bosom of the deep, with good wages accumulating, than it is to risk the uncertainties of a naval conflict. Under no other view of the case would it be possible for a few to be so successful against so many, capacities being equal.

August 4th.—Election day in Kentucky. So brave and chivalrous a people as Kentuckians have ever had the name of being should feel ashamed to leave on record for their posterity the history of the manner in which the Commonwealth is now governed. A free and law-abiding people as they have been, it is difficult to conceive how they can submit to the dictatorship practiced over them by the powers that be. A military stewardship has superseded civil laws and rights, and the freedom of speech is a mooted question.

Telegrams inform us that the *Union cause* has carried in Kentucky by 20,000 majority. Appropriately we might ask, why not twice that? since there was allowed to be no other cause, for he that dared go to the polls and cast his vote in opposition to the Administration did so at the peril of his liberty, as soldiers and bayonets were all about to warn the people that the Administration *must* be supported—right or wrong. Though the Federal Constitution says the right to speak and to publish one's thoughts is a sacred one, not to be interfered with, yet thousands have been and are languishing in prison because of using that right.

When will this reign of anarchy, misrule and deception cease to exist? It appears not till the whole American government is revolutionized. Those who have been deemed wise and reasoning men rush on madly and blindly into the *maelstrom* that must lead to inevitable ruin. The masses engaged in this mighty and brilliant conflict are actuated by good motives, but very many of the leaders—those in whom the people put their trust—act with sinister designs, and care not how many they drag down, if they can thereby elevate themselves. But there is an All-seeing Eye that will finally rule the destinies of nations, punish the guilty, and reward the just with life everlasting.

At noon to-day the remainder of Morgan's *horse-thieves* were shipped for unknown quarters, the boys in blue intimating that they were going on exchange, but the prevailing opinion was that it will be an exchange from prison to penitentiary.

The fellows left in gay spirits, laughing at the idea of having their heads shaved and becoming convicts, and promising to remember their ungenerous benefactors at a future day.

One poor fellow was sick in the hospital, and the officer who called out their names ordered him "to be brought dead or alive." My heart burned within me and my tongue craved to tell him what I thought of him. A number of privates of Morgan's command who have been captured at various times and sent here, fixed up to go out with them, expressing a willingness to follow the command anywhere; but they have to tarry yet a little longer.

This evening we had a fine and refreshing shower, making the heated air far more pleasant. The changes of weather here are sudden and singular; in the morning the sun may rise upon a cloudless sky, and before noon the rain will be pouring, and, though to-day is almost insufferably hot, to-morrow may be bleak and chilly.

To-day, 5th instant, the Island Queen, which makes regular excursion trips, passd close round the island with a cargo of heaven's last and best creation, and they seemed to be astonished that the rebels looked so well and perfectly contented. I dare say they imagine not of the restless, latent fire that is burning in the bosoms of these true but unfortunate sons of the South. Perchance at a future day their brothers and sweethearts will have occasion to tell them that the fellows who seemed so tame and harmless on Johnson's Island made them smell frost in the shape of gunpowder and lead pills.

An exciting yacht race came off in Sandusky bay this forenoon, and many tall sparred and heavy reefed vessels are now cruising about 'twixt us and the city, some of them having no visible means of livelihood.

This morning's *Register* had at the head of its telegraphic column, in brazen capitals, "Yancey is dead," and the whole abolition crew no doubt felt as that paper, and rejoiced at his exit, for he was one of the first and staunchest champions of Southern rights and Southern independence. In his fall we have lost a bright star in the constellation that forms our first Congress. His wisdom and foresight have had great instrumentality in organizing and building up our new government, and the void made by his death will be deeply felt by the whole South.

The same telegram said General John B. Floyd was lying dangerously ill at his home in Abingdon, Virginia. The noted ones of earth, like all things else, are passing away.

While our friends at home are worrying themselves and sorrowing about our misfortunes and want of comforts, we are perfectly easy and contented, and perhaps more safe and comfortable than the majority of them, for we have no cares, and being all birds of a feather, speak what we please. We have plenty to eat brought to our very door at no cost, nor do we trouble ourselves as to the morrow. How many at home can say they are even half so well off?

He that will can find consolation in almost any situation, but the soldier is better prepared than the civilian to be contented anywhere and any way, for he has, in a great measure, given up his liberties to enhance the interests of his cause, hoping for remuneration in time to come. He learns to regard whatever comes, whether good or bad, as necessary for the advancement of his cause, and with humble patriotism meekly submits.

Perchance this very day the folks at home had a good dinner, with some of my old friends around the board, all concurring in the wish that I were there to enjoy the meal with them, no doubt picturing in their minds a disagreeable, loathsome situation for me. But I am sure they did not relish their meal more than I did the splendid repast just finished, which seemed all the better because of our own manufacture.

To-day we had for dinner, besides our regular bill of fare, green apple pies, honey, pickles and ice water, and old Kentucky ham, butter and biscuit graced our board at tea time last evening.

Then we often have baked beef and potatoes, and every few mornings some splendid hash, seasoned with red pepper and onions. Where's the lord, with his gorgeous mansion, rich china and silver plate, and servants in livery, that, according to station, outlives us? Indeed, does he live as well? We enjoy ours—not he.

This day two months ago we entered these high, white walls, and we've hoped and we've dreamed of freedom again, but the day of delivery seems rather to recede than approach us. When at home in civil life the idea of going into a prison to stay shut up from the world for months was terrible to me, but, of a truth, one can get used to almost anything.

It was two years ago on the 2d since I left my home in Kentucky to try the unknown realities of military life in the South. Then I left a smiling and prosperous land, teeming with grain and fruits, the light-hearted farmers rose with the lark, and all the households were happy. The demon monster, civil war, had not yet reached her borders, and there were many—yes, very many—who were carried away, and took unction to their souls by the deceptive and absurd policy of "armed neutrality."

The history of past rebellions of a similar nature convinced me that our lovely State must, sooner or later, feel the venomous sting of war, and, as my feelings and sympathies were not in a passive state, I conceived it my duty to give my mite of strength in the cause I believed most nearly right. So, consulting none others than my conscience and sense of duty, I bade good-bye to home, friends and all, and wended my way to a Southern camp, and have, in the short space of two years, seen and experienced more than a life-time of civil existence.

Then there were free intercourse and traffic among the people, and railroads, stage lines and the public highways were safe for travelers. How now? Then the once "dark and bloody ground" had not felt the hostile tread of devastating armies, nor had there been a clash of arms on her soil. But now all those dread realities have been enacted. The rich and blooming fields of my native State have been changed into desperate battle grounds, her noble sons have met in deadly array, and stained mother earth with their life's blood in attestation of love for country and principle. Fathers have been left to mourn, mothers to weep, and sisters to pray for the success of the cause in which their brothers are engaged. But I'll turn away from so unpleasant a picture and silently contemplate the bright side of the panorama that we hope will pass before us bye and bye.

August 8th.—This day has been appointed by

President Lincoln as a day of fasting and thanksgiving for recent victories. I feel sure the occasion is not now reverenced with that unanimity of sentiment which was felt upon annual thanksgiving days a few years ago. Then we could thank God that we had been so prosperous and so wisely governed. Now, though we adore and reverence His goodness and kindness none the less, our thanks are turned into supplications to avert from us the evils of wicked men, who, for self aggrandizement, would sink a nation.

Yesterday was pay day for our cooks. I have mentioned somewhere else that, in the beginning, we hired a couple of Lieutenants of our mess to cook for the whole, paying them per month $15.00 in greenbacks, or four times that much in Confederate. They having faithfully served us for two months, begged to be relieved from further duty in that line. No one seemed anxious for the office, so Captain Jim. Law, of Georgia, took the responsibility on himself and hired two cooks, and matters roll on smooth as ever again.

Captain Law is an important personage in our midst—the soul of honor, good nature and drollery; he seldom buttons his shirt collar, it being either flung to the breeze or confined with a shoestring, and whenever about the cook room, handling the dish rag, he is sure to put it in his pocket, instead of where it belongs, and it is an uncommon thing to find him wearing more than one suspender at a time.

The other day the sutler brought in new peaches and fresh corn, the first of the season, and delicious to the taste, but gouging on the pocket book. And, too, the pump man from Sandusky repaired our old pump and put in a new one close by, watered by a leaden pipe extending out into the lake, so now we can get lots of good water without waiting long, and our water is cooler, purer and better than might be imagined.

Some days ago, being desirous of sending my likeness to my mother and some other friends, I made written application to the commandant of the post for permission to go over to Sandusky City to have some taken. Next morning the application came back endorsed "disapproved," nor was I in the least disconcerted, for I expected even the same, but I thought there was no harm in asking as long as there was a possibility of success.

For several days past Lieutenant Smith, of my brigade, has been busy making a watch fob out of a piece of gutta percha rule; it is ornamented with silver and pearl sets of a variety of shapes, and is a beauty. He has sold it for $10.00, a big pile in this institution. On the 17th of May last this same Smith, with twenty-three men, kept Sherman's army corps from crossing at Bridgeport, six miles above Big Black bridge, Mississippi, from eight o'clock A. M. till two o'clock P. M. He had so fortified the place, and so manœuvered his men, as to make the impression that he had a large force. It may well be imagined that the General was chagrined to find his prize a corporal's squad instead of a brigade. From that time forward the Lieutenant has borne the title "Kirby Smith."

The eyes of the Northern Confederacy open wider, and they begin to think and reason for themselves more earnestly as their blood and treasure flow more freely. A Northern paper says: "The North has twenty-one millions people and all the means to equip and subsist a most powerful army. The South has eight millions of people, and no means, except as they invent or produce them, to carry on a hostile war.

"Aside from their resources at home, the North can communicate with all the civil powers of the earth, and procure the greatest and best warlike inventions and auxiliaries. The whole Southern coast is blockaded, with no means—except as a vessel now and then runs the blockade—of getting foreign help of any kind. Now, if, with all this disparity of facilities, they fail to subdue and bring back the rebellious States, who is to blame?"

A great statesman once said: "The battle is

not always to the strong, but to the active, the vigilant, the brave and the just."

About twenty officers of Scott's cavalry, lately captured in Kentucky, came into prison yesterday, and among them was Lieut. Bearden, formerly post adjutant at Knoxville, Tennessee, and with whom I have had many a festive time thereabout. Capt. Gammon and Lieut. Fain, of my command, have each just got a full suit of Confederate gray from a cousin in Louisville, Kentucky. Said she: "'Tis my greatest and almost only pleasure to aid a Southern soldier." The boys will ever remember and love her for her kindness.

If I could truly delineate the manners and customs, or portray the occurrences of a single day in our prison, it would, without doubt, be full of interest to an outsider. The great variety of talent, wit, peculiarities and eccentricities discernible in different localities and countries is here more fully portrayed than in the outer world, for the reason that the panorama of life is longer and more constantly before our view, the characteristics being developed on a smaller space of ground, but there being all the resources necessary to call them forth. Here, as everywhere else, there are some characters of more than ordinary prominence, who attract the attention and remarks of all in their vicinity, some by one peculiarity, some by another.

The personage that tickles me most is one Capt. Youngblood, of the artillery service; he is highly intellectual, fluent and witty; once edited a little newspaper in Alabama. He can tell yarns on himself and the world at large in a more ludicrous and laughable manner than any clown I ever heard, and he can draw a crowd as infallibly as water runs down hill.

Our mess is not without its man of celebrity. Captain Thomas Burgess Brantly, my next door neighbor and frequent visitor, is the distinguished character alluded to. He was born and reared on Tar river, North Carolina, and now hails from the home of the Arkansaw traveler. If life, activity and a flexible tongue are precious endowments, Brantly is rich. He is generally first up and last to bed, and *ad interim* is diffusing merriment and laughter all about; he is not dangerously affected with piety, and is always ready to tell a good joke or hard yarn on himself. Said individual dances, sings, visits, talks, laughs and has a happy time generally, nor is his fame circumscribed by the narrow limits of our mess.

In Block 3 a Georgia Lieutenant did carry the day, but can't raise a crowd any longer. In Block No. 1 Charley Stout, once of Dan Rice's circus, carries the palm of victory in the humorous line. For the present I'll pass over the lesser lights.

If a civilian should some evening come to our island and peep over the walls after the declining sun has shaded the square between our two rows of buildings, he would not imagine us to be prisoners, for he could scarcely conceive how those in bondage could be so full of fun and contentment. The scene is not altogether dissimilar to that of a lot of schoolboys at recess playing all sorts of games.

We get up when we please; some rise with the sun, and some are driven from their bunks by the announcement of breakfast. No one is allowed to leave his quarters till the garrison flag is hoisted—a little after sun up.

When we have anything extra from the regular soldier fare we cook it ourselves; at least a half dozen extra cooks are around the stove at every meal, baking biscuit, making hash and other things. Notwithstanding the jam and crowd, everything goes on smoothly and agreeably; as in milling business, first come, first served.

About half after seven we have roll-call; the drum beats for all hands to turn out, a Yankee corporal for each of the thirteen blocks comes in, gets us into line, calls our names, and then counts us, to make certain that no one has dug out. All titles are dispensed with; the loyal corporals don't recognize any of the Rebels as Captains,

Colonels or Generals, nor are we in the least troubled over it.

At eight o'clock the garrison have guard-mounting, attended by drum, fife and brass band. About the same time the sutler comes in with the morning papers, butter, eggs, onions, cabbage and a variety of notions. We dine about noon; but before that—an important item—our mail comes in at ten o'clock. Just after dinner Mr. Sutler brings in yesterday's New York papers, which we buy in great numbers and read with avidity. All the afternoon a beautiful span of spirited bays are busy hauling in wood for the various messes to cook with.

I forgot to mention that early in the morning the ice-wagon comes in, and a little later the milk-vender, each giving us a very good article at a fair price, and their supply is seldom equal to the demand. And I didn't say that our rations are brought in and issued to the various messes about nine o'clock each day. We generally sup a while before sundown, then collect in groups on the various wood-piles, stair-steps or shady plot of grass, and tell of adventures in the wars, travels, incidents, manners of society and characters of the people where we have been, and get off good jokes on each other.

The fellows from the different States—all the States South are represented here—try to get a run on the boys from some other State by telling jokes and yarns on them, and it is a remarkable fact that, though it is the profession of soldiers to fight, they seldom fight each other.

After the drum beats for retreat and the flag goes down, which is about sunset, no prisoner is allowed to leave his quarters. At nine o'clock the garrison band regales us with several spirited tunes, and at the tap of the drum, at half-past nine, all lights in the prison must be extinguished. After that, all within our walls is dark and silent, save the rays of a dozen lamps reflected over the prison yard and the lonely tread of the sentinels on the parapet.

This, the 8th day of August, the officers of Price's army taken at Helena, Arkansas, on the 4th day of July, arrived from Alton prison, several of them, Col. Johnson, of Arkansas, among the number, wearing, as ornamental appendages, a ball and chain, for the offense of trying to escape from prison. They had made a hole through the ceiling and roof of their quarters, but some traitor or spy informed against them, and a detachment of Yankee boys was paraded to greet them as soon as they made their exit through the hole. Several cases of small pox came in with them, and were quartered in a tent in one corner of the prison yard.

They did not give the Alton House a very good name, and promise never to patronize the institution again if they can consistently avoid it, for they don't admire the situation of the concern, nor the compactness and hight of the yard fence, and last, but not least, the landlord and his sub-officials did not distinguish themselves for hospitality and generosity.

This appears to be a general sunning day, the whole prison yard being spread with bed-ticks and blankets, and a health-officer is going the rounds inspecting rooms, cooking departments, slops, and everything that might get out of order. Lime is occasionally distributed to destroy the stench of decaying matter and purify the air, and, all things considered, the whole premises are kept remarkably clean and healthy. Captain Scoville, who has charge of the internal affairs of the prison, visits all parts of the institution frequently, and is very kind in listening to the various questions and supplying the wants of the prisoners.

When a lot of prison birds come in, each is given an empty straw tick, and they go out in squads to a barge of straw at the landing, and in a little while come back with their ticks stuffed full, and in the same squad may be noticed the General, the Captain, and the private.

Several evenings in each week the big gate facing the lake is opened and Confederate detachments of perhaps a hundred allowed to go and bathe in the lake, and, as most all are glad of the opportunity to get out of the walls and into the water, we have to take it by turns. 'Tis a pleasing sight to see them, like so many ducks, splashing about in the water, and riding the waves, if the lake is rough. Several fellows with blue jackets and silvery bayonets sit on the shore during the performance to see it well, but not too well, done, for well they know that there are ducks here who would risk swimming three miles to Sandusky if they knew of any birds of a feather there to receive, clothe and help them on to Canada.

Last night there was a laughable, ridiculous occurrence in camp. Along about midnight the sentinel on post number five cried out, "Halt! Who goes there?" There being no answer, he challenged a second and a third time; click, click, then bang went his fusee, his heart perhaps nearer his mouth than the bullet went to the object aimed at. Still it stood like a ghost. So his neighbor on post number six cracked away with the same result. And now, with feelings perchance alike the bold soldier boy for the first time in battle, he lustily yelled out for the corporal of the guard, who came promptly, espied the object, but could not make it out till he took a lamp, came inside the square, and marched up to the bold figure, which was our new pump, put in the other day—"that and nothing more." Harper's sketch man ought to get hold of the story. The boys christen the affair "the skirmish with the pump."

CHAPTER VII.

Southern Hotel, off Sandusky, Ohio,
August 12, 1863.

Yesterday evening, as the slanting rays of a glorious sun were gilding the loftiest branches of the oaks in rear of our barracks, a puffing steamer hove in sight, and, passing through the opening in the blockade near the lighthouse, directed its course directly toward the island, and came within a few hundred yards of the shore, which is less than thirty yards from our prison wall. It was a gay excursion party, and all of them saluted the Southern boys, who were out watching them, but whether in esteem or derision must be for a longer head to say.

Last Sabbath there were divine services in front of Blocks Nos. 4 and 13, a large concourse listening to each sermon. Colonel Lewis, of Missouri, a Southern Methodist, who has just arrived, is said to be possessed of more than ordinary merits as a preacher, and will most probably deliver us a religious discourse next Sabbath.

The other day I had a letter from my brother at Camp Morton, Indiana, stating that he and four others of my company were left there sick when the balance were sent to Fort Delaware. Two of them are yet ill, and Page Gregg, poor boy, has gone to his eternal home. He was just past eighteen, and was kind-hearted and submissive to his every duty. Away down in Tennessee is a good father and a devoted mother, who put their precious boy under my charge, but cruel war has snatched him both from my guardian care and their loving embrace.

A letter from Lieutenant Hoggins, *alias* Dick Taylor, informs me that the last squad of Morgan's men sent from here are now in the penitentiary at Alleghany, Pennsylvania, and that, so far, they have been closely confined, two in a cell, but that they are anything but downcast because of their situation.

To-day there is no news of stirring interest, and the probability is that active military operations will be partially suspended for a time, as all the main armies have very lately been actively engaged, and it requires time to recruit, repair damages and make additional preparations for another campaign.

Now I will give a few more sketches of professional life in prison. Nearly every vocation in the glossary of human labor has its representative here. The lawyers have no clients at all, for we have nothing to squabble over, and are inclined to be peaceable and law-abiding anyhow. The doctors kindly dispense their charity to those sick in hospital, where there are now about thirty patients, half a dozen having died since we came here. In our midst we have some natural artists and draughtsmen. One firm has out its shingle, "Drawing or Painting of any Description," and have executed several admirable and accurate colored drawings of the island and prison. Captain Barron, of my regiment, has somewhat of a talent for making pictures, and passes a greater portion of his time in sketching and painting.

The other morning at the express office I saw a fellow who was trying to DRAW, but could not. The matter had resolved itself into this shape: A box came by express for Lieut. Minor, which, upon being inspected, prior to delivery, was found to contain a package of tobacco, a box of cigars, and 24 bottles of something for the inner man. Officer said he must deliver it to the surgeon as contraband. Minor said, "Can't you let us have just one bottle?" Officer said, "Can't do it," and Minor's chum then chimed in, "Well, then, can't you manage to bring a bottle up to our room after a bit?" That evening there were some mighty jolly fellows up in Block 2, and, as no effect comes without a cause, one can imagine the sequel of the matter.

An order has been received from the War Department forbidding the sutler to sell us any boots, and prescribing what shall be sold, which ain't much. But when a fellow has the shinplasters a Dutch Jew sutler don't stand very heavy on orders.

Ofttimes has it been demonstrated that necessity is the maternal ancestor of invention. We Dixie boys are fully aware of the scarcity of many little articles of prime necessity among the ladies of the South, and we don't forget that, as in the past, so in the future, we may at some time be dependent on them for socks, gloves and other things.

Yesterday I bought some needles, pins and other little tricks designed for Southern maidens who have been friends to me, and I will aim to out-Yankee a Yankee in getting my chattels through the lines.

I have laid away a little sack of coffee for a good old mother I know in the South, and, if she now knew what was in store for her, I know her mouth would water, for she ain't had a drink of the pure stuff for many a day.

Last night six rebel officers came in from Fort Delaware, and this morning several others from another quarter. The Federal authorities announce that it is the intention of Mr. Lincoln to collect all the rebel officers at Johnson's Island, and hold them here till Mr. Davis makes an appropriate reply to his communication with regard to exchange and retaliation. We have no voice in the matter, and can only await the result of coming events. True, we have a longing to be on Southern soil and breathe the air of freedom once more, but, if the honor of our government and the furtherance of our cause demand it, there is scarcely an one here that would not, without a murmur, suffer many more months of martyrdom.

The sutlers surely imagine, and have some assurances, that they will drive a fat trade for some time to come, for they are building an addition to their store house; and, though only commenced yesterday, it is now almost finished, for the prisoner boys, anxious for something to do, pitched in and made light work of it. Hereafter there will be two departments—one for dry goods, the other for groceries and vegetables, and two clerks will preside over each.

Last night we, that is myself and room mates, put our dirty clothes to soak, this forenoon we put out our washing in good style to dry, and to-morrow, like the old folks at home, we will iron out the wrinkles.

The loyal forces here don't put much confidence in us representatives of the Southern Confederacy, nor do I blame them, for the fellows are continually trying to play off pranks on them. We are not allowed to have any intercourse with the sentinels on guard, and those who come inside the prison on duty are forbidden to carry out anything for a prisoner, and are closely watched by the head officials; still, a contraband letter or something else will find its way out every now and then.

A slop cart comes in every day to haul out, in barrels, the refuse of the kitchens. For some days past we have noticed that a guard accompanies the slop man, and curiosity tempting us to pry into the why of the matter, we learned that he had entered into an agreement with one of the Southern chivalry to cover him up in a slop barrel and haul him out. When the plot was almost consummated somebody "let the cat out of the wallet," and Mr. Rebel had to be dumped out.

On lightning wings the news comes to us that the Federal godhead, cabinet and wise men of the North are caucusing, scheming and concocting plans whereby the rebellious States may be brought back into the sisterhood. Supervisor Halleck has, by some mysterious means, found out that the populace, and many of the leaders of the South, are willing to play quits and come back. The real motor power of their deep solicitude is foreign fear rather than domestic love. A war with France or England could be easily gotten up; they feel that a divided house can not stand, and they conceive that, though we still shoot at them, we love them better than a foreign people, and they further conclude that we, being weak, and both of us in imminent danger from abroad, would gladly go into an alliance for mutual protection. Mistaken souls! they dream not of the reality.

There are to-day two Republican and two Democratic parties in the North, consequently a complete jargon and confusion. The Radical Republicans would have peace on no other basis than the immediate and complete extinction of the institution of slavery; the Conservative Republicans hate slavery, but are willing to gradual emancipation: the Unconditional Union Democrats are willing to abide by the edicts of the Grand Mogul, *compelling* their consciences to admit that it will all be well; the Simon-pure Democracy would have the Constitution carried out in spirit and in truth; they believe that the people are the government and the public officials the servants, not the masters of the people, to preserve in purity and operate in good faith that Magna Charta of liberty and government bequeathed to them.

The President, not yet quite lost to all sense of national honor and justice, has not pitched his weight into either balance, though his sympathies are Republican. The gordian coil is so momentous, complex and intricate that no mortal genius can unravel it; an omnipotent, higher Power must be appealed to for a righteous solution of the problem.

The eyes of the whole world are now gazing on us, and the universal press is teeming with speculations as to the probable result of the present state of affairs, some seeing a bright future for one side and some for the other.

August 14th.—For several days past Captain Brantly and myself have been reading a religious work urging objections against the doctrine of punishment in the world to come, and advocating that of Universalism. Night before last we had a discussion on the subject in my room, Brantly continually protesting that he was no Universalist, still he could not see how a greater portion of their arguments could be got around. When the drum tapped for "lights out," we stopped just where we began, perhaps neither wiser nor better.

Last night there was prayer meeting in the mess adjoining ours, Lieut. Methvin, of Georgia, conducting the exercises, and Captain Hodge, of my regiment, leading in prayer. The brilliant divine from Missouri, Colonel Lewis, now belongs to our mess. Yesterday we had a splendid mess of string beans and beets for dinner at our house, the first of the season for us.

A little incident has just occurred calculated to mollify the monotonous routine of our thoughts and emotions. Two sisters of Lieut. Brand came from Missouri to see him, which, of course, was contraband, unless it could be done by getting on an eminence some where close by and peeping over the wall with a good pair of opera glasses, which expedient was adopted as a " dernier resort." Of course, they love all the rebel boys; it was a novel thing, and there were many gazers, and not a few expressions of kindly feeling and sympathy were exchanged by gestures, waving of handkerchiefs, and wafting kisses on the breeze.

An order has come from the War Department, restricting the amount of clothing for prisoners to one suit of outer and a change of under clothing, but the chink can come along as usual, and with it a sharp fellow can get anything. Some of the rioters in New York are reaping the fruit of their work; numbers are being arrested daily and tried, and a part of them find lodgings in Sing-Sing for from three months to three years. The great rebel privateer Alabama is again spreading consternation and destruction amongst the American shipping; a large merchant vessel has been seized and converted into a war ship, and not a few have served as bonfires to light the ocean all around.

This day I was the happy recipient of a letter from my mother, full of sweet and consoling sympathy. Oh! what a blessing it is for one locked up in prison to have such a mother, one whose every word and every sentiment is calculated to make a son happier and better. And I am just in receipt of a half-dozen New York *Ledgers* from home, which will keep me busy and contented for several days.

All the fore part of to-day I have been engaged in making potato pies after a fashion of my own; we had one for dinner, which was pronounced as good enough for anybody. I spend some part of most every day in cooking, for it furnishes employment, and then I like the sequel. I fix up most of my dishes after a style known to nobody else; in fact, they are experiments with myself, but I seldom fail to get up an eatable dish, though in the case of a certain "bread pudding" not long ago, I made almost an utter failure.

Although I can wash first-rate, I never tried to iron a linen shirt till yesterday; my starch was too thick, my iron too cold, and instead of turning to a glossy surface, the stuff formed into little rolls and balls under the iron, and when I at last gave up in disgust, the garment looked worse than when I began. I have a sutler's ticket which will surely make the shine come upon my linen next time.

This evening, when the sun had so far declined as to make a shade on the east side of our barracks, about one hundred of us, including generals, colonels, captains, sergeants and privates, engaged in an exciting game of town ball, furnishing fun and exercise till the flag went down, when perhaps four score voices yelled out all over the prison, "Rats, to your holes"—not very classic, but suggestive language. Sometimes we have foot races, and at other times the boys wrestle—in fact, anything is done that will give exercise and keep up an excitement.

August 15.—The daylight is gone, and a serene, starlit sky is looking down on us and our islet home, and a phosphorescent blaze from the lighthouse over on yonder point lights up the lake between here and there, and a dozen reflecting lamps cast a soft light all over the prison yard.

Some of the inmates are sitting out on the verandahs discussing war and home topics; others are in their quarters, some sitting straddle of a bench playing poker or seven-up, while others stand by gazing on. Some are sitting or standing in groups singing a familiar hymn or a favorite war song, while others are writing to the dear ones at home, and still others are reading trashy novels; some are fast asleep, while others are merrily scuffling around and over them.

And now, while all these states of being are

around me, I, in the quietude of my own little room, will proceed to write up my day's journal by the flickering light of the stump of a candle, which is glued to our little shelf as a candlestick; nor have I any table upon which to write, except a piece of plank and my lap.

Neither the grape-vine nor the electric telegraph worked much to-day, and we were very well satisfied, for it is so awful hot and sultry that the fellows were too lazy to talk about it. It is a great fashion for the Southern gentry here to go *en dishabille*; many of them don't wear shoes half the time, and coats are seldom seen, except hanging on a nail. Those who have good clothes take more pride in looking at them than in wearing them, which was not the case with them in palmier days.

Just before the call to quarters this evening one of our notables made his appearance upon the upper balcony of Block 3, and as the fellows could see he was ripe for something, they called for a "hard shell" sermon from the honorable gentleman. Without much persuasion, he launched forth on one of his rich sermons, which soon brought out a considerable crowd, who would sometimes burst forth in shouts of applause, then again in laughter, and when he had finished three rousing cheers went up for "Youngblood." Then, as an afterpiece, he told one of his lawyer-preacher stories in his own style, and the merry crowd dispersed to their homes to laugh and grow fat.

And something occurred in the evening to put them in a humor for laughing. Uncle Tommy Stevenson, or "Old Pap," as he loves to be called, who, by the way, is our postmaster, and has been here about a year, got a suit of clothes yesterday from Missouri, and this evening he came out dressed in grand style, presenting a visible contrast to his usually sloven garb. The prisoners flocked around him as little boys would about a monkey, and beset him with all kinds of questions and jokes, and it was fun to him to humor them to their heart's content. So goes life in the prison land.

August 16.—This is the Sabbath day, and the last one in which I shall write in this journal, for I am near unto its end. Whether or not it may prove interesting to those into whose hands it may fall I can not tell, but to me its contents are, and ever will be, precious; for 'tis full of real life incidents, inseparably connected with a great era in my life—incidents that, though their existence shall fade away, their impressions can not, for they are indelibly stamped on my memory, and the effects of some of them are in my heart. Though the future is, perchance, fuller of events, and mighty ones, in which I may be a participant, still none can erase those already imprinted on my mind and remembrance.

From seven to twenty I was most all the while in the schoolroom, and had every reasonable facility for acquiring knowledge, but all that theoretical learning is not worth the stern practice of the past two years. Then I saw the world, its people and machinery, political and physical, through the dark and uncertain medium of fallacious and prejudicial history. The virtues of the good were over-estimated and the wickedness of the evil exaggerated. Then I, as the rest of mankind who had not seen life in all ranks and phases, had too great credulity in the prominent men of our land; I believed what they thought and said was surely so.

Now I have learned to believe that there are none without deficiencies, and that if you would truly know a man, you must weigh him by some adequate standard; for some, one test will do; for some, it requires another. Extensive observation has convinced me that interest and self-aggrandizement are two powerful elements in the characters of most men, and that those traits have had a full share in bringing on and keeping up this strife.

Sabbath afternoon, 16th of August. — This morning the Rev. Mr. Samplin preached for us, and this evening there will be services in front of

Block 13. Our ministers invoke the blessings of Heaven upon our cause; and pray that wisdom and strength may be given to our President; and they urge the propriety of observing the 21st instant, a day appointed by President Davis for "fasting, humiliation and prayer." It may be that the authorities will forbid an open expression, but the workings of our hearts are incomatable—not to be ruled by force.

All around the prison now is calm and still, like a city on Sunday; the mandates of the Good Giver of all are not wholly forgotten, though 'tis true that soldiers become more careless of life and less considerate, or at least seemingly so, of hereafter than circumstances demand. But the army, when properly disciplined, has not that demoralizing influence accredited to it by the world. In fact, many men see their own bad traits so disgustingly portrayed in the conduct of others that they repent and are reformed.

This struggle has heaved up oceans of hidden, mysterious character and talent. Many, very many, hitherto unknown to the world have proved as shining jewels, and not a few have been weighed and found wanting. Verily, it is a time that tries men's souls.

AUGUST 18—A RETROSPECTIVE GLANCE.

I can not look back over the soldier life I've spent and think of the thousand happy associations

I've found, of the many nice cities I've seen, of the beautiful uplands and delightful valleys, and of the picturesque hills and grand, rugged mountains where my feet have wandered, without feelings of regret—regret because a great many of them have passed away from my sight forever.

Let him who will soliloquize on the dangerous, turmoiling and comfortless life of a soldier, and feel in imagination and proclaim aloud that there are—there can be—no joys attached to such a mode of existence. I speak not from conceptions, but from a taste of the stern realities, and can say, with a free conscience, that the past two years of my field, camp and social experience have been quite as agreeable as any like period in my former life.

I entered upon this struggle, as I did my collegiate course, determined to persevere unto the end, and take all that came as that which was to be, murmuring not at hardships or disappointments. My rule of action has worked happily, and now I'm ready, so soon as relieved from duty here, to strike out on another year's campaign in Dixie. My heart is as light and my faith in the justice of the cause as strong as the day I entered the lists.

From Camp Boone, Tennessee, in August, 1861, by a circuitous and zigzag route to Vicksburg, in May, 1863, is the line of my adventures, and my chain of memory lingers and finds something 'round which to entwine in every vale and along the banks of every rippling stream on the route.

Many hundreds with whom I have traveled and toiled through those scenes are gone; yes, their bones lie bleaching on the banks of Green river, Kentucky; on the plains of Donelson, Shiloh, Perryville, Murfreesboro, and around the classic fortress of Vicksburg, and wherever any army camped, the rough oaken slab tells of the resting place of him that was stricken from life by disease.

If our hearts are not adamantine, can their sympathies help still clustering 'round those spots made hallowed by the blood of our loved comrades, and is there not a monument of memory reared on each battle-field and in each graveyard?

Pleasing recollections do now, and ever will, cling around those in social life about whose homes I happened to be and whose generous hospitality I enjoyed. There are very many mothers and sisters in the South land who, by their kindness, have endeared themselves to me by links that neither time nor distance can sever.

'Tis now just three months since our capture—since we were transferred from the Department of General Pemberton, first to that of General Grant, then to that of General Burnside, and prospects bid fair that we are now permanently located, though the rumor is afloat this morning that news has come from Washington pointing to a speedy exchange or parole. Some fix the further time of our stay here at one month, some at six, some twelve, and others for the war. Express letters, with money, are coming in at a rate that indicates the majority are fixing up for a long stay, and I would not be surprised if their heads were level on the subject.

Let us here take a glimpse at the panorama of war presented to view. It would seem that Generals Grant and Pemberton had agreed mutually to suspend hostilities for a time, for they are inactive, and many officers and men are being paroled, and Commodore Farragut and a host of Yankee Generals are now on a visit North. Perhaps the tide of battle will swell again and sway toward Mobile before the close of the year.

The armies of Lee and Meade are comparatively inactive, but watching each other with eagle eye. Bragg and Rosecrans, though they seem to be dormant, are, no doubt, making strategical moves. Generals Burnside and Buckner are each standing off watching for a favorable hour. The cavalry everywhere, save in West Tennessee, seem to be doing little else than picketing and scouting. Generals Beauregard and Gilmore, at Charleston, are "pegging away," each confident of success. The Trans-Mississippi Department is in full blast, and the probabilities are that some definite results will be accomplished there the ensuing fall.

It would be futile to speculate where the vast tide of battle, stretching in two great military lines, almost from the Atlantic to the Pacific, will tend, or what the result will be, for no man knoweth.

The Federal nation believe that the defeat of the rebellion is now a fixed fact, and the Confederate nation is as much determined to be free as the day the first blow was struck. We must leave it to high Heaven to determine the justice of our cause, and to mete out the rewards we severally deserve.

CHAPTER VIII.

JONESBORO, WASHINGTON COUNTY, EAST TENNESSEE, }
July 1, 1865.

Almost two years have rolled into eternity since I finished up my first sketches of "Camp, Field and Prison Life," but in the meantime, as subsequent chapters will show, I have not been asleep, neither have I been idle. All through the year 1864, and up to date, I have kept brief notes of what was transpiring all around, promising myself, at an opportune time, to write them out in a more elaborate form; and to-day, as I look over those suggestive jottings, the panorama of prison life for 1864 is as vivid as though it had passed away but yesterday.

The first manuscript was written to fill up the lonesome, vacant hours generally attending life in prison, and this is penned under similar influences and circumstances, the difference being that then I was a prisoner of war, now I am a prisoner of State. Then I had a host of companions and a large boundary for exercise; now I'm all alone, and my extreme limits are a room, perhaps sixteen feet square, with a small door and two diminutive windows, so checkered with iron bars that only a moderate portion of light finds its way in to me; and, although my situation might seem extremely disagreeable, almost terrible, to those hearing of it, I am resting comparatively easy and content, "waiting for something to turn up."

It may be well to tell, just now, why I am here. In the spring of 1862, while serving in the Department of East Tennessee as a military detective and general police officer, I was ordered by Col. William M. Churchwell, Provost Marshal of the Department, to come from Knoxville to this county with a detachment of six men, and arrest and deliver at his headquarters a man who, he said, had been repeatedly reported to him as notoriously disloyal and dangerous to the Confederate cause. I came on the cars to Jonesboro, one hundred miles, and went, at night, twenty miles, through a rugged, mountainous country, crossing a swollen river at a dangerous ford, took the man into custody, stated to him what was my duty and what his, under the circumstances, and promised him the kindest treatment in our power if he did not rebel or attempt to escape, but notifying him explicitly that if he attempted to get away it was our duty and orders to fire on him

He acquiesced in all I said and made fair promises, but afterward broke to run, and was fired upon, receiving a wound in the calf of the leg and one in the small of the back. I thought the wounds were more serious than they proved to be, so I took him to his house, sent for a doctor, and we made tracks from that quarter, feeling certain that the "mountain men" would collect and overwhelm and murder us if we tarried there. Fearing misconceptions and misstatements of the facts in the case, I published immediately in the Jonesboro *Express* a detailed account of the whole affair, and no one seemed to censure me for my conduct, in consideration of the circumstances, nor did the Provost Marshal think I had acted improperly when I reported the matter to him.

Time passed on; I went to the Department of Mississippi and was captured in May, 1863; spent nearly two years in a Northern prison; was released on parole, and, the war having ended, I, on the 1st day of June, 1865, started from Western Virginia to my home in Kentucky with a gladsome heart at the idea and prospect of meeting those who, after four years' absence, seemed dearer to me than ever.

After a tiresome journey on foot of one hundred miles, I reached this point on the 7th day of June, little suspecting any evil ahead, feeling unconscious of having committed any wrong. I repaired to the home of Mr. Slemmons, whose good lady had been like a mother to me in days of yore, and expected to take the cars next morning for home, by the way of Knoxville, Chattanooga, Nashville and Louisville. When I entered the town all the children, white and black, playing in the streets, recognized me, though they had not seen me for three years, and my presence was soon published all over town.

In a little while I was waited upon by Mr. Shiply, county sheriff, and, by the way, a clever gentleman, who requested me to appear before a magistrate to answer to the charge of "assault and battery, with intent to kill." I went straightway, and the only witness was one of the men who had gone with me to make the arrest. He made no gross misstatement of facts; then I had my say, which was mainly to corroborate and explain what he said. I claimed that I was acting strictly under orders, and that if there was any wrong, a higher power was responsible. Mr. Magistrate could not see it in that light, and said that, though I was acting under orders, and was justified by Confederate laws, it all amounted to nothing now, for the Confederacy was "played out," and those laws were illegal, and that he must consider it as an offense against the civil laws, and so deal with it. When his august majesty put the matter in that shape, I had no longer any ground for defense, and went to jail in default of $2,000 bail.

The next number of the *Jonesboro Union Flag* contained an article headed, in flaming capitals, "*Arrest of the Notorious Capt. Wash!*" Among other things it said: "This individual made his appearance on our streets and seemed to take the liberties of a martial knight, which was a specimen of the most audacious impudence that has occurred during the war, when it is remembered that this is the same notorious individual who, in 1862, took a posse of rebel guerrillas, went into Greasy Cove, in this county, and, at the house of an old and esteemed Union man, Mr. Tinker, literally shot him to pieces." The public will know how to appreciate the foregoing when they learn that its author was connected with the same office when it belched forth Southern sympathies and plead for the Southern cause. In olden times the renegades from any cause were its most inveterate and ignoble enemies, and history seems to be continually repeating itself. The sequel to my Jonesboro imbroglio will be found in the closing chapters of this journal. It is enough here to say that, in three weeks, Tinker was in the mountains bushwhacking again, and was killed by some North Carolina troops perhaps a year after.

As it is now almost certain that I will have to tarry here several weeks, I will neither cry, swear nor laugh over it, but calmly settle myself down, and employ a greater portion of my time in writing out, from the sparse notes in my memorandum, my recollections of the year 1864.

But, before entering thereon, I will remark that I am kindly cared for by my custodian and his lady, and receive many favors and delicacies from the ladies about town. And in regard to the situation of the country generally, I would observe that East Tennessee is, probably, in the most unhappy predicament of any section in the South. The railroads are open throughout its extent, and goods of every description are plentiful, nor are many of the people actually suffering for food, but the antagonism caused by bitter partisan feelings, and the countless instances of abuse, insult, cruelty and inhumanity perpetrated by both parties—the offender and the offended often being old neighbors and friends—has produced such a state of feeling that hundreds of families, who are now in exile, must remain away, and many others must leave, if they would prosper or be happy.

If matters go on as at present, almost the entire property of nearly all the prominent rebels will be confiscated or taken by damage suits brought by Union men who have in somewise fared badly at the hands of the Confederates. I am happy to say that in Virginia, where I have been since the downfall of the Confederacy, such is not the case. The citizens there are generally on as good terms as before the war, and the amount of litigation is comparatively small.

And now, before going back to bring up the incidents of 1864, let us take an inventory of my visible household and personal property. I look around me and behold: for my bed, two blankets; for my pillow, a haversack, containing a change of under clothing; for my water bucket, a half-gallon tin measure, now sitting on a brick. I have but one chair, which seems to indicate that I don't propose to have much company. My hat and coat hang on the nail where I placed them the first night I took lodgings here, to stay till I get ready to leave. The foregoing, and a small stock of stationery, two novels and three newspapers, complete my stock on hand. Imagine the grated door and windows from the interior of any ordinary county jail, and you have the picture complete.

When I glance through my note book at some of the items that helped to fill up the year 1864, there comes rushing to my mind and before my mental vision ten thousand things not recorded in my book, but which made a vivid, unfading impression on my recollection, and to-day I have a pleasing remembrance of many of those prison scenes and associations.

But there are not many pleasing recollections connected with the very beginning of 1864. The first item jotted down in my diary is: "January 1st. Coldest day of the season, and the coldest for several years; wood rations short, and saws and axes in demand." Without doubt, it was the coldest day I ever experienced; it was impossible to keep warm either by going to bed or hovering round our stoves, they red hot. The most violent exercise had but little effect in warming the body or hands, and wherever a drop of water touched it congealed instantly, and I knew of several bunks being burned for fuel. Everybody, both gray jackets and blue jackets, kept indoors, unless compelled to be out, and the sentinels, who were often relieved, paced their beats at a double quick all the time.

The 2d day of January was almost as frigid, the thermometer standing 10 degrees below zero, or 42 degrees below the freezing point. Sandusky bay was now tightly frozen over, and there was a world of ice all around us. Our mail came over on the ice, and that night several fellows whose proper place was inside the pen, proposed to take advantage of the temporary crystal bridge connecting us with the main land, change front to rear, and make a demonstration on Canada. It was so intensely cold that the guards generally kept close in their sentry boxes. Four valorous lads from the cotton States eluded their vigilance, scaled the walls, and made tracks for the British Possessions. One lost his gloves, and his hands were so frozen that, at the end of a few miles, he had to give up; another got sick from extreme exertion in the cold, and laid by several days at the house of a Copperhead near Toledo. When he resumed his journey, and took the train for Detroit, which is near the Canada line, a detective, who was on the lookout for just such fellows, nabbed him, and the next day he was at his old post, taking a free lunch with Uncle Sam. The other two had better luck, and in a few days sent us glad tidings of their safe arrival in the domain of Queen Victoria.

January 3d, Colonel Cluke, of Kentucky, died very suddenly in his quarters—disease not clearly defined; nor was that the only case in which a prisoner had been cut down, almost without warning. In fact, many of the diseases about prison seemed to assume a different type from the same diseases in camp or in civil life.

On the morning of the 4th the wind commenced blowing from the east, and by noon the ice had been driven from the open lake on to the blockade east of our prison, till it was piled up from ten to thirty feet high, and perhaps a mile long. In the afternoon a number of Yankee soldiers went out on a skating expedition, and to view and explore the magnificent scene; and from our position the scene had a striking resemblance to the pictures and tales of explorers among the icebergs in the arctic regions.

That evening a large amount of express matter, that had been accumulating at Sandusky for some days, came in, and, as was always the case, it was thrice welcomed. After supper I went to the hospital to see some sick friends, and I noticed three corpses in the dead room. The extreme cold weather seems to have increased the mortality, which, for a month before and after that time, was greater than for any like period while I was there. The following day, when I went to visit some friends at Block 12, I found them building ladders and plotting to escape that night. The ladders were made of benches stolen from the mess rooms. Just about the time the scheme and preparations were complete some traitor in our midst informed the authorities, who caused the ladders to be confiscated and the scheme abandoned. During the day the weather moderated very much, and the snow fell to the depth of four inches.

The 6th was clear and cold, and the daily papers from all parts of the country came filled with descriptions of the effects of the bitter cold weather; many trains were blocked up in every quarter, and both persons and stock were frozen to death all over the land. Many sleighs, horses attached, came over on the ice that day; some parties came on business and some for curiosity and pleasure. The post commandant received orders to make out a roll of five hundred prisoners for exchange, and who will think strange when I say the whole prison was wild with excitement and joy.

And here let me record an act of Yankee kindness and generosity. That day Major Scoville, prison superintendent, presented to the members of my room two dozen delicious apples. Nor is this the only time I will have to mention kindness at his hands; never have I met with a more kind Federal officer. In this connection I will note an incident, containing some of the milk of human kindness, which took place at the incipiency of my imprisonment. It was before I got any clothing, money, papers or anything else, and I was longing for something to read, to take my thoughts off of unpleasant things.

I learned that Major Scoville had a library at his office, and seeing that he was inclined to be accommodating, I asked him if he would bring me in something to read. To my pleasant surprise, he asked me to go out with him to his office and make a choice from his library, which I did. While I was scanning the books, preparatory to a choice, he went back into his little bed room and brought forth a silver cup and an old-fashioned jug, saying, while a pleasant smile wreathed his countenance, that it contained a little "old rye" for medical purposes, and that he seldom drank with rebels, but, if I said so, we would see what it was good for. When it is known that I am a creature possessed of more curiosity than anything on earth, except a woman, the world will not judge me harshly for being tempted to test the merits of Scoville's best.

I believe it was the 7th of January that the sutler was ordered to close out straightway; we could not see any reason, except as a retaliatory measure. One thing which is not down in my note book, but which I remember well, is that Mr. Sutler left me with $2.50 worth of his checks, worthless when he went away, and it was at a time when money was money with us.

Our fuel was hauled to us in the shape of cord-wood, and each morning a Yankee corporal would bring in and distribute to each block an ax and a saw, which were carried out at night, for fear we might devote them to unruly purposes.

One evening Colonel Johnson, of Arkansas, and a Captain Somebody, disguised themselves in loyal apparel, and when the time came for the axes and saws to go out, each collected an armful and marched along. Leaving the tools at the proper place, they left the island and struck out afoot to visit some of their friends in Canada. But they had not gone far beyond Sandusky before they were recognized as Southern gentlemen and furnished an escort back to our home in the lake. At most of the Northern prisons it was a custom to punish prisoners for attempting to escape, but with us they were generally simply relieved of what they had contraband and turned loose—always inside the pen.

No papers were allowed to come into prison on the 8th of January; we didn't know why, unless it was that they contained news too good for us unpatriotic fellows. That day there were a hundred conflicting rumors on the subject of exchange—one which was ever and anon in the minds and on the tongues of a great many of those fellows who had been caught in the overt act of trying to break up the government, and had therefor been consigned to short rations and narrow limits. It seems that at that date full power had been given General Butler to effect an exchange, and we were eagerly expecting something good for us to turn up. And, to add to the stir in camp, a rebel Lieutenant who had applied to take the oath, was detected by his comrades and kicked out of prison by his room-mates, and a squad of loyalists had to come in to quiet down the excitement 'mong the Southern boys.

On the 9th the excitement and flurry rose again to even a higher pitch than the day before. The Sandusky *Register*, which, though we hated it, we were always glad to get, contained a telegram saying that all the prisoners were to be removed from Johnson's Island to Fort Delaware and Point Lookout. In a very short time groups of secesh could be seen all over the prison pen laying plans for escape on the way, and some almost conceived that they were actually gone, so sure were they of getting away. But full many a time did our hearts swell with joy and hope only to collapse again in bitter disappointment; and well do I remember that on that day, as well as the whole week previous, I in vain watched the mails for letters. My correspondence was one of my most potent sources of comfort.

The succeeding day Colonel L. M. Lewis, of the Seventh Missouri, preached for us. He was one of our most talented companions and decidedly the most interesting divine in prison. He roomed next door to me, and was, for a time, my tutor in French. The same day Captain Barnes, of the Masonic fraternity, was buried by the Order, of which Colonel Lewis was President. And here I will record my good opinion of that Order. From early childhood I had imbibed a dislike to anything hidden or secret, for I imagined that whatever was meritorious would not suffer by being brought out into the light. But now I take it all back, and give my testimony in behalf of Freemasonry as a good and valuable institution. During my stay in prison I had ample chance to watch its workings.

A little flock of perhaps three hundred of the Order had been gathered up from every quarter and sent to stay with us. They were regularly organized for such charitable ministering as was in their power among the fraternity. If one was sick the brotherhood were detailed to wait upon him, by day and by night, till he got well; and if he had no means, a collection was taken up from the scanty purses of his comrades to procure whatever dainties or comforts were to be had; if he died, they gave him the most decent burial possible. At first they proposed to procure a metallic case for every member of the fraternity who might die, but soon found it inexpedient, for want of means. In many ways did the Masons prove themselves worthy, and many an incident have I heard of humanity, prompted by a Masonic brotherly feeling, on the field of strife; sometimes it would be the victorious Federal showing kindness to the unfortunate Confederate, and sometimes the rebel soldier dealing out kind words and sweet comforts to his Masonic brother though a foeman in another cause.

My memorandum says that on the 12th an escaped rebel was caught, and that I had an argument with a Yankee Major. Of course it was Major Scoville, and the subject abolitionism or treatment of prisoners, for we often had friendly discussions about those matters.

The day after that a brigade of veteran troops arrived from the Army of the Potomac, and many were the surmises as to the object of their presence. It appears that the authorities were fearing a revolt among us, and were preparing to make our stay doubly sure. The whole brigade crossed Sandusky Bay on the ice. The day was balmy and magnificent.

I took two books that I had just finished reading to the "circulating library," and traded them off for others. That day Captain Broughton, of Texas, my bunk mate, returned to his quarters from a long stay in the hospital, where he had almost breathed his last with the small-pox. He remained in his room several days after being taken sick, and I slept with him till the small-pox broke out on his skin—until then we did not know what ailed him. For several days after that everybody, my room mates included, was very shy of me, but I was not in the least alarmed, nor did I ever have the least symptoms of the disease.

There was a fresh fall of snow on the 15th, and the lads with their lassies from Sandusky City were sleighing on the ice all around our place of abode. Our mail and express matter came over on the ice, and I received the photograph of a good lady friend. The papers said Gen. Longstreet was advancing in East Tennessee, and that there had been a fight at Strawberry Plains, which was one of my old camping grounds, and that day we got an extra good ration of wood, which was not an unpleasant item with us. The next day was delightful, and Brig.-Gen. Terry, now commanding post, came in to inspect the prison; he talked mighty nice and promised better rations, but took care not to send them.

Next day was Sunday, and the snow having melted, the whole prison yard was a pond of slosh. I spent the day reading E. Bulwer Lytton's "Caxtons," and there were pleasant but false rumors about the sutler returning. On Monday a United States army surgeon inspected the prison, and passed a high encomium on the cleanliness and neatness of our room, and in fact our domestic arrangements were in better and more systematic shape than most any other room in prison.

That day I built a new patent right chair, we installed a new cook, and my notes say that we *enjoyed* slim rations and increased appetites, nor do I doubt it, for it was a universal complaint.

It snowed almost incessantly during the day and night of the 19th, and the ground was covered to the depth of ten inches next morning, and all hands were full of glee and in a humor for snow balling, at which we had a regular old-fashioned good time. The garrison guard, which was fifty-four men daily, was now increased to eighty-four at night. As a hungry wolf is more bold and aggressive, I reckon they reasoned likewise about us.

On the morning of January 21st the officers of Terry's brigade made their first appearance in the prison at roll call, and they introduced a new order of things: every fellow had to be at the beginning of roll call or lose his day's rations, not a pleasant thing, as his neighbors had none to give or lend. That day Captain Sullins, of the 1st Alabama, whose room was next to mine, died, after a week's illness, and Colonel Pierson's report of his administration on the island appeared in the *Register*. He said that, up to date, there had been over 6,000 prisoners on the island; 149 had died, 3 been executed, 1 shot by sentinel, over 300 released on bond, oath and parole, and there were then remaining 2,612. That day, for the first time, a four mule team came into prison, and everybody ran out to see it.

It was about the day aforementioned that we had a grand snow ball battle, like real war. Maj.-

Gen. Trimble commanded the Conservatives, and Brig.-Gen. M. Jeff. Thompson was in command of the Radicals, "so-called." Gen. Thompson was captured, but subsequently exchanged. Captain Youngblood, a Dutchman of singular and rare genius, was Thompson's chief signal officer; his spy-glass was made of two bottles tied together, and he tore off his shirt-tail for a signal flag, and while he was signaling the positions and movements of the enemy he took special pains to always keep himself in a safe locality. The adversaries pitched in manfully, nor was it altogether sham-like, for many a fellow came out of the rencounter skinned, bruised or lamed.

Col. Lewis preached the succeeding Sabbath, and the audience was so large that many had to leave for want of room. That morning's mail brought me $2.00 worth of postage stamps, a scarce and precious article just then, from Jas. A. McBrayer, who had been 'way down in Dixie, and knew how to sympathize with a fellow in durance vile, far away from home. As usual for Sunday evening, there came extravagant rumors, or "grape," as we termed it, that Gen. Longstreet was going to surrender, and that Mr. Beast Butler would have us all out in a month. Nobody knew the source of the report, but hundreds of credulous fellows felt good over it. It was ever the case that we had most news when there was least means of obtaining it.

On the 24th of January I resumed the study of French, which I had been pursuing for several months previous to Christmas. Colonel Smith, of Tennessee, Lieut. Tobey, of Arkansas, and several others, were in a class with me, and Major Mitchell, of South Carolina, a highly accomplished Southern gentleman, who had been educated in Europe, was our preceptor. All parties took a deep interest in the study, and we recited once a day wherever we could find a fitting place. For some time after that I corresponded with Rev. Father Lavialle, President of St. Mary's College in Kentucky, who wrote me letters in French for my instruction and improvement.

Judge Breare, Lieutenant of an Alabama regiment, was elected chief of our mess on the 26th January. He made an interesting, witty, little speech, assumed the official robe, and waded into active duty. "Chief of Mess" is one of those offices full of labor and responsibility, with no pay and but little thanks, but Breare was eminently "the right man in the right place," enjoyed his authority, and gave satisfaction. For some time we had been suffering from scarcity of water, but now an arrangement was made, leaving the big gate leading to the lake open four hours each day, and we could get plenty of crystal ice water.

Mr. Johnson, owner of the island, was now our sutler, and I heard but few fellows bless him, except with execrations. He had gone to the expense of getting a lithographic view of the prison, Sandusky and vicinity, expecting that it would take like hot cakes among the prisoners. But his judgment was faulty, for but few of them wanted to see the place longer than was absolutely necessary; besides, $3 was an exhorbitant price. It was reported that he refused to sell goods to any one unless they bought a picture, and the boys all resolved to buy nothing, and, whenever his clerks came in, a yell would go up all over the prison, " Here's your picturs." He soon found it would not pay to treat us otherwise than as honor and honesty demanded.

The 29th day of January was beautiful overhead but terribly sloppy under foot, and our bridge over to the city was becoming monstrous treacherous. The telegraph that day said that Longstreet had flaxed the Feds. out at Dandridge, Tennessee, and that Knoxville was alarmed. At night some naughty rebels broke into the sutler's store and bought some things when he was not there; supposed to be in retaliation for high prices and meanness.

My diary says that on the last day of January a heavy Dixie mail came in, and of course everybody was expecting a missive from the dear ones in the Southland. Alas! too many were bitterly disappointed; but some got cheering news from home, and others heard that poverty, sickness, and even death was reigning amongst the loved ones, and still they had to remain in prison and suffer the mental agonies consequent to such news.

CHAPTER IX.

WASHINGTON COUNTY JAIL,
July 4, 1865.

To-day, while so many thousands of the American people are celebrating and enjoying the annual return of Independence Day, here am I, a victim to the unjust hatred and unchristian prejudices of a victorious foe. Were I as unreasonable as they, I might invoke temporal troubles and Divine wrath upon their heads; but rather will I ask our Heavenly Father to soften their hearts and enlighten their minds to a sense of propriety and justice. To-day is a great jubilee in Jonesboro; most all the men, women and children for ten miles around are in town, bells are ringing, processions are marching, cannons are firing, orators of the day are making spread-eagle speeches, and picnic dinners are spread all around. Everybody parading the streets, without reference to age, sex or color, has a little Union flag pinned somewhere, to denote *super-loyalty*. I can see much that is going on from my little, grated window.

The former secesh generally keep close in their quarters, for, even if they received no direct insult or injury, no welcome would be extended to them. I, too, expected to have been enjoying this festive occasion with friends at home—no Union, no rebel, but all united in fraternal bonds of sympathy and interest, in forgetfulness of the unhappy past, all hearts glad and all tongues rejoicing that peace was come. But fate has decreed that still more trials must I undergo, and yet longer must I remain from the dearest place on earth. 'Tis not pleasant, but I will try to muster up courage to face it all with resignation, and content myself with the hope and prospect of a better day coming. The 4th day of July, 1863 and 1864, were spent in prison, and there is a saying, " the third time is the charm." We will see.

The month of February opened rather inauspiciously; there was much wind and rain, and large masses of floating ice were driven from the bay into the open lake. On the 1st day of the month the beef issued to us was so poor and mean that most of it was thrown out into the street, and we had fast day, *nolens volens*. It was on the 3d of the month that Major Scoville, who had been absent for a week at his home in Cleveland, Ohio, re-appeared in the prison yard; everybody had some business with him, and it was a notorious fact that he promised to fulfill almost every request that was made. He would take a minute of a fellow's name and wants, and leave him in a state of mixed bliss and suspense, for sometimes the articles would come and then again they wouldn't, in which latter case Mr. Scoville would get numerous irreligious blessings. For myself, I can say that he never failed to grant the many favors I asked for in the course of almost two years.

We had much war news on the 5th day of February, and among other things came an order from Mr. Lincoln for a draft of 500,000 men on the 10th of March, and those who know the state of the public mind at that time can well imagine with how little favor the mass received it.

Just a few days previous Hon. Jas. B. Clay, one of Kentucky's most gifted and honored sons, died at Montreal, Canada. Upon his shoulders had fallen the mantle of one of that trio of America's greatest statesmen. He loved the old Constitution and all pertaining thereto, and he left this world in sorrow because it was being dishonored and trampled under foot.

It was upon the date above mentioned that the "Little Eastern" came over from Sandusky for the first time in the new year, and it was at the same time that General Terry came into the yard and scourged the sutler about the picture business and other improprieties. And on that day a Choctaw Indian, captain in the Confederate service, died in the hospital, and was buried by the Masons in a metallic case. They put a nicely painted head and foot board at his grave, with his name, rank, Masonic emblems and wild scenery carved thereon.

The next day we had snow and mud, and got but very little wood, but, to cast a pleasing shade over the gloomy aspect, an immense pile of express came in. *Dr. Foster* (?) a Yankee of small caliber but wonderful pretensions, had a rich time confiscating liquors and other forbidden things, but still much contraband slipped in.

Captain Lister, of our mess, played sharp on the Yankees, in this wise: He had sent out to the post commandant, for approval, a permit to receive certain articles of clothing from a lady friend in Kentucky. In the body of the permit he left a small blank place. It came back approved, and he inserted, "one pair boots," and sent it on the way rejoicing. It will be remembered that boots had been pronounced contraband, but the permit was approved, and he got them. Before long the fellows from down East detected the *modus operandi*, and after that filled up all the open spaces with red ink lines.

On the 8th our grapevine telegraph was in fine working order, and there were many pleasant stories afloat about our emigrating, and, sure enough, next day, 400 rebels *did leave for somewhere,*

Lieutenants Bouldin and Allen, of my company, among the number. Of course, there was great excitement in all quarters, and some of the fellows leaving put on several suits, fearing that otherwise their property might be confiscated. Some others were left in a peculiar predicament, for, expecting to leave, they gave away their surplus clothing, and then had to stay. The prison pen was perceptibly thinned out, and for several days there was a gloom over everything. That day I visited Captain Hodge and Lieutenant Taylor, of my regiment, who were sick in the hospital, Captain Hodge being painfully afflicted with inflammatory rheumatism.

The 12th Ohio cavalry bid adieu to our island home on the 10th, and the Sandusky *Register* was kept out—news contraband. That day the most prominent and ardent Southern rights men in our prison convened and organized a society, known as the "Southern League," intended to strengthen and make more lasting the bonds between Confederate soldiers. It flourished for several weeks, then died a natural death.

The next day's news from the front was that there had been fighting on the Rapidan, the secesh getting the best of it, and Longstreet seemed to be flourishing. A Federal officer issued some clothing to our mess, most of it being captured goods of an inferior quality. Colonel B. Howard

Smith, of the 5th Kentucky cavalry, was paroled —a rare instance—and Lieutenant Alexander, of the 62d Tennessee—I am sorry to record it—took the oath of allegiance, and departed from the atmosphere that was tainted with secessionism.

My diary for the 13th says that mountains of ice were stretching along the horizon out in the lake beyond the breakwater. I have before spoken of the blockade in the lake, close to our prison home, and will here explain what it is. All who are familiar with American history have a knowledge of the naval conflicts on the lakes between the United States and Canada. Who has not heard of "Perry's victory" on Lake Erie? Sandusky Bay is nearly the shape of a horse shoe, and, by the way, Johnson's Island, which is about the center of the bay, is similarly shaped. The bay is a safe and commodious harbor, and there Commodore Perry rendezvoused his naval fleet. Across the opening of the horse shoe he made a blockade, by sinking stones and logs, until it reached, in many places, the surface of the water. An opening just wide enough for ships to pass through was left at one end, and guarded by a strong battery. A similar battery was there during our stay on Johnson's Island, so our friends down South, who wondered why friendly crafts did not come to our rescue from Canada, can see that we were in the stable, the door locked and the keyhole guarded. More than fifty years have rolled round since that blockade was constructed, and to-day it is plainly visible.

The 15th was a beautiful, spring-like day, the ice was leaving the bay, and the boat came over from the city, bringing lots of express, and among it was a box of books for me, from Frankfort, Kentucky, sent through the kindness of my friend Marvin Averill. Among the books were a New Testament in French, Life of Stonewall Jackson, Southern History, Life in the Old World, and Intellectual Development of Europe. There was a sudden change the next day; it was bitter cold, our communication with the city was blocked, no mails, high winds, my health splendid and appetite keen.

Two ladies, from Kentucky, came on the 18th, with a permit from the Secretary of War to see their brother, who was sick in prison; and a woman had become so uncommon a sight inside our walls that the boys rushed out by hundreds to see them, and truly they looked so good and sweet we could not help loving them.

I received, per express, on the 19th of February, a photograph album, instead of an autograph album which I had ordered, and my note book said, "I am negotiating for rings for some friends at home and in Dixie." Ring making proved to be a lucrative vocation, for many an ingenious fellow made from $1.00 to $3.00 per day. About that date we heard that the prisoners sent off a few days before had arrived at Point Lookout, several having made their escape. And now the bay was frozen over and sleighs were crossing.

On the 20th I made a wholesale purchase of rings, to send by mail to friends in various quarters. Just then rings and autographs were all the go, and nearly every lady in the Northern land, whether loyal or secesh, had a ring of prison make, and for a month a stream of autograph albums were going the rounds of the prison for signatures. I had the fever, too, and got some 600 names, with rank, command, and address. And quite a number of Federal officers and soldiers were getting the autographs of their rebel acquaintances. That day a Confederate captain disgraced himself by taking the oath, and was farther degraded by being driven from prison by his comrades after night. The next day Brigadier General Shaler, who was now in command of the post, issued an order, promising protection to all such, and threatening offenders with punishment, but the boys laughed at the idea, since "it is necessary to catch a dog before you hang him."

The succeeding night I sat up at the hospital with sick friends, not closing my eyes during the whole night. There were some very sick men in the ward where I stayed, suffering from a variety of diseases, such as prison fever, rheumatism, chronic diarrhea, diphtheria, and abscesses from old wounds.

How the 22d was passed in prison may be gathered from the following, which I transcribe *verbatim* from my diary.

"Washington's birthday—brass band playing Yankee Doodle and Hail Columbia—rebel band (violins) play Bonnie Blue Flag and Dixie—Yankees make speeches under the old flag, and swear anew their allegiance to the same—rebel orators, Colonel Lewis and Captain Fellows, vow to live and die for Dixie—the mass approve, and shout loudly—Yankee chaplain listening to the rebel speeches, but gets disgusted, and officer of the day disperses the Confederates."

Another memorable event of that day was that I went on detail as cook, after having been off of that kind of duty for four months. I found washing the dishes to be the most bitter pill, but persevered, and all came to be easy enough.

My memorandum for the succeeding day reads, "Mild as full-blown spring—Captain Thomas Burgess Brantly catches, kills, skins, fries and eats a rat, and I get a hind leg to pick—excellent, tastes like squirrel. No less than twelve men breakfast on a rat, not from necessity, but curiosity. Lieutenant Colonel Lyle, of 4th Alabama, dons blue clothes and walks out with squad of Federal officers going from roll-call, is recognized at the edge of the ice and brought back. So goes prison life."

The next day was delightful, and the birds were singing everywhere. At night two prisoners tried to scale the wall in rear of block 4—both caught—one got over, but soon found himself in the calaboose. For some days previous a revival had been going on in the dining-room of mess 1, block 4, and quite a number went up to be prayed for.

Several days of bright, warm weather having put the prison yard in nice order, continuous streams of Confederates could now be seen promenading from morning till night. And General Shaler had an order read before all the messes, saying: "Sentinels are positively ordered to fire on all prisoners trying to escape." The idea was so juvenile that the boys could not help laughing at it, for they thought that was the understanding all the time. About that time General Polk was falling back before Sherman at Meridian, Mississippi, the Army of the Potomac was quiet, and no extensive cavalry raids were going on in any quarter.

It was on the night of the 26th that I visited a room occupied by Arkansians, or "cane biters," as we politely termed them. I went to hear some music, and, out of the ten Arkansaw travelers present, seven were fiddlers, and the whole lump being jolly fellows, we did have a gay and festive time. Dr. Brantley, who ate the rat, was the trump of the whole pack. The next night I attended a revival in our mess room, and saw great religious enthusiasm manifested. Lieuts. Crouch, Gibson, Lee and McGill, of our mess, were converted. I watched the subsequent course of many of those who professed a change of heart, and in most instances they seemed to walk more circumspectly before men, and gave evident signs of more reverence for their God.

A glance at my diary shows that March opened with bright auspices for Southern arms. The Northern press reported a brilliant success for the Confederates at Lake City, Florida, and General Forrest had driven General Smith back to Memphis with heavy loss. On the 3d the Federal chaplain brought in for distribution religious books, papers and tracts, requesting the boys to read them and form their opinions at will. Some refused even to listen to the Abolition sentiments in them; others were more reasonable, and glad to get them for what good there was in them.

Complaints about short rations were now going up from all over the prison. A Federal officer came in and weighed some loaves of bread, finding them deficient, which deficiency, of course, went into the pockets of the post commissary. The bread wagoner was caught selling the precious loaves, and the tricky secesh were constantly trying to steal bread from the wagon while on its round of delivery; in fact, there was a perfect bread mania.

My diary for March 5th reads: "In prison nine months to-day; weather like Southern spring time. I have written home for clothing and provender. My mamma writes to me about love matters; I am promised the type of an old sweetheart, now married; small-pox in the home-land; rations getting better; potatoes issued; new cups, knives and forks furnished; boys sending out rings and autograph albums by express; sudden and exciting reports of exchange."

After that I have no record till the 9th, when there were signs of spring-time everywhere. The ice was all gone, and our pumps in running order again. A ventilator had been put on the top of the hospital, and the post chaplain was coming into the prison more frequently than usual, seeming to be more interested in the welfare of his secesh brethren. That day a rebel broke a lamp over Mr. Sutler's head because he sold it to him and then refused to sell him oil. The officer of the day hunted "the man who struck Billy Patterson," but, of course, nobody knew who it was. Maj. Scoville visited our room and laughed heartily over the matter.

The papers of the 10th said General Grant was

made Lieut.-General, that 700 prisoners were exchanged, and that the rebels had put Kilpatrick's men in irons for retaliation. On the 12th Lieut. Clark, of the 55th Georgia, moved into our room. Rations were now getting better, loaves of bread larger, and constant improvement was going on in the prison yard. A raised gravel walk was being made through the center of the yard and in rear of the buildings. Two four-horse teams were kept busy hauling wood, one removing slops and filth, and another was constantly hauling in rations. The 13th was a rainy, sleeting, snowy, gloomy Sabbath day. The next day I got the first number of the Louisville *Daily Journal*, which a friend sent me for one month, and there were many reports concerning exchange, and the privileges of the sutler being enlarged. Just now there was a great rage among the Yankee women for rings made by rebel officers, and they were going off like hot cakes at from 50 cents to $2.00 in greenbacks.

Just about that date, one morning as a starchy Federal officer was going out from roll-call, some fellow popped him in the back with a snow ball, by which heinous misdemeanor he was grievously offended, and proposed to have the cells at the guard house chock full of rebels if the chap was not brought to light, but he gradually cooled off, and then didn't feel so bad.

On the 16th a new sutler came into the prison, with permission from the Secretary of War to sell anything to eat on surgeon's recommendation, and it was no difficult matter to get sick, so as to require some of the sutler's stuff. A few days previous I had sent out for examination and approval my journal of prison life, desiring to send it to my mother, and that morning Lieut. Williams, United States army, informed me that Gen. Shaler was reading it. It may be that it let him into some of our ways and thoughts until then not known, but I was not aiming or desiring to do anything prejudicial to the interest of those around me.

I visited the hospital on the 18th, and found a good old captain praying and singing in the various wards; sickness was on the decline, erysipelas dying out, no small-pox, chronic diarrhœa being most fatal. And I noticed a little house just erected in rear of the hospital, in which to lay out the dead. The succeeding day Col. Printup, of my room, got a splendid box of eatables from some lady friends in Richmond, Kentucky, and it made all our hearts glad, for we shared everything in common in our room.

Here I will insert a little scrap going to show that one never loses anything by treating his enemy kindly. After Richmond, Kentucky, was captured by Kirby Smith, in 1862, and the army was moved on to Lexington, Colonel Printup, with the 55th Georgia, was left in command of the post at Richmond. He treated the Federal prisoners there very kindly, and would not allow his soldiers to disturb the citizens, but extended protection to the loyal and disloyal alike, and everything was smooth and harmonious. Time went on, our army retreated from Kentucky, and in September, 1863, Printup and his regiment were captured with Brig.-General Frazier at Cumberland Gap. The officers were sent to Johnson's Island, and Colonel P. brought with him a letter signed by several prominent Federal officers and loyal citizens, recommending him for parole or the kindest treatment possible. As I have before said, my room was one of the most comfortable in prison, of which fact Major Scoville, prison superintendent, was aware, so he came to us and asked us if we would take Colonel Printup into our room, telling us why he took a special interest in his welfare. We thought that an officer who had manliness enough to treat his enemy kindly when a prisoner would do to risk, nor had we afterward cause to be sorry.

My memorandum says March 21st was cold, the bay frozen over, and we got no mail, but lots of grapevine telegrams. My week as cook expired, and Lieut. Clark was inaugurated. The next day I got a pair of shoes from "*Gen.*" Frank

Berger, and my note book says that I tried to steal a pair of pants from him, but failed. I had a chat with one of the veteran soldiers who was at work in the yard; he said bounty would not bait him any longer, that he was going home in a few weeks. Our chief cook fixed us up a delicious bread pudding for dinner, and a burlesque picture on the bulletin board attracted a large crowd, though it was cold as blazes.

On the 23d General Shaler sent back my journal of prison life, saying I could not send it off, for it was too *rank with treason*, but the fact is that by perseverance I did manage to ship it to my mother after a while. That day I received a letter informing me of the resignation of my Colonel, J. H. Crawford, and that my first Lieutenant, T. T. Bouldin, had left Point Lookout for Dixie-land. The next day was beautiful and delightful, and in the afternoon a host of Yankee Lieutenants and Sergeants came in to muster all the rebels, taking full name and rank of each, for what reason we could not tell, but hoping it was looking toward exchange.

An impudent, disloyal fellow assumed loyal garb and walked out with said officers, but was taken up like a stray calf, and turned back into the pen, minus his shoulder straps. Nobody ever knew how so much Federal attire found its way into prison, but I believe the motto up North is, "money makes the mare go."

The Yankee carpenters were at that time building an addition to the hospital for the accommodation of the surgeons and cooks. General Grant had just taken command in the East, and gold was rating at 169. On the 26th a steamer came from the open lake and plowed its way through the slush ice up to Sandusky City, and the same day the "Little Eastern" made its way to the island. On the next day, which was Sunday, eleven Confederate officers were baptized in Lake Erie, a large crowd of ladies and Federal officers being out to witness the novel sight.

The following day was a glorious one in our prison life. Sutler Terry, brother of the General, opened a large stock of goods in the prison, and the crowd, jam and squeeze to get to buy exceeded most anything I ever saw. He sold out half of his stock the first day, realizing over $2,000. Though rather contraband, he had plenty of good brandy, at $5.00 per quart, and many a Southern gentleman got "how come you so." One fast mess paid $60 for a case of champagne, and felt richer after than before spending their money.

It was the day after that I got, rather unexpectedly, from home, a box of clothing and eatables, and Captain Broughton, of my mess, also received a box of good things to eat from a lady friend at Russellville, Kentucky. She only knew him through a friend of her's, who formed his acquaintance at Hopkinsville, Kentucky, while the 7th Texas was stationed there, in the fall of 1861.

The good ladies of Kentucky are loved and blessed by many a poor, unfortunate rebel soldier that they never saw or knew, except by the story of their privations and sufferings.

CHAPTER X.

Ark of Safety, Jonesboro, East Tenn., *July 6, 1865.*

On the 1st day of April General Heintzelman visited our island, and many little sail-boats were beginning to appear on the lake. For some cause no sutler had been in the prison for several days, but it did not matter much, for a half dozen sub-sutler shops, kept by rebels, were open, and there was a great rivalry among them for the trade. Captain Wood, of Tennessee, had one open in our block, and advertised to sell anything on commission.

Nothing short of an actual sight of the thing would give a just idea of how nearly our prison was like a diminutive city—not town—for there you never see that variety of petty speculations and engagements.

We did not forget that it was April Fool's day, and many good jokes and sells were got off by the Confederate fraternity. I made a sawdust pie and presented it to Major Stuart of Arkansas, for trimming my hair. His appetite was sharp as a razor, and his mouth watered, till he waded through the tough crust into the sawdust; then his feathers fell. The boys plagued him about it for a month, and he was constantly trying to get the turn on me, but I was always on the lookout, and he failed.

During the early part of the month the air was balmy, and the lake smooth as a mirror. There was a dancing school going on at Block 13, and, to vary the programme, one fellow stuck a knife into another. The papers reported that Colonel Ould, Confederate Commissioner of Exchange, had gone to Fortress Monroe in our behalf. On the 4th Colonel Gregg and Captain Hodge, of my regiment, took dinner with us, and "we put the big pot in the little one," and had something extra. My note book says, "On the 6th there were bright prospects for exchange, and the rebels were all jubilant." Yes, and a hundred other times did the prospects brighten, but only to glimmer and fade again.

And now here comes some fresh "means of livelihood." A shifty Southerner bought a pair of scales and erected a weighing machine, and would tell any fellow his hog weight for a three cent postage stamp—I brought down 160 pounds at that date—and about the same time another institution was opened for the purpose of making a speck of change. Lieutenant McLoughlin, of Alabama, set up an oyster saloon in mess No. 1 of our block, and for awhile drove a thriving trade. From my memorandum it seems that I was a little indisposed about that time, which was something unusual, for I enjoyed excellent health most all the while.

The 8th day of April had been appointed by President Davis as a day of fast and prayer, and we observed it with due solemnity. The Confederates most all dressed up, and we had preaching. As to fasting, the majority approximated to it every day. I had now received no letters for a whole week, when one came from Miss J. G. B., full of good cheer and encouragement, and asking for a history and description of "Asa Hartz"; nor was she the only one that made inquiries about "Asa." His real name is George McKnight, and he was a major on the staff of General Loring. By his wit, poetry and fascinating letters he had got half the damsels in the country crazy about him. One of his poetic effusions, "My love and I," contrasting their situations in humorous and witty terms, went the rounds of the whole Northern press, and he received clothing and eatables from all quarters in profusion. The truth is he had most reputation where he was least known. "We 'uns" didn't lay much stress either on the man or his poetry. Truly did distance give enchantment.

April 11th two ladies from Kentucky came into prison to see a sick friend, and, as was the case every time a lady appeared inside the walls, it created much interest and excitement. The same day several Northern ladies were on the parapet taking a view of rebeldom. They didn't portray much sympathy for us, and we reciprocated the compliment in like coin.

The next day two "galvanized rebels" were ordered to leave the prison because they were in the wrong pen, having satisfied us that they were abolitionists at heart. They received no sympathy or countenance from any honest rebel, and so disagreeable did their situation become that they made application to be put in the cells with the condemned prisoners, which was granted. Ours was a genuine Southern institution.

The succeeding day I got a letter from my brother at Camp Morton, saying our mother had been to see him, but was denied the privilege, only being allowed to write a note. She took him clothing and provisions, all of which they promised to deliver promptly, but some of the articles, including all of the delicacies, he never got. That day General Terry was in to inspect the prison, and the inmates were curious to know his ideas about exchange, which proved to be not very flattering.

At that time the news from Washington represented warm times in the Federal Congress. Mr. Colfax moved to expel Mr. Long, of Ohio, and epithets of traitor and liar were freely used. Right or wrong, the Confederate nation glorified in seeing the strife of words and feeling among them. Gold had gone up to 172.

On the 14th of April about forty Confederate officers, from the Trans-Mississippi Department, were brought in, most of them having been captured at home, which was anything but a recommendation among the mass of the prisoners who were captured on the battle-field. The same day two regiments of the veteran troops left for the front, and subsequently suffered terribly in Grant's May campaign.

At three o'clock P. M. of the same day the "rebellonians" gave a performance at Block 9, said "rebellonians" being a minstrel concert troupe not to be grinned at. They had displayed much talent and enterprise in getting up so creditable an entertainment under so many adverse circumstances. The house was crowded, the music was splendid, and the theatrical scenery and acting, though somewhat rustic, gave evident signs of genius. The price of admission was 25 cents, reserved seats 50 cents. Several Federal officers were present, and seemed to enjoy the jokes and burlesques got off on the Yankee nation. I afterward attended the theater at Richmond, Virginia, and yet think the "rebellonians" excelled them in interest.

What might now seem a very trivial matter, but then merited noting down, was that on the 16th of April we had corn bread for dinner, it being the first we had tasted for six months. And still there were exciting debates in the Federal Congress, and gold was fluctuating between 176 and 180. Just then there was a howl going through the Northern press, calling for retaliation for the killing of so many colored troops by General Forrest's men at Fort Pillow. The matter was grossly exaggerated everywhere, and the real facts in the case never told. General Forrest felt himself justified, and right-minded people to-day, who know the circumstances, do not condemn him.

My memorandum book says April 18th was a beautiful, life-giving day, and that I got a sweet letter from my mother and one from a good lady friend in Missouri. The next day was one of grand excitement on Johnson's Island. There came an order from the Secretary of War to remove all the sick and wounded prisoners to Point Lookout. In the shortest possible time there were a thousand before unheard of ailings, and in many cases the diseases were so deep-seated that the surgeon could not find them. The armless and legless were jubilant for once.

Dr. Woodbridge, United States army, was very kind, and did all he could for the sick, and everybody liked him. The next day 175 sick and wounded did leave for exchange, and we who had to remain were truly glad to see the poor fellows off. My room mate, Captain Broughton, and five others from my mess, went. Many letters were smuggled through in hat crowns, coat linings, boot soles, and every other fashion. Several loads of straw for our beds came in that day, and I noticed the inmates of Block 1 placing nice sod around their quarters.

April 24th we received the largest Dixie mail that had ever come to the prison. Up to that time I had gotten no letters from the South, though I wrote many, and it was a general complaint that not one-fourth of the letters written in the South ever reached us. From noon till night of the next day the winds howled and the lake surged so that no bark could ride its bosom. The scene was wild, rugged, magnificent, exceeding in grand beauty anything the artist could paint.

That very same day Plymouth, North Carolina, with a garrison of 2,500 troops, was captured by some gentlemen of disloyal persuasion, and gold closed in New York at 184 About a dozen prisoners arrived, all laboring under the impression that they were on the way to Dixie, but, as soon as the poor fellows got into limbo, their eyes were open to the delusion. The Federals told us away back in the beginning of June, 1863, that they would only keep us a couple of months, but they forgot and added nineteen thereto. In that squad of prisoners was a Copperhead youth who was sentenced to confinement there for expressing Southern sympathies at a Northern college.

And now the tocsin of war, which had been almost slumbering, began to sound again. Grant was preparing for war on a momentous scale, and Lee was arranging matters to checkmate him. All the regular troops were being sent to the front, and the garrisons filled with militia. Governor Brough, of Ohio, had just called out the militia for one hundred days' active service. And just then news came from the far South to the effect that Mr. General Banks, whom the Confederates regarded as their Commissary General, was in a bad fix, his army whipped, and his gunboats and transports aground in Red river. About the last of April some reckless, thoughtless or mean prisoner tried to set fire to the eating room of mess 1, block 4, but fortunately the fire was discovered and extinguished.

The 1st day of May was pleasant and warm, the 2d it rained and snowed, and the 3d I received four letters, one being from my grandmother, and one written in French from Father Lavialle, of St. Mary's College.

The next day was one that kept us secesh full of life and fun, though to the outer world it might seem that it was calculated to depress us. A host of "National Guards," citizen soldiers and other gentry, of every age, size and appearance, visited the island to get a peep at the compound essence of the rebellion. Perhaps fifty of them were on the parapet at one time, curiously inspecting the appearance of things on the inside. The fellows yelled at them in all manner of ridiculous styles, actually making them ashamed of themselves.

Maybe a rough looking old customer, with a tall hat on, would make his appearance, and instantly a hundred stentorian voices would ring out, "Come down out of that, old man; I know you are in there, we see your legs working;" then somebody would chime in, "Bring home my churn," or, "I want my stove pipe," and very soon some other would sing out, "What are you doing with my camp kettle," or, "Send me my tar bucket." If a fellow of uncommon size or appearance came up, in a little while a dozen rebels would be spying him through stove pipe joints, black bottles, or other contrivances, and they would motion for him to advance or recede, or move to the right or left, so as to get him at the proper focal point. These and many other means

15

of annoyance were resorted to, and seldom did the loyal folks fail to make a speedy exit. When ladies came we went out to look at them, but tried to be more respectful in our manœuvers.

About that time the rebel General Marmaduke captured 1,000 prisoners from General Steele in Arkansas, and several different tunnels were under headway in various parts of the prison. The Feds. had been smelling a mice for several days, and concluded to dig a deep ditch all around the inside of the prison wall, which they did, seriously interfering with the programme of those having a finger in the tunnel pie. It was just about then that several soldiers of the garrison got drunk and were put under arrest. The discipline was very rigid, and I never saw the same number of men better trained to duty and obedience.

On the 6th of May I jotted down in my diary: "The armies are all moving; Meade has issued an address to encourage his soldiers, and already it is breathed that there has been a dreadful conflict of arms; 'tis a vital hour, and there is no talk of anything else in prison. Most all the Confederates express confidence in the issue; some feel it, some do not. I hope, but fear."

The 8th of May we had a thunder shower, and all the trees budded out. That morning Lieut. Williams, of the United States army, who had been calling our roll for some time, and whom we all liked for his kindness, came in to bid us adieu before leaving for the front. We gave him a letter of recommendation for good treatment in case he should be captured, and promised to reciprocate his kind deeds if we should ever have charge of him 'way down in the land of cotton.

The same day Captain Day, of the 55th Georgia, died, and that night the veterans, who were going to leave for the front, had a torch-light procession, and their hearts seemed to beat time to the music of the fife and drum and brass band.

At the self-same hour some rebels, Dr. Brantly & Co., were at the opposite side of the pen, trying to bribe a sentinel to let them over the fence; he said he was willing but afraid. The Dr. Brantly mentioned is the same individual of whom I have before spoken under the cognomen of Captain Thos. B. Brantly. He once peddled bread pills for six weeks in Texas, claiming them as a catholicon for every ill; and, after he had humbugged the people to the tune of several thousand dollars, he left off and went to trading ponies with the Indians. The Doctor was superintendent of one of the tunnels mentioned a little ways back, and he had held some office in no less than five subterranean companies, all of which failed. At last he gave up in disgust, and said that if he could not get to take the oath (and go to Dixie) he would hold on awhile, which he did.

From my sketch book I copy as follows: "May 11th cold, and heavy gale, breakers lashing the shores, and white-caps running high over the blockade; great battle progressing in Virginia; voluminous and conflicting telegrams; Confederates, as yet, equal to the task; sixteen Yankee Generals *hors du combat;* General Shaler, who commanded at Johnson's Island last winter, a prisoner. Sundown—Great excitement all over the pen; Grant reported in full retreat, and Forrest said to have taken Decatur, Alabama, with 4,000 prisoners; Grierson killed." Some of the foregoing proved very true, and some not so much so.

My diary for the 17th reads thus: "So foggy we can't see the lake—we had codfish for breakfast—rebels playing hob with Federal transports and gunboats—the armies of Steele and Banks nearly destroyed and demoralized—about 500 wagons and ambulances taken from them. 'Tis one year ago to-day since I was captured—the great fight in Virginia continues, without material success on either side—Longstreet wounded—Buckner commanding his corps—Breckinridge has threshed Siegel in Western Virginia, and gold is feverish at 176."

We scoured our room on the 19th, and that day there was a general muster and inspection of the prison, and some New York papers published a bogus call for 300,000 more troops. The next day we (my room) bought a half barrel of shad, eighteen pounds of butter and ten dozen eggs, which helped our commissary department along most wonderfully. Corporal Berger made the purchase in Sandusky, by special permission of Major Scoville. That evening the sloop-of-war "Michigan" steamed proudly into Sandusky bay, and anchored just off our island. She looked warlike, but as we were (under the circumstances) inclined to be peaceable, nobody was scared.

About the 23d Grant and Lee were manœuvering before Spottsylvania Courthouse. Sherman had advanced to Rome and Kingston, Georgia, and General J. E. B. Stuart, Lee's great captain of cavalry, had just been killed in front of Richmond. Two days later Major Scoville was relieved from duty as prison superintendent, and some prisoners came in from Johnston's army.

On the 27th Lee and Grant had left Spottsylvania and were still making strategical moves, and Sherman and Johnston were likewise engaged in Georgia. The news from Mr. Banks' department got no better fast, and he was superseded by General Canby; Nathaniel Hawthorne and Joshua R. Giddings had just passed away from earth.

The last day of May there was a great commotion among the little Yankee nation on Johnson's

Island. The previous night several Southern gentlemen had tried to scale the walls, and several tunnels were discovered and nipped in the bud. It seems that the impression prevailed on the outside that some rebels were on the wrong side of the prison wall, and the loyal forces hunted all over the island, skirmish fashion, but found no game. And there was a rigid inspection of all the blocks. Just after dinner they called us out into line, as if for inspection and muster; then guards were placed between us and our quarters, and the corporals were ordered to make a close search of all the rooms and bring all the contraband to light. The result in our block was, a wooden gun, that the boys had made to practice with (for we taught the military art clandestinely), several fruit cans fixed up for life-preservers, one pair of *muddy* pants, used in tunneling, and one ladder, supposed to have been intended as a stepping-stone to Dixie. At other blocks the harvest was equally as rich and ludicrous.

CHAPTER XI.

In Jail, Washington County, Tennessee,
July 8, 1865.

On the first day of June, 1864, there came to my address the first number of the *Courier des Etats Unis*, a French paper published in New York, for which Lieut. Tobey, of Arkansas, and myself had subscribed, and in reading which we whiled away many happy hours together. Lieut. T. belonged to our French class, and was one of my warmest friends and most constant companions. Though he was born and reared in the State of Maine, he was as true as the truest to our cause, entertaining liberal and conservative views about all subjects. I did not then, nor do I now, think much more of the Southern radical "fire-eater" than of the Northern radical republican; both overdid the fair thing.

The sutler's shop was moved out of the way preparatory to enlarging the prison yard, and Major Hall was announced as prison superintendent on the 2d, and several hundred Dixie fellows were playing ball, and quite a number were amusing themselves at marbles. On the 4th an order issued from headquarters was put upon the bulletin board, positively restricting the length of letters written or received to one page of ordinary letter paper. For some days after there were many catastrophes in the letter business, scores of them being suppressed because too long.

And just then there was another rumpus between the loyal and disloyal gentry on Mr. Johnson's Island. Some of the latter attempted to make an underground railroad, beginning at a point under the center of the dead house in rear of the hospital. The affair was detected by *Gen.* Frank Berger, and there resulted a vexatious but fruitless search for the man that dug the hole in the ground and the instrument with which he dug it.

Colonel Hill, post commandant, made an order on the 8th, holding messes responsible for any damage done to the buildings or tunnels dug from under their respective blocks, requiring the members of messes to inform against those who did either. The penalty was to be the cutting off of rations. The prisoners *en masse* were indignant at the very idea of such a requirement, and no one thought for a moment of obeying.

That day a terrible calamity befell us in the shape of an order from the War Department forbidding any more coffee, sugar or candles to be issued to us: the act claimed to be in retaliation for the treatment of Federals in the South. For some days there was a legion of long faces over the matter, and some of the fellows thought they would surely starve and die, but I never knew of many deaths resulting therefrom.

The next day a box of sundries came to the hospital from Mrs. Martha Lillard, of Anderson county, Kentucky; its contents were from various kind ladies who sympathised with the suffering Confederates. Hardly a day passed but that some donation of clothing, delicacies, and other little things needed by the sick, came from some society of charitable, big-hearted ladies in Kentucky, Baltimore or elsewhere.

The day following we got a large mail from the South, and at six o'clock in the evening a dozen prisoners came in from Johnson's army. From that time forward the arrival of prisoners was not an event of much note among us, after the excitement of looking for friends and inquiring about the state of things at the front. My notes of the 11th say that Morgan was at Lexington and Georgetown, Kentucky, playing smash. It is presumed that every one has read or heard of his artful and ingenious escape from the Ohio penitentiary, where I last spoke of him.

The news of the 12th was that Grant and Sherman had come to a halt, Marmaduke had blockaded the Mississippi, and gold stood at 199. The intelligence the succeeding day was that General Morgan had captured General Hobson and 1,500 men at Cynthiana, Kentucky, and that Frankfort had been put under martial law and the State papers moved to the fort. That day the loyal postmaster very unexpectedly sent in several confiscated letters, which was naturally calculated to make us think more of him; and the Southern rights men were playing town ball, baste, marbles and knucks all over the pen—that day I played my first game of knucks in prison.

At that time Grant seemed to be changing his base, and Forrest had defeated Sturgis in Mississippi, driving him back to Memphis, and capturing 2,000 men and 14 pieces of artillery. General Grant moved his army to the south side of the James river on the 17th of June, and the next day C. L. Vallandigham suddenly turned up in Ohio, after an exile of several months. The people everywhere received him with enthusiastic joy, and the press was soon in a mighty stew over the matter, some advising the President to ship him off again, while others suggested that it would be best to let him alone, which was done.

On the evening of the 18th we were allowed to go swimming in the lake, for the first time in the season. The water was warm, and it was delightful sport. There were about 200 of us in the water at once, and a loyal cuss was on picket in a little boat out in front of us.

On the 19th the ice wagon began its summer visits, and we gladly welcomed it. We got ice at five cents per pound, and from five to eight pounds daily was enough for a mess of from six to ten men, so the tax was not very heavy— nothing compared with the luxury. The larger messes of from twenty to fifty kept their water in barrels, and bought ice accordingly.

At that date we were getting five daily papers in our room, the New York *Herald*, Chicago *Times*, Cincinnati *Commercial*, Philadelphia *Age* and New York *Times*. They preached all kinds of doctrines. About twenty of Morgan's officers, captured at Cynthiana, arrived at prison on the 22d, and from Major McAfee I learned that my cousin, B. A. Wash, was among the captured, and had been sent to Rock Island, Illinois. It was about that date that we heard General Polk had been killed in Georgia, and just then the Yankee sentinels seemed to be exceedingly particular, and even insulting; for what reason we could not tell.

June 23d there was a grand review of the troops on Johnson's Island, Major-General McCook being present, and gold was ebbing and flowing between 220 and 235; but that did not hinder the rebellonians from getting up a good performance, and any number of the fellows from down South had the change requisite to see and hear the show.

General Archer, who had been with us since the battle at Gettysburg, was, at noon of the 24th, ordered to prepare to leave immediately, and it was whispered around that he was to be sent to the front to be put under fire, in retaliation for some Federals who were quartered in Charleston, within the range of the Union batteries. He never went farther than Fort Warren, from where he was soon exchanged, promoted to a major-general, and died soon after.

Also, on the 24th, twenty officers came in from Johnson's army and from Western Virginia. Several of my acquaintances were among the latter, and from them I learned that the skeleton of my regiment was in the fight at Staunton, and that Major Rhea was badly wounded in the face.

It was about the 27th that Grant's 2d army corps was routed, and several of Sherman's supply trains burned in Georgia by the rebel General Wharton. The next day we got news that Sherman had been repulsed, and gold had gone up to 240.

The day following perhaps a dozen more Morgan Rangers came to take lodging with us, Lieutenant Oliver, of my native county, being of the number. And that day Captain Jonas, of Arkansas, returned from a parole of one month. He had been to see his parents, in Illinois, who were old friends of President Lincoln. At that time the Yanks were blasting some wells and sinks in our prison yard, and frequently did fragments of stone fly uncomfortably close to rebellious heads.

On the 11th day of June the 171st Ohio, which had been sent to Kentucky to look after the Morgan raiders, returned to the island. And the same day seven of General Morgan's surgeons were sent to our prison, preparatory to going South. By a mutual agreement, surgeons and chaplains were to be released unconditionally, but, from bad faith, they were frequently kept imprisoned for several months.

July 1st I received a letter from Lieut. H. M. Baldwin, battery M, 5th United States artillery, dated "Two miles from Petersburg, Va." Henry Baldwin was my class-mate in college, and we were ever the best of friends, each always emulous to excel the other in merit. On the day of graduation he stood at the head of the class, and I was not far off. In parting we severed a tie of sweet friendship, neither dreaming that we would ever be in hostile array, the one against the other, for, though living at the North (New Jersey), he was conservative, and I was no fire-eater.

In truth, neither of us then (May, 1861) thought

of entering the army at all, and I presume that, at last, the same took him in as did myself—he found that the conflict of North and South was inevitable, and felt it a duty to take sides. Nor do I think it unreasonable that he chose the side he did, because, let men say what they will to the contrary, surrounding influences have a mighty control over our thoughts and actions.

Lieutenant B.'s letter expressed the same personal feeling as the day we parted, and I'm sure I felt none other. He told me of many of my Northern school-mates—some killed, some still in the battle, and I could give him similar intelligence about the Southern boys. My only other Northern class-mate, Geo. M. Steever, was killed at Vicksburg. Poor George was the youngest of our class, had a brilliant mind, a kind heart, and but few cadets had more friends than George Steever.

Secretary Chase resigned the 1st of July, and two Southern gentlemen sojourning up North tried to scratch out under a lamp, at the stilly hour of midnight. The sentinel kindly warned them that he had his eyes open, and politely requested them to return to their quarters and wait till exchange day. They saw the point, took the hint, and went instanter. The next day I received, per express, a package of nice books from Miss Julia G. Barry, who is one of the best rebels old Kentucky affords.

Prisoners were now coming in at a rapid rate, and our pen was getting crowded beyond its proper capacity. Lieut. T. F. Hooper, of Georgia, came into our room by order of Major Scoville, but he did not prove an agreeable room mate, and did not stay with us very long. He had been raised in affluence and indolence, consequently petted and spoiled, and seemed to ignore the fact that there were any duties to perform, or that he was under any obligations to his fellow prisoners.

Our room was an institution carried on in a systematic way, every one having his share of the duties to discharge. Hooper generally took care to be out of the way when his time came, and, as we were unwilling to wait on him, and neither weak hints nor strong ones had the desired effect, it became disagreeable, and nobody shed tears when he was sent South with a squad of invalids. During the night of the 3d a part of the ditch which had been dug inside the prison wall caved in, and the sentinel over it fired several shots into the inanimate earth, thinking it was some Southern fellow trying to go home.

At my Northern prison home on the 4th day of July, 1864, a salute of thirty-five heavy guns was fired at noon, and the island was chock full of women, children and colored people. Some of them came to see their soldier friends, but a large per centage was attracted by a curiosity to see how "Southern chivalry" looked and lived up North. Several excursion boats went out from Sandusky that morning to spend the day at Kelly's Island, or some other romantic place, in feasting and dancing. The steamers came as close to our prison fence as possible, some three hundred yards, with the stars and stripes flying, the bands playing, and the ladies waving their handkerchiefs, but we guessed that it was not a token of love for us. In our prison all passed off quietly and soberly that day.

I find inscribed in my diary for July 6th: "The Alabama sunk off Cherbourg, France, by treachery of a Federal cruiser. Uncle Abe proclaims martial law in Kentucky. I have no letters from home for a month; am getting uneasy. Geo. P. Morris, the journalist and poet, is dead." The next day I got a box of provisions from my grandmother, which had been broken open and several articles extracted, but I had no right to complain of bad luck, for I had been very fortunate in receiving my express matter promptly and in safety. On the 8th my heart was eased and gladdened by the receipt of a letter from my mother; she had written, but her letters miscarried.

Little did I dream, one year ago to-day, that the country would now be situated as it is, and that I would be in a common county jail, charged with an infringement of the civil laws. But the future ever was and ever will be wrapped up in mystery. To-day we know not what will be our portion for to-morrow. And it is a merciful provision of Providence, for, could we see the dark and troublous paths before us, too many of us would grow heart-sick, despair and want to give up our mission on earth, and lie down and die. As it is, the little monitors of hope and faith give us incentives to struggle on for something yet ahead—we know not what, but it is an element of man's nature to desire still something more, no matter what or how much he may possess.

But that is digressing from the narrative of my prison experience. The 12th day of July was a rather memorable one on Johnson's Isle. The whole west wall of the prison yard was moved back some sixty paces, and those who inhabited the inside were discussing the propriety of revolting. But nearly the whole garrison was under arms and watching our manœuvers, so the wise and prudent ones among us said it was best to be right easy. Some monstrous brave fellows, with more courage than discretion, ranted around and called for volunteers to charge the loyal troops, but "burnt children dread the fire," and we *all concluded to remain a few days longer.*

The next morning the rebel boys were out bright and early surveying the hitherto forbidden ground, just like a lot of mules or cattle, when first turned into a new pasture, will run all over it. Very soon little plots of ground were being staked off for gardens, and in a few days a score of patches were planted out with every variety of seed. The owners spent much of their time working, watering and watching over the crops, and some of them received the reward of their labors.

About the 14th of July the Confederates were threatening both Washington and Baltimore, being within a few miles of each, and Maj.-Gen. Franklin, of the Union army, was captured, but subsequently escaped. On the 16th several fellows went out *after dark* and took the oath, the treatment of some other chaps of their stripe having made them somewhat cautious. The next evening the "Michigan," which had been off somewhere on a cruise of observation, came and cast anchor at her usual station, right close to the beloved (?) sons of the South, and about dusk a Dutch officer of the day came in and ordered the rebels to keep close in their holes till daylight. Subsequently the order was slightly modified, but the Yanks, for some reason, "had the devil in them," and several shots were fired during the night, but no harm done.

I received, per express, on the 18th, $50.00 from my mother, and at the same time she sent, at my request, $10.00 each to my orderly sergeant, Red Anderson, at Point Lookout, and Squire John

Murrell, a citizen prisoner at Johnson's Island, from East Tennessee. The guerrillas were now swarming round Louisville, and the rebels were reported as entering Eastern Kentucky, but it turned out to be a scare.

July 20th President Lincoln made a call for 500,000 men, but volunteers were hard to get; in fact, that system had most played out, and nearly all their recruits were conscripts, which means a little worse than no soldiers at all. Maj. Scoville was now sick, and there was smart sickness in our hospital, but not of a fatal kind. That day I observed several Southern gentlemen of secesh persuasion making turnip patches, and among them was General Trimble, of Maryland, who had one foot shot off at Gettysburg, and was going on crutches. I went to the circulating library and exchanged "The Wandering Jew" for several smaller volumes that I had not read.

The circulating library was an institution after this style: A request was made for all the prisoners to send all the books they had read and did not desire to keep to the room of a certain officer, who was to act as librarian. For every book contributed the donor was allowed to read so many volumes from the library thus accumulated. Soon a miscellaneous collection of from 500 to 800 books, magazines and novels was amassed, and formed a very popular institution. Those who had no books to give or exchange could, for 50 cents a month, have free access to the library.

That day, while at the library, I accidentally met Lieutenant Tom Brown, of the 26th Tennessee regiment, with which I was once connected, and in which I was wounded while commanding Captain Morrell's company at the battle of Fort Donelson. Though Lieutenant Brown had been in the prison several months, neither of us knew of the other's presence.

The next day I received a letter from Colonel H. V. N. Boynton, of the 37th Ohio, who was at his home in Cincinnati recovering from a wound received in Georgia. Colonel Boynton graduated at the Kentucky Military Institute the first year I was there, and was afterward one of our professors for a couple of years.

My notes for the 25th speak of a chair factory in the prison pen, and all that kept many other professions from being engaged in was a want of means and facilities for procuring and contriving the necessary implements. At half-past nine o'clock that night a sentinel shot into Block 5 and wounded one man in the arm and another in the shoulder. That was the hour at which lights were required to be extinguished, and the guard claimed that he fired at a light, but fifty men who were in the room declared that no light was burning. Colonel Hill investigated the affair, but we never knew to what conclusion he came.

Captain Wells, who was acting Superintendent of Prison during the illness of Major Scoville, took out some bad bread for inspection and to give the baker a warning. It seemed to have the desired effect, for the bread began to get better right away. That day a new police sergeant was assigned to our division of the prison, and he tried to be more strict than his predecessor in the matter of police and cleanliness of rooms.

The next morning at roll-call our mess voted that all hands should turn out promptly at roll-call, as the punctual ones were often kept standing in line a long time because of the laziness or tardiness of a few fellows. Some selfish, unreasonable individuals tried to resist the will and action of the majority, but when their rations came in jeopardy they succumbed, and all went on swimmingly.

The day before we had got news of a bloody fight before Atlanta on the 22d, in which General McPherson, of the Northern army, was slain. General Joseph E. Johnston had been superseded by General Hood because he was unwilling to carry out the policy of the President instead of his own. The whole South did then, and does yet, condemn that as one of the blindest acts of Mr. Davis, for General Johnston was everywhere regarded as one of the master military spirits of the South, and General Hood was known to be imprudent, though brave to a fault. By bold and reckless manœuvering and fighting he soon reduced to a mere skeleton a magnificent army. I have always regarded the day of Johnston's supersedure as one of the darkest in the war for Southern independence. His retreat from Dalton to Atlanta was a briliant military feat in every sense of the word.

While all this was going on General Jubal Early, who had temporarily retired from Maryland, was again invading Northern soil, and Senator Mallory, of Kentucky, was killed by guerrillas near Louisville. Both Kentucky and Missouri were now swarming with bushwhackers and robbers. Many of the roving bands gave no quarter to their enemies, nor did they receive any. A few years hence it will seem strange that peace and harmony could have come out of such a chaos. On the 30th all the 128th Ohio went to bury Gen. McPherson at his home with military honors. The last day of July was the hottest day of the season up to date.

I will now close this chapter by giving entire the programme of the concert given by the Rebellonians on the evening of the 22d, simply adding that it was a complete success, the gross receipts being over a hundred dollars.

REBELLONIANS.

MANAGER..............................LIEUT. H. CARPENTER
MUSICAL DIRECTOR..................LIEUT. A. E. NEWTON

FRIDAY, JULY 22, 1864, 3 P. M., AT BLOCK 9.

COMPANY:

Capt. C. Sherwin, of Tennessee.
Capt. W. Harris, of Mississippi.
Capt. G. H. Henchy, of Louisiana.
Capt. W. S. Otey, of Arkansas.
Capt. J. C. Ward, of Virginia.
Capt. B. Palmer, of Tennessee.
Capt. J. B. Withers, of Virginia.

Lieut. A. E. Newton, of Mississippi.
Lieut. H. Carpenter, of Louisiana.
Lieut. S. G. Cooke, of Mississippi.
Lieut. D. Dunham, of Florida.
Lieut. P. E Maher, of Alabama.
Lieut. J. J. Loughlin, of N. Carolina.
Lieut. Chas. P. Crandell, of Maryland.

PROGRAMME.

PART FIRST:

1. Overture ....Band.
2. Opening Chorus...Company.
3. Who Will Care for Mother Now?.................................Henchy.
4. Gentle Nettie Moore ....Withers.
5. Eupidee..Carpenter.
6. Annie of the Vale ....Maher.
7. Cavalryman's Song ....Sherwin.

PART SECOND:

1. Ballad—Dear Mother, I'll Come Home Again..................Henchy.
2. Off to Richmond Like a Flam......................................Sherwin.
3. Picayune Butler...Otey.

PART THIRD:

The performance will conclude with

THE FASHIONABLE BALL.

ZEKE, a rustic...Sherwin.
CYRUS—of undoubted musical ability...............................Otey.
MR. GINGER BLUE, } exquisites of the first water.. { Carpenter.
MR. WASHINGTON GREEN, }   { Palmer.
MISS PHILLIPS—A Terpsichorean divinity ....Henchy.

PRICE OF ADMISSION, 25 CENTS. RESERVED SEATS, 50 CENTS.

☞ Tickets for Reserved Seats can be obtained from the Manager on the day preceding the performance, at Block 11, middle room, up stairs.

CHAPTER XII.

AT HOME, IN THE CALABOOSE,
July 10th, 1865.

As August came tumbling in, so did the rebel prisoners. Sixty-two Confederates, captured at Atlanta, July 22d, made their appearance the 1st day of the month, said they had been furloughed and had come to spend the balance of the summer with us. Among them I found my old friend and class-mate, Major Dick Person, of Memphis. About that date it was that Ulysses Grant, having in vain tried every means reasonable to catch Robert Lee napping, undermined and aimed to blow up the old gentleman at Petersburg. The result was that scores and legions of Mr. Grant's colored folks got so badly hurt that they never spoke again, and Mr. Lee and his boys were in a humor and condition for laughing rather than crying.

Eleven rebel surgeons left for the South on the 4th of August, and I had my bunk widened so as to take in my old friend, Major Person, to sleep with me. Stoneman's cavalry were almost destroyed near Newnan, Georgia, on the 6th, and Early was reported entering Maryland with 35,-000 men, but the strength of the command was greatly exaggerated. And the Northern papers said Mobile was in Federal possession, which same yarn had been perpetrated forty times over concerning Richmond and Charleston.

The following day the authorities commenced hauling in sand and lumber to build a couple of cook and mess rooms, of sufficient capacity to accommodate the whole prison, it having become necessary to take the old cook and mess rooms as quarters for the large number of prisoners then on the island.

Here comes a bold and successful attempt to escape from Federal clutches. In the afternoon Lieutenant Murphy, of our mess, while walking with a companion in the lower part of the prison yard, noticed the detailed soldiers coming and going with the sand wagons, and, having a pair of blue pants at his quarters, concluded that maybe he could go, too. So he donned his blue, put on a rusty woolen shirt, got a police shovel, rolled up his sleeves, rubbed some dust over his face, arms, and clothes, then, with his spade on his shoulder, he marched out behind the first wagon that had no attendant. And now, to carry the joke out, he had to resort to one still more bold, so he went straightway to Colonel Hill's office, and, with a monstrous long face, told him that he had just heard that his mother, who lived near Sandusky City, was at the point of death from a sudden illness, that his Captain was not at his quarters so as to give him a pass, and he prayed the Colonel to give him leave to go to his mother immediately.

The ruse worked, and it happened that Major Scoville, who knew him well (for that was his second visit to Johnson's Island), crossed the bay in the same boat as himself. He afterward wrote to the Major from Canada, telling him of the fact, and that he thought it best to keep his presence dark in consideration of the circumstances. For several days we kept his absence covered up in this wise: When his name was called on the roll some one would say he was sick; then, after roll-call was over, some fellow would detain the Federal officer till another would go and cover up in Murphy's couch, and when the roll-man would go round to see the sick man (Murphy), he would find him "*mighty bad off, aching all over,*" and grunting with pain.

Thus things went on till the third morning, and when Mr. Lieutenant called the name "Murphy," no answer came. He asked where Murphy was; the boys said they didn't know, but reckoned he was in Canada. It was several days before we could convince him but what we were joking.

Lieutenant Murphy soon sent us his photograph, and at the end of two months was in Dixie-land.

My notes for the 7th say: "Seven rebels in blue pants follow lumber wagons out." The prison pen was now in a great fever for Yankee trowsers, and a new sutler came in, we being happy of the chance to bid Mr. Johnson good-bye. The boys prepared to go out by the wholesale on the 9th of August. More Yankee garb was raked up than I dreamed was in prison, worn-out blue pants being worth more than new ones.

It may seem incredulous, but I saw eleven rebels go out on two wagons, and they looked very fair specimens of the laboring Yankees, with ragged pants, rusty shirts, slouched hats, and arms and face begrimed with dust and sand to make up for the want of sunburn. Adjutant Newman, of my regiment, was among them, and he looked so completely Yankeefied that I could scarcely recognize him, though sitting but a few yards off watching the manœuvers.

At last one fellow was detected, and spoiled the fun of himself and those who had gone before. Lieutenant Selecman, of Savannah, Missouri, after attiring himself in proper costume, procured a shovel and bounced into the first sand wagon that came in and commenced heaving out the gritty stuff with all his might, the sweat making huge white streaks through the dirt on his face and arms. The sergeant in charge of the work, happening to look at him closely, could not exactly recognize him as one of his detail, but the fellow assured him that such was the case, telling him to what company and regiment he belonged. But when asked his Captain's name it was a stunner, and he had to capitulate.

The sergeant then remembering that he had seen quite a number going out with the wagons, began to feel a little suspicious, and went to the sentinel at the gate and ordered him to let no one go out with the wagons till further orders. He then invited Lieut. S. to visit Col. Hill's quarters with him, to which the Lieut. readily assented, but on the way he changed his notion and made tracks around several blocks to his quarters.

In a half hour the whole garrison was out and the entire island alive with blue-coats hunting seceshers. At sundown seventeen of the royal stock were turned into the pen wearing gray pants instead of blue, and some of them without any hats at all. Next day the balance of them, I don't know how many, were brought in, but very few having got away, for the shores of the island were kept picketed day and night, and it was the next thing to impossible to find means of escape. From that day forward a corporal, with a squad of men, was kept at the big gate, whose duty it was to examine every wagon that passed in or out, and to allow no one to pass either way that they did not recognize as authorized to do so. Of course, we had a rigid inspection, muster and search the next day, but the gentlemen from the lower country anticipated it, and not a contraband thing was comeatable.

About the 11th of August General Stoneman, with 500 men, was captured near Macon, Georgia, and on that day gold stood at 257 to 260 in New York. I noted down on the 14th of August: "Sunday—Yankee carpenters working on new mess hall; a corporal's guard brought in to make Block 13 respect the Lieutenant calling the roll; some rebels gone to Canada; more strict at roll call, preaching and prayer meeting."

The rebel Colonel Adam Johnson was on the Ohio river, in Kentucky, with 1,200 men, about the middle of August. The 16th was a chilly day, and some twenty "fresh fish," as we called them, came to stay with us. And it seems that every means of escape had not yet been tried, for my journal for the 18th has the following: "Colonel Baxter dyes a rebel uniform blue, assumes a Federal Major's dress, and goes out at the small gate, representing himself as a New York officer; is detected and brought back."

On the 20th of August two disagreeable, heavy strokes fell upon us at the same time. There came an order from the Commissary General of

Prisoners cutting off all provisions from either friends or the sutler, which produced many grim faces, brought forth many a sigh, and something more than a few left-handed blessings upon whoever had a hand in striking the Southern chivalry such a cruel blow.

Then, to add fuel to the fire of discontent, Col. Hill, for the sake of innovation, and to crush out our means of traffic with each other, abolished the system of the sutler giving us checks bearing a stated value, and taking an order for the same on the post commandant, who had all our money in charge. Instead, a complicated schedule or requisition was gotten up, which had to be filled out and approved by the roll caller, superintendent of prison and post commandant; then, being presented to the sutler, he furnished just the articles on that particular requisition, of which we acknowledged the receipt at the price set opposite each article, that being his order on the commander for the amount.

None but those who have had experience know of the thousand and one inconveniences to which prisoners were subjected. Some fellows were always troubled and constantly mad about these little annoyances, but I took it all as something that was to be, and seldom was my equilibrium of temperament ruffled by anything of the kind.

August 21st was a disagreeable day, and that

night was rainy and stormy, and my diary says that three Southern gentlemen, desiring to go South, crawled down a slop ditch that night, prepared to saw out, but the sentinel spying them, called for the corporal of the guard, who marched them to the guard house, where they nearly froze before morning, in their wet and muddy apparel.

During the afternoon of the 23d, while promenading the prison walks with a friend, I met Lieut. Isham Dudley, of the 4th Kentucky, who had arrived some weeks previous, and could give me much information from my old friends of the 4th, with which regiment I was connected at the time of its organization at "Camp Burnett," Tennessee, in the latter part of August, 1861.

On the nights of the 23d and 24th Lieut. Clark and myself *drew* about 100 feet of plank from where the Yankees were building the new mess halls, to make us a studio in the garret loft of our block. A guard was kept over the plank, but we tricked him thus: One of us would go just at dusk and get him at one end of the pile of plank, and detain him there by getting his interest or sympathy aroused by whatever kind of talk was necessary, and, in the meantime, the other one would be dragging a plank from the other end of the pile. Then we would change positions and occupations without any seeming concert of action, managing to get several fine plank each night. It was no trouble for us to make a saw of a case knife; so we measured, sawed and put aloft our lumber while the sun was down.

On the evening of the 25th I wrote in my diary: "Our studio finished; just the thing." And here I will give a little pen picture of it: Just over the outer foot post of my bunk we sawed a hole two feet square in the ceiling through which to pass our lumber and our carcasses *en route* to our studio. As the hole was five feet above the top of the post, we had to first poke our head and arms up, and then draw up the balance, after a manner more easily imagined than described. The joists were now under us, and the rafters and shingles close overhead, and it was pitchy dark. We groped our way to the gable end of the building, and, with case knife saw, soon made an aperture the size of a 10 by 12 pane of glass, which glass we put in after the most approved fashion. I shall not tell where we got the glass. The next thing was to make our floor, which we soon had down in good shape, ten feet square. But now we had no furniture, so we went to work with borrowed tools, stolen nails and confiscated lumber, and, in a reasonable time, a respectable table and two fair stools graced our platform. Then we took a block of wood and bored a hole in it for a candlestick, and then it was I wrote "our studio is finished."

The question may be asked if it didn't "cost more than it came to?" I answer no, for it was a real gratification to do it just because it was "against the rules of school;" then it was a quiet, retired, pleasant nook to study in, such as one could not find in any room of the prison. Then, again, we could study or read there till midnight if we chose, which we often did. All lights in the prison had to be out at half-past nine, and all that we had to do to make it seeming darkness up in our cuddy-hole was to hang a blanket over our little window. Lieut. Clark was studying Spanish, and I was driving away at both French and Spanish, and to-day I would not take a peck of shinplasters for what I learned then and there.

A few days after we made our "home in the loft" Major Scoville, who was often in our room, asked what was the meaning of that hole in the ceiling. We told him it was to let the heated air from our stove escape, and changed the subject soon as possible.

For the 27th August my diary contains: "Excursion party on the island; cannons fired; two hundred rebels in bathing; fifty yards of the prison fence blown down by wind storm; a large squad of secesh threaten to charge out, but it's all smoke and no fire." For the 28th I jotted down: "Lee and Grant, and Early and Sheridan having some heavy fighting—both parties seem to be whipping."

On the 30th I started a letter home, in the name of a rebel who was sick, for some eatables. We had to resort to all sorts of tricks to evade the cruel and unnecessary restrictions of the powers that were. If we could not be sick ourselves we could get some fellow who was sick to assume our name long enough to get a permit for a box of good things from home or elsewhere. After we got the permit signed and started, it was all right, for when the box came it was easy to claim that a fellow had got *most well* since the things were sent for.

A short time after that Lieutenant Clark, who was so bony and ugly that he always looked sick, played off on the Yankee doctor, in my name, with a bogus case of chronic dysentery, and got an order to send to one of my friends for some needful restoratives. I have heard Dr. Eversman, chief surgeon of the post, remark that out of 100 "sick letters" presented to him for approval, 80 per cent. called for "chronic diarrhea," the applicant often being as fat and blooming as a morning rose.

On the 1st day of September I wrote in my memorandum, "Wheeler moving on Nashville from Murfreesboro—Atlanta reported captured—white fish issued to us instead of bacon—nothing to fry it in, and we are displeased—an order comes forbidding us to write more than two letters a week, and we are displeased again, but many of us see a way of getting round it, for there are other names except our own, and some of us can write running hand, back hand, and another style."

The next day, Friday, at 2 P. M., a Kentucky rebel soldier, named Nichols, was hung on the island. He had been sentenced by a court-martial in Cincinnati, on the charge of being a murderer, guerilla and robber. The proof seemed clear, and, though we felt sad, we could not but justify his fate. At the hour of execution the prison guard was doubled. His cousin, Lieutenant Nichols, a prisoner with us, allowed to go out and see him that morning.

Saturday night there came along a little incident that, at home, would not have been noticed, but which I jotted down as follows: "We have big ratastrophe—kill two." That night three large rats came into the room, and one of the boys, being awake, closed the door on them. As it was hot we had left the door open and the top sash of the window out. Their scampering and lunging to escape soon waked the whole room, and two of the fellows, being somewhat nervous and tired, wanted to let the rats out. But as the majority ruled in our room, and we wanted to have some more fun, the animals had to stay. It was a jollification from 3 o'clock till daylight, the rats racing over the floor, table, stove, shelves and beds, and frequently finding the end of a leap right in our faces. One huge fellow crawled on my bunk near my head, and made a clear leap through a second story window. At daylight, after chasing the other two for awhile, we captured and beheaded them. So much for the rat story.

Notwithstanding the following was the Lord's day, our prison witnessed a "ratastrophe" on a far more magnificent scale than the one just named. I was an eye witness and noted down at the time, "Sunday, 2 o'clock P. M.—About fifty rebels, with a little dog, ratting—catch forty—some of the fellows going to make chicken pie, and others squirrel fry of them—lots of rats and fun." To give some idea of the respectability and rank of our "rat club," I will just mention that Colonel John A. Fite, 7th Tennessee regiment, was its President, and Lieutenant Billy Foote, son of Governor Foote, of Nashville, his chief-of-staff.

On the 5th day of September I got leave from Major Scoville to send home for some winter clothing, which, after many vexatious obstacles, my mother succeeded in getting to me in November. At that time my friend, Lieutenant Nick

Fain, of the 60th Tennessee, was sick in the hospital, and sickness was on the increase. Two days later we heard that Atlanta had certainly gone up, and that General John H. Morgan had been killed at Greenville, Tennessee.

Now came one of those troublous, exciting eras in our prison existence. The new mess halls were finished, and all the cooking stoves were ordered to be moved to the appropriate department of the same. The cooking facilities of at least 1,200 men were now crowded into a place about 40 feet square. Imagine twelve large cook stoves in that space, with about fifty cooks, and the rations, wood and water to cook for a thousand men interspersed, and you have a very slight idea of the disadvantages. That broke into the domestic comforts of the institution more than anything ever before had done, and I knew not an individual who was not displeased by the new order of things. But necessity compelled them to accept and accommodate themselves to it.

There were a dozen or more small, private cook stoves in the prison, and they were also ordered to be moved, but, by skillful and judicious manœuvering, some of us managed to keep our stoves in our rooms. For a week we hid the vessels of ours and hired a fellow to cook for us at the mess hall, then we cooked a little for breakfast and kept the stove cold all day. Before long we went a step farther, and cooked dinner, too, but, for a whole month, did not let a Yankee catch a pot on our stove, or us washing dishes. If our dinner pot was on, and they came on an inspection tour, it had to go under the table and be covered up. And "we 'uns" were not the only chaps that had to make hay only while the sun shined.

In the great future all these facts and incidents will seem strange, almost mythical, to the reader, but it is a true picture of every-day life on Johnson's Island.

And now came the exciting question of who should occupy the cook and mess rooms just vacated. The rooms, being small, were desirable, as winter was coming on, and it was almost impossible to keep warm in the large rooms during cold days. No one could change his quarters without leave from the prison superintendent, to whom at least two hundred applications were made, almost every one adducing some special reason why he should have preference. I must say that the assignment was a partial affair, the friends of the superintendent getting preference over those worse situated.

My journal says that on the 10th Capt. Blair's room of our mess took in four additional men, for the sake of getting to cook in their room on a small stove; it also notes that the press reported

Early as continually retreating in the Valley, that gold stood at 225, and that the letter of acceptance of General McClellan, who had just been nominated for President, was warlike. I copy from my diary for the 14th: "One hundred privates sent here from 'Camp Chase' to do police duty; circular from General Trimble concerning police matters and the general interests of the prison; at nine o'clock P. M. we make a raid on the hospital wood-pile."

Now, about that last item. We (our room) were taking the squirrel's plan, and laying away a store for the cold blasts of winter. They issued us wood in limited quantities, but furnished the hospital without regard to quantity, and we could see no impropriety in appropriating a stick or two every night or so, which we laid away in a nice pile in the loft close by the studio. Every few days we would take a little of it down and saw it up with our regular rations of wood, then store it away in the garret over our room. By the 1st of November we had a solid half-cord of nicely prepared *extra* stovewood. It made us feel independent, and many a time in the dead of winter made us feel comfortable while the less provident were suffering.

Twenty-five sick were sent off on the 16th, and at the same time Colonel Lewis, our most eloquent preacher and most prominent Mason, left for special exchange, and six naval officers also went on exchange, pursuant to an agreement between the naval departments. The next day two rebel captains who had been nurses in the hospital, and who had managed to procure Federal corporals' uniforms, forged passes and walked out at the gate, big as General Grant, but the Yankee hospital steward, *Doctor Foster(?)*, recognized them, and they were earnestly, though kindly, solicited to metamorphose back into Confederates, which they did without much delay.

About the 18th of September the steamers Island Queen and Philo Parsons were captured on Lake Erie by Confederates from Canada, and the next day several conspirators were arrested in Sandusky City, and for several days the gunboat Michigan was searching about the lake for piratical crafts. One of the Sandusky conspirators was formerly a lieutenant in the Confederate army, and known by many then on the island. My journal reports heavy fighting on the Potomac and on the Weldon railroad about that time.

Major-General Hitchcock came to the island on the 22d, and that day I bathed at the wash-house and had my clothes washed on a machine. Washing was carried on as a business. A fellow would get permission to buy a machine from Sandusky, and engage to do the washing of certain ones every week; then he would hire sufficient help to collect, wash, iron and deliver the clothing. Prices were moderate, and the work generally faithfully performed. I did my own washing at first, but after hiring a few times, lost all taste for the business. But I never objected to doing my share of the cooking.

On the 23d Generals Hitchcock and Heintzelman visited the prison quarters and inspected the hospital. That night, or rather next morning before day, Captain Furnish and Lieutenant Maris, of Andrew county, Missouri, who roomed opposite me, had a fight in the dark over a rat. The critter came snuffing around in search of something to eat; Maris concluded to eat him, so fastened the door on him, and Mr. Rat began such gymnastic feats as I have described a few pages back. Furnish wanted to sleep, was annoyed, and asked Maris to let the quadruped out, which he refused to do. Furnish said he would do it himself; Maris said he should not. Up they bounced in the dark, each intent on having his notion carried out; they clinched, they scuffled, they fell, and each was glad to find the other willing to quit. Maris had a finger nail bit off, and Furnish an eye badly gouged. No one knew what became of the rat; he vanished during the progress of the fracas.

CHAPTER XIII.

Headquarters, Up Stairs in the Jonesboro Jail,
July 11, 1865.

I am still an inmate of that institution built at the public expense, and where they propose to board fellows for nothing, "*pro bono publico.*" It is possible that the public may be benefited by my staying here, but *I* can't see it in that light, and I'm very sure that I am making nothing by the operation. Just now, however, I am driving along very quietly and contentedly, and will try to rest easy and let time tell what will be.

It may be an item not unworthy of note that my writing desk is a strip of plank eight by fourteen inches, and that I have to use my lap as legs for said piece of furniture; but such an inconvenience as that is a mere matter of moonshine to a prisoner or soldier.

Now we will leave the present be and wander back to September, 1864. The great Chicago Convention had nominated McClellan and Pendleton, and I yet well remember the anxiety the Copperhead masses of the North manifested for their success, no doubt sincerely feeling that the welfare of the country and the restoration of peace depended upon it. But the most of us Rebs up North felt indifferent, as we could not see wherein our cause would be benefited thereby. It may now seem a strange, unchristian feeling, but then, little did we care how much internal dissension and ruin was worked in the North.

But now my state of feelings are changed, and I trust the same is true of every honest, reasonable man of the South. I would love to see the party wounds healed up, so far as was possible, and the two sections upon terms of friendship and sympathy, at least so far as commercial relations were concerned; and it must inevitably come to that, for neither section can prosper without it, and interest is a great motor power. If we would only follow the golden rule, how like a charm it would work in alleviating the evils that follow in the train of a civil conflict.

The night of the 24th and the morning of the 25th September, 1864, are times never to be forgotten by any one who was then on Johnson's Island, and perhaps there is not one who has since gotten home that has not told his friends of that memorable occasion. During the day of the 24th all was quiet and settled, but at the hour of half-past nine, when perhaps half the prison were in bed, and the rest preparing for it, there suddenly came a black, ugly cloud in the west, and the first thing we knew a terrific tornado was sweeping over our island.

One-half the standing timber was laid flat, and three of our blocks, 4, 5 and 9, and one of the garrison quarters, were unroofed. When the house began to quiver and the bricks and timber to fly we expected the whole building would be a wreck, and each fellow aimed to save himself. Those who had retired had no time to put on hat, coat, boots or pants, and it was pitch dark, except when a flash of lightning lit up the appalling scene. Some jumped from second story windows, others tumbled down the steps, they knew not how. I made a lunge in the dark from the platform at the top of our flight of steps leading to the second story, without even thinking where I would light, but, as it happened, was "right side up with care" when I reached the ground.

Then some took refuge in the slop ditches, some behind stumps, and some actually climbed down into the wells for safety. Others flew wildly across the prison yard, hoping to find a safe place in the open space next to the lake. I ran the gauntlet of the flying timbers, and took refuge behind the sutler shop, 200 yards from my quarters. This is just a skeleton idea of the reality. Many men who had faced the music in a dozen bloody battles said they were never before so terrified; and, to add to the ill-comfort of the occasion, a cold, pelting rain was falling all the while. Several were badly wounded, one fellow having a strip of flesh two inches wide and to the bone taken off his leg from thigh to knee by a flying timber, and many miraculous, narrow escapes were made.

At least one-third of the prison wall was laid to the ground, and during all that storm and confusion the Federal garrison were got into line and so disposed as to prevent the escape of any one. Several cannon shots and many of musketry were fired, intended to intimidate us, but we did not scare worth a cent at that. The raging billows on the lake, and no way of crossing, was what troubled us. Next morning the whole prison yard was a mass of scattered and shattered timbers. A large force of carpenters and workmen immediately commenced a readjustment of affairs, and in a few weeks all was sound again. From that day till this I have felt uneasy when in a house while a hard wind was blowing, and I think it probable that such a feeling will accompany me to the grave.

The morning after the storm there were any number of advertisements for lost articles of every description, and some rich jokes were told. One poor, lean rebel asked a more corpulent companion to lie down on him and keep the storm from blowing him away. And one chap, suddenly repentant, asked a room mate to pray for him, and received the reply, "I don't know anything but the Lord's prayer, and that ain't worth a damn in the time of a storm."

Now, there is something which I forgot in its proper place, or rather it occurred about the close of 1863, of which period I took no notes, and it will go to show that some of us had happy experiences as well as unhappy ones. With the great mass of the human race variety is the spice of life, and we were no exception to the general rule. We enjoyed in more ways than one the case about to be related, and I'm rather sure that the reader is fond of the spice of life, and will now partially enjoy that which we did to its full extent, because we had both *a taste for it and a taste of it.*

There was one Thompson in our prison, who was neither loyal nor disloyal—the good, philanthropic soul couldn't hate anybody for his politics, but loved the whole world. Thompson was "on the fence," not being rebellious enough to fight for Dixie, nor patriotic enough to risk his scalp in the cause of the "glorious Union." Late in the fall of 1863 Mr. T. established a restaurant at one end of block 5, proposing to be excelled by none in all the balance of the great world either in variety, quality or moderate charges. Dear Thompson loved (?) us so that he did not charge us more than a price and a half for anything.

Well do I yet remember that Christmas eve of the aforesaid year was a beautiful, balmy day, and that late in the evening not less than five hundred sons of the South were promenading the prison walks, the theme of all themes being Christmas times in days gone by contrasted with then. Now, friend T. had procured a fine, fat, old gobbler, and, like all restaurant keepers do, hung it out on a nail at the front door as an advertisement, and the news was circulated everywhere that Thompson was going to have a grand Christmas dinner, admittance fee only half a dollar.

Now, how much stretch of the imagination would it require to conclude that the mouths of almost that whole five hundred were watering for some of said turkey? But comparatively few of them were in a fit financial condition for Thompson's feast. As the twilight was coming on we noticed various squads of Southern gentlemen, evidently canvassing for some—not legal but practicable—means of confiscating the fowl. Perhaps a half dozen of us were standing on the platform in front of our block, and, feeling sure that the turkey would go up, we thought we might as well have a finger in the pie as anybody, so we began to caucus, too, and in ten minutes the plot was complete. In my room a half dozen States were represented, but in the one just across the hall from us were only Missourians, and the two rooms were upon intimate terms of friendship and sympathy. We had a cooking stove in our room and a big, tin boiler, and they had a large table. They were to steal the much coveted biped, we were to conceal and cook it, and all hands eat it Christmas day on their table.

"Faint heart never won fair lady," and besides time was precious, for many a Spartan band were making ready to charge upon and "gobble up" the good old gobbler. Lieutenant Maris, who was lately mentioned as having the rat fight with Captain Furnish, was our bravest Spartan of all, for, with Colonel Printup's ample talma and two-story slouch hat, he took a bee-line diagonally across the pen to where the turkey was, gently, but quickly, lowered it from the nail, under the cloak the gobbler went and around the corner Maris vanished, and, by a zig-zag route through the swarm of rebels, reached our quarters, no one even recognizing him except we, us and company. We laid him (the turkey) down to rest till morning, and "all was quiet on the Potomac," but it was not thusly at Thompson's headquarters. It seems that he knew of the conspiracy up to de prive him of his turkey-fowl, and had taken position over by the hospital, opposite his institution, to watch and catch him who might dare to lay hands on his treasure. *Lord* Thompson saw the inanimate creature vanish, and started in pursuit instanter, but, in hunters' phrase, *the fox doubled on him*, and he soon gave up the chase in bewilderment.

The night passed on; Thompson was sad and we were happy. The morning came, and when the first rays of the great day-god kissed the bosom of the placid lake, *our* turkey was boiling away. While we were eating our frugal Christmas breakfast, in stepped Captain—I forget who—but remember that his thermometer indicated essence of corn within. He politely stammered out that Mr. Thompson had understood that his turkey was in our room, and requested him to come over and ask for it. At once we were astonished and indignant at the very idea, and told him to tell Mr. Thompson if he had any business with us to come and transact it himself, that we didn't care about dealing with agents. He said his mission was a peaceful one, and he did not want to be insulted; and we replied that neither did we want to be insulted by being charged with robbery. All this time Mr. Gobbler was blubbering away in the boiler hard by. The adage that "fortune favors the brave" hit our nail exactly on the head.

Major Scoville had, early that morning, presented our room with a turkey for a Christmas dinner, and his name was on the label attached to its feet. With triumphal air we produced it, and told Mr. Captain where it came from, but that we could not vouch for whether he stole it from Thompson or not. He begged our pardon and departed, fully satisfied that the charge against us had no foundation in fact. As the hours rolled gladly by we were making appropriate domestic arrangements to do justice to the fatted fowl. Nor did we covet company one bit that day, but every now and then an unwelcome guest would drop in.

Dinner time came on; the Missourians had their table spread with all the queensware, cutlery and tin cups of both rooms, Mr. Turkey occupied the center of the board, and was the center of attraction. About fourteen of us did ample justice to all the stuffing and meat that clustered about his carcass, and we had a sure-enough preacher to say Amen, it being no other than the veritable Colonel Lewis that I have mentioned elsewhere. He enjoyed the thing from first to last, and said it was the best joke of the season, to which we unanimously replied, Amen.

Gentle reader, or ungentle reader, don't presume this to be an imaginary sketch, for that preacher, who afterward went South and was made a brigadier-general, will stand by every word of it. Now, how many of the world will vote that, considering the circumstances, it was a good joke well played, and how many will condemn us? "*Nous verrons.*"

Sheridan had routed and almost completely demolished Early's army on the 19th of September, and the whole North was jubilant over the matter, thinking it could never be resurrected, and on the 27th our post commandant ordered one hundred guns to be fired in honor of the event. At that date Price and Shelby were advancing into Missouri, N. B. Forrest was going into Middle Tennessee, and gold was rating at 185.

For the 29th I transcribe from my memorandum book: "Short rations; hungry men; grumbling; two rebs. fight at the cook-house—one of them gets hurt; I chief cook this week; Price and Forrest doing execution." The next morning I noted down, "We had biscuit for breakfast. I made a mistake; we had five biscuit apiece, instead of three."

Now, in our room, each fellow cooked a week at a time, the cook for the time being having sole charge of that department, no one having a right to interfere as to when, how or what was cooked.

But each one took a pride in being prompt, cleanly and getting up the best dishes possible from our frugal stock of supplies. If we got a fifty-pound sack of flour we had biscuit twice a week, but if a twenty-five-pound sack, we usually had wheat bread Sunday morning. We did not sub-divide our rations, as did many rooms, but the cook generally aimed to make an equal number of biscuits for every member of the mess. That morning I made five apiece (small ones), but told the fellows there were only three. Each one made way with his portion and was satisfied, but, when told that there were two more for every mother's son of them, they were glad as if they had been golden dollars. We enjoyed every morsel we got to eat.

About the 1st of October I learned from home that a number of our neighbors (who were loyal like myself) had been drafted to fight for the Union. And the same letter said that our negro boys, George and Armstead, had ran off to a recruiting station at "Camp Nelson, Kentucky." Deluded beings! they left a good and comfortable home in search of thoughted freedom, and very soon were both in the grave.

All along in the first days of October the Federals were "pegging away" close to Richmond, and Price had Missouri in a blaze. In the afternoon of the 4th I took some stewed peaches to

Parson Ash, and some flaxseed for a poultice to Capt. Morgan—both in the hospital. The former was a resident of my county; the latter one of my chums in Block 4. The Rev. Mr. Ash was suffering from general debility, and Capt. Morgan from the effects of a rusty nail stuck in his foot the night of the storm. That night Capt. Brooks, Post Quartermaster, died, and the flag hung at half mast all next day.

The prison carpenter, who was working inside the yard on the 6th, left a wide plank leaning against the wall near Block 1. A gentleman who had been raised and educated in, and was battling for, Louisiana, spied it, and at night, with the necessary implements, evacuated the pen, leaving a hole beneath the fence under that plank. In two weeks he wrote to his friends, congratulating himself at the good luck in findhimself in Canada.

October 8th was cold, rainy, sleety and snowy, and the Feds. began to issue wood to the whole prison that day. Several prisoners came in— among them my old schoolmate, Captain Henry Armant, aid-de-camp on General Heth's staff—and fifty sick left for the cotton States. The next day our room bought from the sutler a lamp, with fixtures and two gallons of coal oil, for $8.00.

For October 10th my diary reads: "Burbridge thrashed out at Saltville, Virginia; lots of his

Africans slain; fight at block 9; Colonel Printup gets sugar, coffee and lard through *Colonel* Scoville."

When the prison was first built on Johnson's Island, in the spring of 1862, W. S. Pierson was Major commanding post, and E. A. Scoville was Captain in command of a company. During the summer of 1863 Pierson was promoted to Lieut.-Colonel and Scoville to Major. When the "Hoffman Battalion" was increased to a regiment and called the 128th Ohio, Charles W. Hill was made Colonel, Pierson resigned, Scoville took his place and rank, and Captain Thomas H. Linnell was made Major of said regiment.

A general search was made through the prison on the 14th for saws and axes that had come up missing. During such searches (we being under guard out in the yard), various little articles were supposed to have been purloined by the light-fingered Northern gentry, and so, to keep along even with the Yanks, we had to "play possum." One fellow in each room would invariably get sick and be in bed on such occasions.

The Confederates had now recaptured Rome, Georgia, and "Old Pap Price" was at Boonville, Mo. Considerable express matter was coming in, and that evening Lieut. Wilson, of Georgia, presented us with some parched coffee. If the reader will keep a sharp lookout, there will, before long, be found a place where Wilson was highly complimented, kinder like our friend Thompson was. All jokes are said to be free in harvest times, and why not as well in Christmas times?

Major Person, in the name of Lieut. Lotspiech, got a nice box of good things to eat from his cousin, Mrs. Madeira, of Covington, Kentucky, on the 17th October, and, as what one received we all received, the whole household was heartily glad. The succeeding day Maj.-Gen. Trimble and Brig -Gens. Beall, Jones and Frazier were removed from our prison to Fort Warren. Hood's army was now between Dalton and Bridgeport, Price was at Lexington, Missouri, and gold was at 220. Pestiferous bands of marauders were still carrying a bold front all over Kentucky, the authorities seeming utterly unable, by terrible warnings, to dissipate them.

On the 23d of October we had codfish and flour issued to us instead of pork and baker's bread—some liked the change, some didn't, it being utterly impossible to please all. For the 24th my diary reads: My birthday; I have been in the army 38 months; we had ham, coffee and biscuit for breakfast." During the last days of October Price was about Fort Scott, Hood in Walker county, Georgia, and all was quiet along the James and Potomac. And along about those times Lieut. Clark and I were spending many pleasant hours up in our little studio poring over the Castilian language. We had at first a German, who had resided in Mexico, for a preceptor, but we did not like him, and concluded to go it alone.

November, 1864, opened in a most auspicious manner for room 19, block 4, Johnson's Island, Ohio. On the first day Lieut. Oliver Clark got flour, ham, coffee, dried fruit and butter from Richmond, Kentucky, and per the same express Colonel Printup received a jug of six year old whisky, and one of claret wine, all contraband, but Colonel Scoville let him have it—*for medical purposes*, of course.

We were happy that evening, and my diary says: "Old Pap got drunk." Old Pap was Tom Stevenson, a native of Woodford county, Kentucky, but latterly from St. Joseph, Missouri, and he had been on Johnson's Island since September, 1862, held as a suspected spy. He says that Gen. Price sent him to Kentucky to look around, and that they took him in out of the weather at Versailles. The first six months of my stay up North he was our postmaster and tailor, and, being a vain, pompous, eccentric, spluttering fellow, everybody knew "Old Pap," and had something to say to him. He was acquainted with all our room, and Colonel P., knowing that he admired the critter to desperation, invited him over to take a social glass with us. He came, he saw, and *it* conquered, not exactly verifying Cæsar's laconic dispatch, "*Veni, vidi, vici.*"

We had not yet reached the end of our string of good luck, for on the 3d Major Person received a splendid box from his wife at Memphis. Among many other goodly items was a bushel of sweet potatoes, and, as I noted down in my little book that evening, "we were in town with a pocket full of rocks." It was some *supposed terrible ailment* that produced each one of these boxes, for a well man was not allowed to send for anything.

Maj.-General Marmaduke, Brig.-General Cabell, and four Colonels from Price's army arrived at our headquarters on the 6th, and General Price was now retreating from Missouri at double quick time before the legions of Federal cavalry concentrated on him. All along about that time gold was ranging from 245 to 256, and the weather was cool and changeable.

The 8th of November was election day for President of the United States, and the whole Abolition and Copperhead press was teeming with charges of fraud, and the Federal authorities were very much alarmed about threatened raids all along the Canada border. Troops were stationed at many of the border towns, and a General assigned to the special duty of looking after the Federal interests along that front.

I copy from my diary: "November 9th, much

wind and rain; sudden change of temperature. 10th—Sherman reported moving on Charleston; Hood in Middle Tennessee. 11th—Forty of Gen. Price's officers arrive. 14th—Snow, but pleasant weather. 16th—Sherman's movements mysterious."

I received a letter from Kentucky on the 20th, saying that the guerrillas were troublesome about my native haunts, but that it did not prevent the people from marrying. The same day we had letters from East Tennessee, through which I learned of the whereabout of several members of my company that I had lost sight of. From it I learned that Wm. Holloway, who went to prison with us, and, after eighteen months' captivity, had started home sick, died at Bristol, Tenn. Will. was a good boy and a good soldier, though his neighbors at home told me he was disloyal and would not do to trust. I did not conceal from him what I had heard of his character, and he seemed to take a pride in being faithful and honorable; and such was the case with several others that had been reported to me as not just the right thing.

It was about the 21st of November that Breckenridge gave Gillam a terrible beating at Morristown, Tennessee. His wagon train and artillery, with many men, were captured, and almost his whole army scattered and flew, pell-mell, to Knoxville.

November 23d was a very cold day, and the bay froze over. I employed Captain Lattner, of Louisiana, who had a machine, to do my washing, and my diary records that the whereabout of Sherman are yet mysterious. The fact is that he had left Gen. Thomas to take care of Hood, and, cutting loose from all base, struck out on one of the boldest campaigns of the war, Charleston or Savannah being his objective point.

It was about this era that General Burbridge was having guerrillas shot by the wholesale, and not unfrequently regular Confederate soldiers were led out and cruelly executed, in retaliation for the depredations and crimes of outlaws. There was a reign of terror and bloodshed in Kentucky; may the like of which never come again.

On the 26th my old friends, Major Wm. Smith, 62d Tennessee, and Captain Levi Mobly, 26th Tennessee, arrived at our little home in the lake. That was a memorable, exciting day. Some time previous a thousand bales of cotton had been sent from Mobile to New York to be sold, the proceeds to be spent for clothing, blankets and provisions for the rebel prisoners up North, Brigadier-General W. N. R. Beall, C. S. A., was selected to buy and distribute said articles, his headquarters being at New York. He issued a circular to all the prisons, requesting them to choose a commissioner to receive and distribute what was sent to each place.

The office seemed to be desirable, for the expectation was that the agent would get many favors and privileges not accorded to his fellow-sinners. A number of candidates offered, and wire-working and electioneering began straightway. On the evening of election we had speeches of every grade—sensible, foolish, grave, humorous and witty. Colonel John A. Fite, who has been before mentioned as President of the "rat club," got the position by long odds, and most everybody thought he was the right man, for he had been our very efficient chief commissary, and was not afraid to talk to the Yanks, or even curse them a little, if it was necessary to get our dues.

I sat up with the sick at hospital in ward 4 on the night of the 28th. Hood was now before Franklin, Tennessee, and Sherman's movements were no longer mysterious, he having taken possession of Milledgeville, Georgia. He was now several hundred miles from any base, in the heart of a hostile country, with 70,000 men, and many of the Confederate leaders pretended to think that his doom was fixed, but he managed to reach the sea coast, thus showing to the world what can be done where there is a determination. I will not speak of the unworthy, unchristian incidents connected with that "march to the sea." Would that all such could be blotted from the pages of history and from our memories; then we would be happier.

CHAPTER XIV.

IN JAIL, *July 12, 1865.*

The past few days have been extremely hot, and this abode has not added very much to the comfort of such weather, but I have withstood so much that I conclude I can bear up under anything that would not kill a mule. From my relative situation, being directly between the courthouse and printing office, it would seem that I ought to be able to get justice. Mr. Grissom, of the Jonesboro *Union Flag*, thinks that *justice to rebels* is persecution and suffering equal to what the Union people here have undergone, no matter at whose hands. He grossly prevaricated and magnified the cause and manner of my arrest, but I won't say any more about it here, for I happen to remember that it is sometimes best for a fellow "not to whistle till he is out of the woods."

Now let us travel back to the first days of last December. My note book says there was a big fight at Franklin, Tennessee, and that Thomas had fallen back on Nashville. On the 7th one hundred officers taken at Franklin were brought into prison. I listened to the story of the battle from many of them, and it was surely the most fearful and terrible struggle of the war. At one time a long column of Confederates pressed up to the very earthworks of the Federals, but could not scale them, and there the contending parties laid within a few feet of each other, shooting over the embankment at random. The Southern troops were not reinforced, and had to surrender, as every one who attempted to retreat was shot down. In that battle the noble, gallant, beloved Pat. Cleburne gave up his life.

About the first of the month Adjutant Frank Clewel, 1st Missouri cavalry, who had made several daring but futile attempts to escape, got a special exchange, and at night of the day he left two of the "Southern chivalry" scratched out at the end of Block 1, but were taken in, and a new lamp put up there to caution them against repeating the risk of so unpleasant a defeat.

The end of Block 1 was rather a famous place, perhaps fifty different rebels having tried to escape there. And it was a place of resort to witness dress-parade, look at visitors to the island, and whatever was going on about headquarters. Full many a pleasing hour have I whiled away at that point, watching the movements of the world without.

The 8th was an extremely cold day, and we could almost see the body of ice grow as it extended itself over the bay, and there were three inches of snow on the ground. Colonel Matlock, of Arkansas, died on the 10th. Along about that period of our captivity, Colonel Hill was becoming more popular among the prisoners by issuing more reasonable orders and being more consistent generally.

President Lincoln's message was now before the country. He seemed to have issued it more as a matter of form than anything else, as no new theory or policy was enunciated, but he referred to his former messages and proclamations as still the rule of his faith and action. Chase had just been made Chief Justice and Speed Attorney-General.

The 12th day of December was the coldest, so far, of the season. That forenoon Col. Scoville was in our room, "about three sheets in the wind," and quite jovial. I observed to him that if I had about half that he had under his shirt it would make us both feel better. Said he: "It is a splendid time to take on a little, and, if I don't forget it, I will bring you fellows in a drop after dinner." After a little prison chit-chat and some pleasant jokes he left the room, we not expecting to see him again for, probably, several days, but about 3 P. M. in popped Mr. Scoville again. We had several visitors; he said he wanted to see the members of the room privately, and they left, we supposing it was some warning or special news for us, but he simply hauled out a bottle filled from the jug under the bed in his quarters, which jug I had tapped in the summer of 1863. He just remarked that we must keep the thing dark. Were I given to lying, this would certainly be classed among the untruths, but it's a fact, and one more incident showing that we had some generous Abolition foes.

The night of the 12th was almost as memorable and alarming as that of the storm. At about two o'clock in the night some thirty rebels attempted to scale the wall in rear of the hospital. They had prepared themselves with nearly a dozen ladders, some clubs, rocks and one or two pistols, and all started at the same time for the fence, one hundred yards in rear of the hospital. The moon was shining bright as day, the sentinels saw them, and a half-dozen concentrated where they aimed to strike the fence. Hostilities commenced immediately; several rebels got to the top of the wall, but were knocked back, and one Federal was hurled from the parapet.

Some fifty musket and pistol shots were fired, but, miraculously, only one man was killed. Lieutenant Boles, of Louisville, Kentucky, was shot from a ladder half-way up the wall. But few of the prisoners were aware that such a break was contemplated, and it may be believed that we were terrified by being aroused from our slumbers by such a racket right in our midst. In a little while the whole garrison was out, and a number of cannon were fired, evidently to make us lie still. That dried up all talk about charging the fence.

The next day a prisoner fell from the platform of Block 9 and was mortally injured, and that evening I noticed four corpses in the dead-house. My notes for the 15th are: "General Beall in New York—issues a circular to Confederate prisoners to find out their most pressing wants as to clothing and provisions; we almost a unit for grub; exchange going on at Charleston; Sherman fighting in front of Savannah; Warren makes another raid on the Weldon railroad; Nashville besieged."

On the 16th our mail came over on the ice, Hood and Thomas were fighting at Nashville, and Colonel Boles, 2d Kentucky cavalry, was elected to assist Colonel Fite.

I will here say that, after all the talking and fixing, never a rag nor a morsel had we received when I left Johnson's Island, the last of the succeeding February, though some clothing had been received at other prisons.

It was the 18th that we heard that Hood had

been defeated, with a heavy loss of men and artillery, and was retreating. His army was almost ruined during his Middle Tennessee campaign. The next day the loyal people cut a port-hole in the wall at the southwest corner of the prison yard, for our benefit, of course. At about that time they commenced the erection of a large fort on the island, northwest of the prison; also another at the southwest, on the highest point of land, and about the center of the island. Their proceedings seemed to indicate a want of faith both in us and the people over north of Lake Erie; and who that knew of the immediate past could blame them?

The 22d was snowy, windy, and bitter cold, the thermometer being many degrees below the freezing point, which makes anything but a pleasant state of weather. That day Captain Sanford, Inspector General, came round to determine the number of blankets in prison, and who had them. Now came a necessity for a little juggling, as we anticipated that his aim was to take away from those who had more, and give to those who had less, than a prescribed number. My bunk mate and I had each a pair of our own besides the government allowance. We were sure that was over the general average, so we took off and hid a part of them till the inspection was over.

The temperature next morning was no better, and the sergeant was allowed to call the roll in our quarters. That day Lieutenant Lear, who had been kicked out of block 11 for stealing, was allowed by the prison superintendent to make himself a little cuddy-hole in one end of our garret loft. It seems that he did not steal from necessity, for he had plenty, but it was his natural inclination, and he was known to capture little things after going there. No one who would associate with him was respected.

The succeeding day 280 of Hood's officers, taken about Nashville, came over on the ice to reinforce our already populous garrison. Among them were Major-General Ed. Johnson and Brigadier-Generals Henry R. Jackson and Tom Smith, the last almost a boy. The whole crew of them gave evident signs of hardships and suffering, many being almost destitute of clothing. All the old prisoners who had surplus clothes were requested to divide with them, and a generous, sympathizing spirit was displayed, the recipients, in many cases, hardly knowing how to express their gratitude.

That day we took into our room Lieutenant Fite, of Memphis, and Lieut. Yarbrough, of Georgia, both of them proving congenial room mates. And that day Colonel Scoville came in and took Colonel Printup to dine with him. For a rebel to eat on the outside was a rare privilege, seldom granted. We thought and we talked a heap about, but couldn't prepare much for, Christmas..

At Christmas of the preceding year we were, many of us, in good fix to enjoy the holidays, as there were but few restrictions from receiving anything from our friends up North. But the latter days of 1864 were almost "dry as a powder horn." On the former occasion there were lots of good things to eat, and a right smart sprinkle of something to exhilarate the inner man; on the latter both were almost "scarce as hen's teeth."

For Christmas day I copy from my diary: "Old Pap comes over for a dram (though he don't say so), but it is like trying to coax blood out of a turnip—Colonel Mike Woods, 46th Alabama, gets a special exchange—Yankee chaplain brings in good things for sick rebels—nobody drunk, for the best of reasons—I am on cook detail this week—we had ham and biscuit for breakfast, pudding for dinner, and will have "fish in the dab" to-morrow morning—I made "fish in the dab" out of our lake shad, and all the scraps of bread, meat, onions, &c., that we had, conglomerated into a batter and fried or baked. I flavored it with sage and pepper, and the boys said they didn't want anything better. We never wasted an ounce of anything edible.

A goodly number of express boxes was delivered in prison on the 27th, some of them without permit, and that day the post commandant issued an order suppressing from prison the New York *News*, Chicago *Times* and Cincinnati *Enquirer*, they being Copperhead, almost rebel, papers. Sherman had now taken Savannah, and "*Beast Butler*" and Admiral Porter were hammering away at Wilmington. About that date the rebel General Lyon cut the Louisville and Nashville Railroad at Elizabethtown, Kentucky, and Gen. McCook was after him.

On the 30th a number of rebels applied to work on the forts for the sake of getting full rations, as such a course was being pursued at other prisons. Gold was then at 216. I had just got through my Spanish grammar, and had spent most of the Christmas reading a novel written in French, and entitled "Rosa, or Filial Piety."

Now, for the closing hours of the year I will transcribe from my diary: "31st December—last day of the old year; mighty dry Christmas; Col. Printup has a box on the outside and I one in anticipation; prison superintendent has on a full load of '*eau de vie*;' weather moderate; Yankees skating; our prospects for another year's sojourn excellent. Good-bye 1864."

But something took place during the small dying hours of the year which, though I took no note of it, I can not forget. Lieutenant Wilson, of General Frazier's staff at Cumberland Gap, and who belonged to the same regiment as Colonel Printup and Lieutenant Clark of my room, had gone to the hospital as a nurse for the sake of something good to eat. Now, Lieutenant W. was all sorts of an antic, jolly fellow, and had a rooster chicken which he had raised around the hospital. We often talked to him about purloining his fowl, but he said we could not steal it in the day time and that it roosted so close to the sentinel's beat that we were afraid to go for it after night, so he was not uneasy.

After supper on the 31st we were discussing what we should have for a New Year's dinner. Some one proposed Wilson's chicken; "agreed," vociferated all hands; but then came the question, "who was to bell the cat?" We discussed the matter in all shapes till bed time, when it was agreed that Colonel P. should furnish his large talma cloak as a disguise and covering, that I should seize the prey, and Lieutenant Clark dress and cook it.

The other boys went to bed, not to sleep, and I sat in the dark by the stove till the sentinel cried out, "half-past ten o'clock and all is well." Then I donned the apparel of somebody else and started out on my errand, the boys giggling and saying they would come to my rescue if a gun was fired. Boldness was my game now. I went to the hospital, where lights were allowed to burn all night, surveyed matters, and, as it appeared that "all was well," struck a bee-line for Mr. Rooster's pole. The sentinel, supposing me to be one of the hospital attendants, scarcely noticed me. Mr. Chicken said something, I didn't take time to listen what it was, but, giving his neck a twist and a squeeze, and tucking him under the ample folds of my "Scotch plaid cloak," I retreated in good order through the hospital to room 19, block 4, where the boys piled up encomiums on my valor, and the beauty, fatness and goodness of Lieutenant Wilson's last chicken.

We had hot water in the pot on our stove, Clark bounced up to his business, and we tried to have a little light on the subject by kindling a small blaze in the stove, but the guard yelled forth, "Put out that light in Block 4." So, in pitchy darkness, we picked, cut up and salted away our game. Thinking Wilson might miss his fowl and get out a search warrant, we concluded to make the first meal of the new year on fried chicken. By daylight we were up and doing, and when the sun came peeping into our prison home *we* could exclaim, "chicken enough," nor was there a bone, feather or other vestige left to indicate that violence had been committed within the realms of our little kingdom.

CHAPTER XV.

Jonesboro, East Tennessee,
July 13. 1865.

What I write hereafter must be from memory, as I took no notes of transpiring events after 1864. The months of January and February were in many respects similar to the same period the preceding year. Though our aggregate number was increased one-fourth, the amount of sickness had decreased, and the hospital comforts and accommodations were much improved, and our rations of wood were better, both in quantity and quality. The large rooms in most of the blocks were cut up into smaller ones, and the number of stoves in prison greatly increased; the majority of us having spent one winter there, were somewhat acclimated, and had a better supply of blankets and clothing.

All in all, I passed the winter off quite agreeably; in fact, I was never much bothered over my Johnson's Island imprisonment, for, during a stay of twenty-one months, I was never sick enough to go to the hospital, and was seldom troubled by the gnawings of hunger or home sickness, which were general complaints. I was most always employed at one thing or another, and never failed to bathe all over twice a week in summer and once a week during the winter, hot or cold, rain or shine To that I mainly attributed my good health, and for my comparative state of contentment I felt that I was indebted to the fact of keeping my physical and mental powers employed and absorbed in the present, instead of indulging in miserable idleness and longings for what could not be obtained.

It was, perhaps, the first of February that Gen. Grant was called before the Cabinet and Congress to give his testimony and views about the exchange question, which resulted in his being empowered to prosecute an exchange of prisoners at discretion. So many attempts at a general exchange, which we all thought would succeed, having failed, very many of us had become incredulous to anything we saw or heard on the subject.

As a matter of policy by the Federal Government, all exchange—except a partial one of sick and wounded and a few specials—had been staved off for nearly two years, and now not less than a hundred thousand Northern and Southern soldiers were undergoing the sufferings and cruelties of prison life, which were greatly augmented by a barbarous system of retaliation inaugurated by both sides. The prisoners had prayed, and the people had prayed, in vain for an exchange, and thousands of the poor, deceived patriots breathed their last in prison walls. No less than fourteen thousand Federal dead now lie at Andersonville, Georgia, alone, and the bones of thousands of brave, noble Southern youths are to-day mouldering around " Camp Chase, " Camp Douglas" and other prison pens of the North. And I remember that we left many a little mound on Johnson's Isle. Sleep on, noble comrades and kind friends, till the Master bids you rise and appear at the Judgment bar with us all!

A gradual exchange commenced about the middle of February. The commanders of the various prisons in the North were ordered to make out rolls of prisoners in detachments of five hundred, taking first, as a matter of policy, those from the States of Missouri, Kentucky, Arkansas and Louisiana. The Confederate officers were to be taken in squads of one hundred, according to priority of capture.

I will not undertake to describe the state of feeling on Johnson's Island about that time. Just imagine a lot of men who have been in prison from one to two years, and now inflated with the hope and prospect of a ride to Dixie-land; then think of a host of others who have not been incarcerated so long and know they can not go for, perhaps, several months yet, and you may have a dim conception of the reality. One hundred officers were shipped from our prison on the 18th, and the same number on the 21st of February; among them nearly all the officers of my regiment.

The scene reminded me of the parting of students at the close of a collegiate year. Friends were saying good-bye, never to meet again, and many pleasant, happy associations and ties were being severed forever, but the regrets at saying farewell were less visible, since, much as we liked the presence of our friends, we were happy with them, because they were going home to Dixie. Even yet I was not confident that I would go, and neither built hopes nor made preparations for a change of base.

A roll of two hundred was made out on the 23d, and the next morning they bade us adieu. Almost every man captured previous to or at the time of myself had now gone, and I began to feel anxious in the matter. All those who had left had to walk to Sandusky on the ice, and, as it was getting warm and cloudy, with a prospect of the ice breaking up, Col. Hill concluded to get another batch of one hundred over the ice bridge before night, to which end all hands and energies were set to work. The officer of the day, with a list of perhaps a dozen names, would come in and call them out, when the fortunate ones would rush anxiously to the small gate, where they were received by a corporal's guard and escorted to headquarters to settle their accounts and sign a parole not to attempt escape *en route* South.

My name was not called till two P. M., and at four we had to leave the island. In those two hours I had a hundred things to do and have done, and was almost too full of excitement to do anything. I had dwelt there so long it was like a family fixing up all in an hour to move far away. And, though I wanted to be free and see my friends in the South, I hated to leave my prison associates, and cut short off the pleasing correspondence I was having with my friends at home and elsewhere. I felt attached to my room, my books, my bunk and our rustic furniture, and I experienced a like feeling for the very prison and even some of the Federal garrison. I parted with them all with the same feelings that I would say farewell to my companions of the camp and field to go to my maternal home. For my room mates and my mess mates I felt a special attachment, and wherever I may meet them along life's journey it will be with a brotherly feeling in my heart. May they prosper and be happy.

At 4 o'clock we had said good-bye to all in

prison, and with our blankets and little wallets of clothing and prison mementoes, such as pictures, letters and prison jewelry, were out in the garrison square receiving rations, and those of us who had been so fortunate as to have the acquaintance and good will of some of the Federals, bidding them adieu, promising to treat them well if we ever caught them down in Dixie land.

The sick and crippled, with the heavier baggage, were hauled across on ice sleighs, and we were strung along for nearly half a mile over the crystal ice of the deep bay. We encountered several air holes, and about the center of the bay was one varying from twenty to fifty feet in width and nearly a mile in length. It was bridged with planks, like a creek on dry land, and it may be well imagined that we felt rather ticklish in crossing such a place, our only possible consolation being that if we went under the blue coats would go with us. We had a merry trip, several fellows breaking through, and many of them getting heavy falls. The distance from our island home to Sandusky city was three miles, and did not look even that far, but when we had walked it over the ice it appeared seven long ones.

That night we stayed in the depot car shed at Sandusky, and the next morning at daylight left for Mansfield, Ohio, where we arrived at noon, overtaking the two hundred who had started the morning before, and we felt as glad to see each other as though we had been parted a year, for indeed we thought that our adieus at the island were final. As we passed through the little towns in Ohio, Federal soldiers, who had been enjoying the ill-comforts of "Libby" and other Southern prisons, would come up, take a peep at us, then curse the rebel government and all pertaining to it, and almost cry with madness because we seemed to have fared better than they did. The boys would laugh at them and turn everything they said into a joke, telling them it was "no use to grieve over spilt milk."

We had to lay over at Mansfield half a day, waiting for a train on the Pittsburg, Fort Wayne and Chicago railroad. Lieutenant Reno, of the 128th Ohio, with about twenty men, had charge of our detachment, and they proved themselves clever, obliging, first-rate fellows. At Mansfield, though a nominal guard was kept around us, we went when and where we pleased, and drank what we liked best. The boys in gray and the boys in blue would imbibe together till they got somewhat mellow, then Mr. Yank would stack his gun in the corner of the car, and they would manfully argue the question of "Union or no Union," each having the privilege of swearing a little, and the closing scene would often be a hearty shake hands and a mutual agreement to disagree.

At dusk the 300 of us left, arriving in Pittsburg at 7 o'clock next morning, where we only stopped long enough to change cars. We now took passage on the Pennsylvania railroad, and traveled on all the Sabbath day, being 195 miles from Pittsburg at nightfall, when we came to the wreck of a freight train, which was not cleared away before next morning, and here we also came up with a train loaded with 500 Kentucky soldiers, from Camp Douglas, most of them having been captured on the Ohio raid.

The blackened appearance of Pittsburg gave evident indications of its vast manufacturing establishments, and for fifty miles out from the city we saw many coal mines, but which were not then being worked much. During the forenoon of Sunday we were passing through the Alleghany mountains, and sometimes would run in almost a complete circle, near the summit of lofty ranges, and, upon looking from the car windows, it would seem as though we were suspended in mid-air, hundreds of feet above a yawning abyss, studded with rugged cliffs and evergreens, with here a and there a drift of snow or an iceberg, which, altogether, formed a scene at once grand, sublime and picturesque

About midday we passed through a tunnel a

mile and a quarter long, on the summit of the Alleghanies, and, after running on a down grade for two hours, we arrived at Altoona, Pa., at the foot of the mountain. We found it to be a flourishing city planted down in a rugged region; I saw not less than thirty engines there, most of them under steam, and the number of cars all about was legion. We were to have gotten dinner at that point, but had been soldiering too long to be much disappointed at a failure; however, the little boys, girls and old women brought pies, cakes, apples and such like in abundance, and nobody suffered.

Our money account at the prison had been kept exceedingly straight, and all our funds, both greenback and Confederate, were intrusted to the officer in charge of us, to be delivered over at the point of exchange. But he had the privilege of giving out small sums along the route, and Lieut. Reno issued quite liberally to the boys, and those who had money spent it freely. Unfortunately, my financial matters had been mighty tight of late, and I was completely "strapped," but friends that I had helped along in prison now returned the compliment.

All Sunday evening we were passing through a beautiful valley along the shores of the Juniata river, whose beauties I had so often seen mentioned and described in fancy and poetic sketches.

Just before nightfall we passed through Huntingdon, a pleasing, thrifty looking town, embossed between the mountains on the edge of the "blue Juniata." And across this, as well as the Susquehanna river, I saw railroad bridges built by Col. E. W. Morgan, of the Kentucky Military Institute, which bridges I had drawn under his instructions while studying engineering at the Institute. I had spent so many hours, days and weeks in the study and construction of those bridges that almost every dimension, arch, timber, bolt and pier seemed familiar and homelike.

As soon as the wreck in front of us was cleared away we rolled on, and Monday noon found us at Mifflintown, Pennsylvania, where we stayed a couple of hours, the Southern gentlemen roaming almost at will over the town, buying things to eat, drink or wear. Many of the fellows ate at a hotel for the first time in two years, and the Federal officer in charge busied himself in having plenty prepared for all who wanted it. Some of the disloyal colonels, majors, captains and lieutenants had a plentiful supply of the "over joyful," and that day felt bigger than any Yankee in Pennsylvania. From the Mifflin Hotel I wrote to my mother the first letter that I had had the privilege of sealing myself for a long time.

All Monday afternoon we were along the Susquehanna, and at sundown were just opposite to, and in sight of, Harrisburg, which presented a stately appearance across the broad river, which was now filled with slush ice. We were now two hundred and fifty miles from Pittsburg and seventy-two miles from Baltimore, our destination. The Pennsylvania railroad, over which we had just passed, is, perhaps, when viewed in all its appointments and surroundings, the best and most attractive road in America. It has a double track for two hundred and fifty miles, is stone ballasted and free from dust all the way, and its capital, running stock and business is immense; then it traverses a country filled with ever-varying, delightful scenery.

I can not say much for the agricultural appearance of the country through which we had been passing. At Harrisburg we had to wait two hours for an opposing passenger train, and, because of frequent stops during the night, we did not reach Baltimore till daylight. At York, Pennsylvania, about three score and ten young ladies made their appearance—some to see the Rebs. and some to sell pies. Some of the fellows would quibble over the price of a ten-cent pie for a quarter of an hour, just to get to talk to a pretty girl.

I can never forget our—some would call it—anti-triumphal march through the streets of Baltimore. About the center of the city we were halted between two blocks of five-story, palatial, granite residences, and from almost every window poked the head of a charming secesh lady; and, by the way, Baltimore never boasted many of any other stripe. So heavily did the tyrant's heel press down on the good people of that city that they did not dare to speak to us or exhibit any signs of sympathy, for fear of arrest. But the dear ladies way up in the windows would mirror the feelings of their hearts in their countenances and waft us kisses from the tips of their fingers, and now and then one would draw forth from near her heart a tiny image of the flag dear to us all, and wave it but for a moment, sending an indescribable thrill through all our hearts.

One lady, in passing along the sidewalk, recognized in our ranks a near relative, from whom she had been parted for many months. Not daring to speak to him, she several times strolled up one side and down the other of the street, gazing at the loved one; and well do I yet remember how full of sweet and tender sympathy was the face of that angelic woman. The provost-marshal noticed her movements, and in a very insolent manner ordered her to leave or take her place in our ranks as a prisoner. Most of us took a mental note of the name and appearance of the inhuman wretch, with a view to the future.

We were taken to the wharf, and still denied

any communication with the world; but the Johnson's Island soldiers, who were still with us, would pass notes or slip in anything possible. In that way Colonel Phillips, of the 52d Georgia, got a whole suit, boots and all, from a lady friend. About noon a boat loaded with privates left for City Point, and two hours later we boarded the steamship Cumbria and glided away down Chesapeake Bay. We had a delightful ride over that beautiful sheet of water, and never stopped a moment till we arrived at the famous City Point, about four o'clock next evening.

We passed some twenty miles off Annapolis, Maryland, and could see its towering spires; then we passed within a few hundred feet of Fortress Monroe, a point not before unknown, but made still more famous by its associations during the war. Just in front of Fortress Monroe is a prison, built, like Fort Sumpter, out in the bosom of the deep. It is called the "Rip-raps," and prisoners sentenced for life are confined there. It was at Fortress Monroe that the celebrated rebel ram Merrimac attacked the Federal fleet and astonished the world by her achievements.

At the mouth of the James river we saw protruding from the water the masts of the famous Confederate cruiser Florida, which had been sunk by the Federals. From there we passed over historic ground every foot of the way to Richmond.

City Point was nothing more than a vast military encampment, with its multiform appurtenances, and there were perhaps a hundred ships, sloops, brigs and steamboats anchored there, all engaged in the Government service.

At City Point we reported to General Grant, and were directed to report to Colonel Mulford, agent of exchange at Harrison's Landing. We proceeded up the James till dusk, when the knowing ones thought it prudent to cast anchor for the night. It did not take us long next morning to glide up to that place made famous by McClellan's peninsular campaign. About noon we left the steamer and bade adieu to our Federal comrades. But before parting with them forever I must say a word concerning each.

The Cumbria had been built in England for a blockade-runner, but, after a few trips, was captured off Wilmington or Charleston, and sold to a marine transportation company. It was rather an unsightly craft, and was divided up into waterproof compartments, constructed rather with a view to stowing away the greatest possible quantity of goods than human comfort. It consumed its own steam and smoke, and ran so smoothly and quietly that its proximity could hardly be detected by hearing.

Having been from boyhood interested in the naval characters of Captain Marryatt's novels, I now took a deep interest in learning something about the ship and all its crew and fixtures, and I found that the queer nautical terms, the sailors' language, and their peculiar characteristics, all comported with the vivid pen-pictures given in Marryatt's sea novels. I went down into the little cuddies in the bow of the ship, where the sailors live, and talked with them, and heard them conversing with each other after a style peculiarly their own. They were ever jovial, free-hearted and witty, and would sell their dinner or anything else for that to which they took a liking. With one fellow, "Dan," I several times exchanged prison rings for his dinner or supper, and for the last meal I took on the Cumbria I paid him a $20.00 Confederate bill, which was good for nothing to him, but he said he wanted it, and I'm sure I wanted the breakfast, even if it was on a tin plate not scrupulously clean. Although they were rough, uncouth, uncleanly, and, in some things, unprincipled, I could not help liking the sailor's character.

When we bade the Federal soldiers good-bye, both they and we thought more of each other than when we started, for they had evinced a kindly spirit toward us, and they could not help admiring the manly, generous spirit of Southern gentlemen. Everything had gone off happily along the whole journey. We numbered altogether three hundred and fifty, one-seventh being of the Northern and the big remainder of the Southern persuasion. During the last forenoon that we spent together promiscuous groups of mottled gray and blue might have been seen all over the ship; some were trading, some telling yarns or their war experiences, and how they had played off pranks on the Feds. or Rebs., while others were gravely and earnestly discussing the war question in its various phases and prospects. The Yanks. had their guns piled away as if the war was over, and we commingled as freely as though we had all been birds of a feather. We thanked the officers for their courteous treatment, and promised to reciprocate in future, should we ever change our relative situations; then we shook hands with our most intimate Federals, and, bidding good-bye to the Yankee nation, went on shore.

At Harrison's Landing, which name will be often repeated in the history of the struggle just past, there is nothing more than a plain brick dwelling and a few inferior out-buildings, surrounded by an open, flat country. From there we had to walk three miles around Butler's far-famed "Dutch Gap Canal" to the Confederate "Flag of Truce Boat" above. Colonel Mulford, with a small detachment of cavalry, escorted us through the Federal lines on the north side of the James. The works at that point were manned by the sable sons of Ham, who looked well enough, and did not offer us any indignity by either word, look or deed.

As we approached *our* steamer the Southern troops cheered us from their fortifications on the south side of the James. Colonel Mulford advanced, riding, with a little white flag sticking in his boot-top, met and shook hands with Colonel Ould, our agent of exchange, and very soon we were told to go aboard, which we did with a leap and a yell of joy, for we were now surely in Dixie land. Colonel Mulford, by his manly, generous course, won our esteem, as he had done of all the prisoners with whom he had ever come in contact.

We were very soon off for Richmond. Several *live rebels with guns in their hands* were on board, and so long had it been since I saw the like that they really looked curious. A Confederate battle flag, which Captain Meyers, of Arkansas, had kept concealed since the Big Black fight, was now brought out and unfurled to the Southern breeze, and we cheered it lustily. After passing several renowned forts and batteries, and the torpedo obstructions in the river, and the Confederate navy, which seemed like a farce in comparison with the Federal, we arrived at Richmond at sundown of March 3, 1865.

CHAPTER XVI.

IN JAIL, *July 14, 1865.*

We naturally expected some kind of a reception at Richmond, but soldiers and returned prisoners were so common there that our arrival and presence was scarcely noticed. I took quarters at the widely known "Spotswood House," where the rate of board was *only $50 per day*, but the fare was excellent, considering the times. About the first one I met there, to recognize, was Colonel W. F. Leathers, of Kentucky, and my recollection is that about a half dozen of us, from near the blue grass region, were instrumental in giving the "hollow horn" to one of his bottles that had a sparkling liquid in it.

On the 4th of March I went to General Ewell's headquarters and procured a thirty days' parole furlough, which I presented to the Paymaster and received six months wages, $780—money earned while I was boarding at Johnson's Island with Uncle Samuel. At the time the Confederate Ship of State went down the Government owed me twenty months wages, $2,600; but as Mr. Magistrate says "the Confederacy is played out," I suppose the debt is illegal and I must let it go by the board.

While at Richmond I attended the theater, the play, "The French Revolution," being in consonance with the times; but I could not help feeling unpleasant, for there would be constantly coming before my mental vision the awful conflagration and appalling loss of life at the Richmond Theater many years ago.

I visited "Libby Prison" and talked with the Federals confined there, and could not avoid sympathizing with them and wishing that their situation was more pleasant. The poor fellows looked badly, but, so far as I could see, were treated as well as the surroundings would permit. I could not condemn and hate them because the Federal authorities mistreated so many of our prisoners, and would have gladly given them comfort, even if my brother and other comrades did receive ill treatment at the hands of heartless Federal ruffians. No doubt there are many who will differ from the feelings and principles just enunciated, but I am glad that it was never in my heart to be otherwise. I feel that any other spirit is unreasonable, unkind, ungenerous and unchristian.

I went to the Confederate Capitol and viewed with admiration the colossal statues of Washington and others of Virginia's gifted sons, and I was happy to see among them the figure of Henry Clay, of whom Kentuckians have a just reason to be proud. The capitol buildings were not particularly prepossessing in appearance, but there were associations connected with the very spot that made me have almost a reverential feeling. I was at the Treasury Department from whence so many millions of worthless currency has been issued. In fact, I was all over the city, and though it had been much hacked up by the war, it still presented many attractions, indicating that, in times of peace, it was a beautiful place.

On Sunday, March 5, I went to church, where I saw both President Davis and Gen. Lee. The very looks of each showed that they were great men, and I could not help venerating Uncle Bob for his good qualities, and admiring him as the greatest living military chieftain of the world. The handsome, gallant Breckinridge, Secretary of War, was there too, besides a half score of Major and Brigadier-Generals, some of them not unknown to fame.

Before arriving at Richmond I thought I would find sights enough to excite my curiosity for a full week, but three days fully satisfied my desires. And we all thought and said, before leaving Johnson's Island, that we would certainly have to get on a little spree and have some fun in Richmond, but, *mirabile dictu*, I saw scarcely a drunken man during my stay in the city, and the only obstacle in the way of procuring liquor was the high price, $5 per drink, which was no obstacle at all to us fellows with pockets full of Confederate scrip

Monday afternoon, March 6th, I bade adieu to my prison companions, some of whom were going to remain and others to go in a different direction, and repaired to the depot of the Richmond and Danville railroad, where I found nearly a thousand paroled prisoners, all anxious to be off for their homes. Several hundred of them had to stay over for want of room, but I managed to get aboard by the hardest. Fifty miles from Richmond we came to Burksville, where the Richmond and Danville road intersects the South Side road, leading from Petersburg to Lynchburg, which latter point was my destination.

We missed connection at Burksville, and had to lie over twenty-four hours. While there I met an old schoolmate from Mississippi, and several soldier friends that I had not seen for many months, among them several men of my own company, who were homeward bound from prison. One of them I did not, at first, recognize any more than if I had never seen him.

And I had the pleasure of giving some intelligence to an anxious mother concerning her son in prison. While they were transferring some baggage from the Danville to the Petersburg train, I noticed a trunk marked J. I. Scales, and, thinking that perhaps it belonged to the family of Colonel J. I. Scales, whom I had left at Johnson's Island, I made inquiry and soon found his mother and sister, who were on their way to Petersburg to care for his brother, General Scales, who had just been wounded. I gave them gladsome news, for they had not heard from him for three months, and he was then sick, but was now well and hearty. My room mate, Major Person, was his especial friend, and he was in to see us the day before I left prison. The mother and sister were over joyful, and thanked me many times over, and it really made me feel good for hours to know that I had relieved their suspense and added to their happiness.

There being no hotel accommodations at Burksville we had to camp out, and I enjoyed it hugely, as I always did enjoy rough camp life. After a frugal supper, we built a blazing rail fire, the fiddle and the banjo were brought out, and we danced after every style. As an interlude, now and then a darkey would come in and "pat Juba," while several other contrabands would dance to it as if life and death depended. Then, for a change of programme, some rebellonian who had taken lessons from the darkies in the cotton field before the war, would pit himself against some ebony friend to dance a jig or the highland fling.

Thus we wore away about half the night, then wrapped up in our blankets and slept soundly till daylight.

When the regular Lynchburg train came it was filled with soldiers going to guard an important bridge against an anticipated Federal raid, and we were promised transportation on a freight train which came along just before nightfall. We left Burksville at sundown, and had not gone more than twenty miles before an accident occurred detaining us all night, and, though the distance to Lynchburg was only 72 miles, we did not arrive there till noon next day. There I overtook Col. Gregg, and a dozen other officers of my regiment, who left prison a week before me, and I supposed were at home.

We found the city of Lynchburg in an intense state of excitement. All the available troops were concentrated there, and every able-bodied citizen was required to go to the city defenses. They were hourly expecting to be pounced upon by General Sheridan, who was at Amherst Court House, 16 miles away, with a large cavalry force, but for some reason Mr. Sheridan, the next day, changed the direction of his devastating line of march.

I can not call Lynchburg an attractive place, though it has some elegant public and private buildings It has a world-wide celebrity as a tobacco emporium, and is the home of some of Virginia's most distinguished citizens. While we were at Lynchburg an order was published declaring as exchanged all prisoners who had been delivered up to the 1st of March, and ordering them upon duty straightway. Most of the officers of my regiment belonged to that class, having been delivered the last day of February, but, having been away from home for about two years and a half, they had no idea of going a soldiering till they had seen their families and sweethearts. Guards were placed on all the trains going west, and ordered to let no one pass whose parole furloughs were dated prior to the 1st of March. That might have been an insurmountable obstacle to a preacher, but our boys all changed their passes to date March 4th, with my own, and went about their business—that is, in the direction of home.

We left Lynchburg Thursday morning, March 9th, and at dusk were at Wytheville, one hundred and thirty-five miles on the way. There about two hundred of us had a memorable scramble at the hotel over a supper that had been prepared for not over fifty passengers, as our coming was not anticipated. We expected to go through to Abingdon, fifty-five miles farther, that night, but at Gade Springs, thirteen miles short of our destination, the train we were on was ordered back to Lynchburg, for fear that it would fall into the hands of Yankee raiders. There we had to get out at midnight and stay till morning, the majority being without shelter or fire, in a sloppy snow.

Four of us went to a one-horse tavern and hired a room with one vacant bed in it; so two of us took the floor with our blankets. Sometime before day I heard a gruff voice cursing the cold bed and troublesome vermin, and after a while he called upon us to splice blankets and sleep with him, to which we assented, provided he would let me in with my boots on, as they were so wet that I could not well get them off. Next morning we found our bed-fellow to be a militia general from the Kanawha Valley.

On the forenoon of March 10th, which I remember was bitter cold, we went on a freight train to Bristol, which is on the Tennessee line. I had been at Abingdon in 1862, and found it a very neat, comfortable place, but now one-half of it was a blackened mass of ruins, the result of a Federal cavalry raid. At Bristol, also, several splendid depot buildings and machine shops had been destroyed by the ruthless invaders. In fact, from Richmond to Atlanta, a distance of five hundred miles, scarcely a depot building had been left standing, and there was hardly a bridge along that whole route that had not been destroyed once or oftener by one army or the other.

At Bristol I met with my Brigadier-General, J. C. Vaughn, his staff, and other old comrades that I had not seen since the memorable day at Big Black in May 1863; and I likewise met up with my orderly sergeant and a half-dozen men just from Point Lookout. We all assembled at Room 3 in the Lancaster House, sent for fifty dollars' worth of brandy, being one quart, and we had somewhat of a jollification, presided over by Captain Bob Houston, Inspector-General of Vaughn's staff.

Bristol is peculiarly situated, the State line running along Main street, and that part of it on the Virginia side is there known as Goodson, Virginia, being named after one of the old citizens.

I took a freight train on the 12th of March for Carter's Depot, twenty miles from Bristol and twelve from Jonesboro, *where I now hold forth.* The railroad is cut at Carter's by the destruction of a bridge over the Watauga river. I had to walk from Carter's to Jonesboro, and at Johnson's Depot, seven miles from the latter point, I came to the spot where my regiment had broken up camp on the 18th of November, 1862, to go South. I had, in a little more than two years, completed a circuit of about three thousand miles, touching at Knoxville, Chattanooga, Atlanta, Montgomery, Mobile, Meridian, Jackson, Vicksburg, Memphis, Cairo, Indianapolis, *Sandusky*, Pittsburg, Harrisburg, Baltimore, Richmond and Lynchburg. The contents of this book are but a drop in the bucket of what I saw, heard and experienced.

CHAPTER XVII.

Prison Home, Jonesboro, Tennessee,
July 15, 1865.

I feel happier now, and the world looks brighter, for the prospects are that to-morrow's sun will not find me here. Only those who have been situated like I am can appreciate what a balm there is in the very thought. I will not dwell upon my thoughts and feelings now, but hurry on and finish my story up to date.

In the spring, summer and fall of 1862 I spent many pleasant hours about Jonesboro, and Gen. E. Kirby Smith having several times sent me to this county on important military duty, most everybody knew me, at least by name. When I returned to the place, after almost three years absence, I had forgotten some and failed to recognize many of my old acquaintances, but olden associations were soon revived, and I spent ten days here in a most agreeable manner—making several very happy additional acquaintances, among them the Misses Luckey, the Misses Maxwell, Misses Wilds and Miss Cunningham, all of them rather of the Union persuasion, but refined, sociable, hospitable—in a word, interesting.

While in Jonesboro I stayed with Mr. Slemmons, whose hospitality I enjoyed on former occasions, and the family were all so kind to me that I felt perfectly at home. Most all the prisoners who came South with me had a home or some special friends to go to. Not so with myself; my home was anywhere that I was kindly received. Several prison friends invited me to go home with them and remain till recalled into service, but I preferred to wander about promiscuously among my old army and citizen friends. I was anxious to make a visit among the good people about Newport, where my company was organized, but the possibility of a second jaunt to Johnson's Island deterred me.

All during my stay at Jonesboro it was reported that the Federals were preparing to advance into this country, so I kept prepared for a retreat, and on the 22d of March walked to Zollicoffer, 21 miles east of this place. One of my Lieutenants and my Orderly Sergeant left me there and went on to Bristol, taking my blanket, canteen and a very good coat. After spending several days with my friends around Zollicoffer I was to rejoin them at Bristol, but have never laid eyes on them from that day to this.

I had camped at Zollicoffer, guarding a bridge, in the summer of 1862, and, as was my luck most everywhere I went, I formed the acquaintance of several very interesting ladies thereabout. In the evening of March 25th, Gen. Vaughn's Cavalry, which had been below Jonesboro, and many citizens, who were afraid to remain at home, began a retrograde movement, and that very night the Yankees followed them to Carter's, nine miles from Zollicoffer, which village was named Union before the war.

Bright and early Sunday morning, March 26th, I struck out a foot up the Holston river. My carpet sack being very heavy—containing a year's supplies—not quartermaster or commissary—I took a change of under clothing in a haversack and left the carpet sack with Miss Kate Worley, two miles from Zollicoffer, telling her I would be back, perhaps in a month, may be not in a year— I plodded on some ten miles up the Holston Valley and laid over one day with Col. Jim Odell, and some other friends of the 26th Tennessee who resided in the vicinity of Meredith's Forge. From there I aimed for Grayson county, Va., 80 miles away, hearing that it was a safe and pleasant place of retreat. I was not with the army, because I was yet on parole and could not take up arms.

I followed the Holston almost to its head-waters in Virginia. Falling in company with some refugoes who had a led horse, I got to ride about forty miles. One night we camped in a school house, and the next we stayed with Mr. Porter, in Smyth county, Va., three miles from "The Blue Spring." Said spring is a basin of water some thirty feet in diameter and of an unknown depth; it is the source of Cripple Creek, which flows into New river thirty miles to the east. On the last day of March we came to the Dry Creek Gap road, in Wythe county, leading over the mountain into Grayson county.

As my fellow travelers were not yet determined which way they would go, we all concluded to stay on that side of the mountain a day or so, to see what would turn up, and straightway we began to hunt some place to stop at. We divided out into small squads. There were four in my party, and wherever we went the complaint was that they had no horse feed, but they would willingly accommodate *us*. Though often refused, I liked the way the people talked. At about the sixth trial we got to put up with Mrs. Gleaves, on Cripple creek, by taking a little stretch of authority and using government hay for our stock. There I learned that a number of Kentuckians were staying in the neighborhood, and that several refugee families from Tennessee, of my acquaintance, were living in the vicinity.

Next morning my companions determined to

beat back toward the Tennessee line, and I, concluding that I could not find a better camping ground, bid them good-bye. The first day of April I went to the house of Rev. David Sullins, whose brother-in-law, Capt. Frank S. Blair, belonged to my regiment, and with whose wife and mother-in-law I had an acquaintance. They asked me to stay with them, but their house being small and they refugees, I did not accept their proffered hospitality, proposing to go that afternoon to apply for boarding in the family of Maj. John Sanders.

During the evening Major Sanders called in, and I told him that I had thought of trying to get to stay with him a few days. Said he, "Come when you please, and stay as long as you please." I afterward found that to be his accustomed blunt manner of expression. The next day I was initiated into the family by Miss Mollie E. Simpson, a refugee from Jonesboro, Tennessee, who was teaching Major Sanders' children, and giving music lessons to his niece, Miss Bettie Brown. Miss Simpson was highly educated, especially in music, and, being rather extra good looking, was a star in that region. In a few days I was well acquainted with the whole family, darkies, dogs and all, and, finding in Mr. and Mrs. Sanders genuine old Virginia hospitality, which always suited me, I was perfectly at home.

I helped Mrs. Sanders plant her potatoes and most all her garden stuff, and frequently worked in the garden during my stay with them, and I have not forgotten that I made for her some chicken coops, and some wire screws to cure gaping chickens. All these things I learned while serving an apprenticeship under my mamma, away back yonder in my boyhood. I dropped a good portion of Major Sanders' corn, and helped him along generally, when I felt inclined—not that they asked me to do any of this, but they would receive no pay for my board, and I felt unwilling not to give at least a partial recompense for the benefits I was receiving; besides, I felt better by employing a portion of my time at light work. With his house as my nominal home, I stayed on the waters of Cripple Creek till the last day of May.

So happily did I pass the time away in the agreeable society thereabout that the two months had passed away almost before I knew it. Col. John Sanders, Major Wythe Gleaves, Mr. Porter and Mrs. Foster all asked me to spend a part of my time at their homes, and I did stay several days and nights at each place. Young ladies were more abundant than young gentlemen, most all the latter being off in the army.

We had many pleasant social gatherings, and went on two fishing excursions to a mountain stream to angle for trout. Though we captured but few trout, we made both trips pay, for each fellow had a pretty girl to wait upon, and the old folks had fixed us up excellent dinners. I remember that the first fishing party was on the 2d day of May, and that just as we had spread our tempting repast on a huge rock, under some beautiful pines and ivys, between the road and gushing, sparkling, mountain stream, about thirty officers of Vaughn's brigade, most of whom I knew, came along on their way home from North Carolina, after Johnson's surrender. We were glad to share our goodies with them, and they were joyful at getting even so small a feast after a comparative famine.

While in Wythe county I visited the celebrated lead mines on New river, which had been worked since the revolutionary war, and still the rich ore seemed inexhaustible. Most all the lead used by the Confederate army during the rebellion was obtained at that point.

I was in a religious community, and there was preaching at one of two churches every Sabbath. I always went, for the ministers, Rev. David Sullins and Rev. W. E. Munsey, were divines of considerable celebrity, and I loved to listen to their fervid religious eloquence. The family with which I was staying, as well as most every other in that community, were strict Methodists, and had family worship each night and morning. During my whole stay at Maj. Sanders' I did not miss prayers a half-dozen times; and here I must tell a good joke on myself.

One night at prayers I was kneeling by the sofa, with my face buried in my hands, and the first thing I knew *I knew nothing at all, being fast asleep.* Prayers were over, and Miss Mollie Simpson rushed up stairs almost dying to laugh. Mrs. S. was tickled at, and Major S. embarrassed by, my posture. In a couple of minutes some noise disturbed my repose, and I bounced up, innocently asking how long prayers had been over. Thinking it might be a tender subject with me, no one mentioned the affair for two days, when Miss Simpson gradually broached it, and, finding that I was not sorely troubled over it, she took a delight in describing and laughing at my appearance. I hardly think I will be caught napping again under similar circumstances.

General Lee had surrendered on the 9th of April, President Lincoln had been killed on the 14th, General Johnston had capitulated on the 26th, and the Confederate armies in most every other quarter had crumbled to pieces, and the men who had for four years heroically fought, bled and suffered in what they thought a righteous cause were returning peacefully to their homes. Ah! what a grand, sublime mental picture is contained in the foregoing sentence! I could feebly portray it, but will not make the attempt.

When I had, on the first day of June, determined to start for my home, and went to thank Major Sanders and his lady for their kindness to me, and say farewell, my heart was too full for utterance, and I burst into tears, and they, too, and their children, wept as if I had been a son and brother, going far away, perhaps forever. I was strongly attached to the family, and my pleasant sojourn and happy associations on Cripple Creek will be fresh in my memory and pleasing in my reflections till I am no more.

I stayed one day with the family of Maj. Wm. Crouch, in Wytheville; then, in company with old Mrs. Blair, I came to Washington Springs, Virginia, where General A. E. Jackson (Mudwall Jackson) lived. I passed a pleasant day with his good lady and his accomplished daughter, who showed me the curiosities thereabout—among other things, a group of mineral springs. Four springs issued out within a few feet of each other, each discharging a different kind of water—one sulphur, one chalybeate, one alum and the other magnesia. I took a taste of each. Mrs. Blair stopped there, and I walked on to Abingdon, where I unexpectedly met my countyman, J. H.

D. McKee, who was also homeward bound, and stayed over-night at his boarding-house.

The next forenoon, being Sunday, June 4th, I footed it to Bristol, and that evening rode on a hand-car to Zollicoffer, and made my way to Mr. Worley's, where I had left my carpet-sack with Miss Kate. She had kept it safe, although the mountain robbers had plundered their house of almost half its contents. I intended to come right on next morning, but my feet were so sore and swollen that I could scarcely walk. So I concluded to lie over two days, Miss Kate promising to have my clothes washed, and let me have her riding horse to go and see my good friends Misses Teed and Sallie, and Misses Maggie and Henrie Thomas, the two families in no wise related, but warm friends.

I found Miss Teed with a new name, Mrs. Boyd, she having married Lieutenant Boyd, of General Vaughn's staff, the very night the rebels were driven back in the latter part of March. The nuptials were not to come off for several weeks, but when he found that the army was retreating he went to her at dusk and laid the matter before her, saying that he did not know when the fortunes of war would bring him back—maybe never. He left it to her pleasure and discretion as to the course to be pursued, and she decided to be his bride before morning. All hands went to work, the cakes were baked, the parson was sent for, and at the strange hour of three o'clock in the morning they were pronounced man and wife. The next morning he rode away, to be gone till the war was over.

On Tuesday, the 6th, I rode over to Blountville to see Major Rhea and Captain Baufman, of my regiment. I had been there in 1862, when it was a thriving, pleasant town; now more than half of it was in ashes, it having been set on fire by shells during a cavalry fight over the town in the winter of 1863.

Wednesday morning I left a part of my clothing at Mr. Worley's, so as to lighten my satchel, and by two o'clock walked to Johnson's Depot, sixteen miles, from whence I came to Jonesboro on a gravel train. The cause and manner of my arrest have been mentioned elsewhere.

Before leaving Virginia I was cautioned by several of the refugee families from Jonesboro not to come through this place, for, said they, "the people and the soldiery are still like an exasperated, blood-thirsty mob, and would not hesitate to take advantage of the least shadow of an excuse to insult, imprison, or even kill you." During the war, and even since its close, I had seen so much needless scare and fear that I did not heed their warnings as the sequel proves I should have done. I thought they magnified the danger because they could not in peace and safety return to their homes, but I found matters even worse than they had represented.

Though the civil powers pretended to be in vogue, a strong guard was detailed the night of my arrest to prevent the lawless, inhuman soldiers from attacking me, but I did not know it till afterward, when I furthermore learned that they intended to beat me up that night, had I not been arrested. I dreamed not of the dangers surrounding me. Even after I was in jail they would have used any treacherous means to harm me. On two occasions, in the absence of the jailer, a soldier has come and tried to get into the jail, each refusing to tell his purpose, more than that he wanted to see me. Of course it was evil. Mrs. Boyd, the jailer's wife and my friend, was spunky, and threatened them with arrest if they did not leave. Now, none of those soldiers (4th Tennessee) ever knew me in person or had a personal grudge against me; it was simply a desire to gratify a fiendish spirit.

A dozen Confederate soldiers have been assaulted in this town for nothing except being rebels, and those who have returned home in the country are frequently driven from church. They do not pretend to come to town, and even many of the Southern citizens stay away, fearing insult or injury. This is not an overdrawn, imaginary sketch, but reality. I wish the facts would bear me up in making a brighter record.

Now I will note down some of the incidents connected with my jail life. I still have a clear remembrance of how matters looked and how I felt when I was first initiated into prison life at Johnson's Island, Ohio, and I can imagine that I will never forget my similar inauguration at Jonesboro Jail.

At about nine o'clock P. M. of June 7th, 1865, Sheriff Shipley, in command of a gallant escort, headed by Jailor Boyd, conducted me up a winding flight of steps, through two doors which I *observed*, though small, were strong. We stooped a little in passing through an iron grating, when we found ourselves in the center of an entirely unfurnished room, but which, a half glance showed, had been made for *keeps*. I was furnished with a pallet and a tin of water; and soon the iron hinges grated, the door slammed, and all was darkness and I alone. Who will blame me for not attempting to describe my feelings just then? But I was tired, and soon didn't know but what I was in bed at home.

Next morning Mr. Shipley and Mr. Boyd came to see me, both offering to do anything they could for my comfort; and I must now say that they have both ever treated me in the most kind and courteous manner. I thought that I could give bail and go right on home; but I was told then, and have since seen, that even the Union citizens, though willing at heart, are afraid to show any sympathy for a rebel.

Confinement and solitude was irksome for a few days, but I gradually habituated myself to the necessities of the occasion, and, though this is the thirty-eighth day of my *positive* sojourn in this little room, the time has not seemed extremely long. I have had books or papers to read most all the time, and have written many a line. A number of ladies have ministered to my wants in various ways. Mrs. Blair and Mrs. Slemmons have sent me many good dinners, the former also sending reading matter and the latter money and stationery. Miss Maggie Williams, an orphan girl with a big heart and generous impulses, sent me a note offering to aid me to the extent of her ability, and an unknown gentleman friend placed $10 in the hands of a lady, subject to my order.

On the 19th June a young lady brought me some gooseberries, pancakes and syrup, and on the 22d I was visited by Miss Amanda Babb, whom I have to thank and remember for several favors. The next day Mrs. Vandyke, with whom I am not acquainted, sent me two books to read.

Dr. "Bill Sketer" Smith, Ex-Surgeon U. S. A., came to pay me a friendly visit on the 24th. I had arrested him in June, 1862, upon a grave charge, by order of Gen. E. Kirby Smith. He was accused of hiring a crazy boy to put an obstruction on the railroad track just before a train of soldiers came along. I found him at home, and, after talking with him for a while, was so well satisfied of his innocence that I did not put him under guard, but rode alone with him into Jonesboro, sending my soldiers back a nearer way. And then I put him upon his parole of honor to report to me at the depot half an hour before the train started for Knoxville. As soon as he was seen at large on the streets a half dozen of the most prominent Southern men in the place came to me and said that if I did not put him under guard he would be gone in half an hour. But I took my own advice, and that night sent Dr. Smith to Knoxville in charge of a single soldier, furnishing him with a letter of recommendation to General Smith, by which he got the privilege of the city limits instead of going to jail. In two weeks he was unconditionally released, as the charge was never verified. Ever after that he was my warm friend, and now offered to reciprocate my kindness in any shape in his power.

On the 25th my uncle, who had been my guardian and protector almost from infancy, and for whom I had sent in the hour of need, came, and *the first shake hands we had after four years' separation was through a grated, iron door.* I invited him into my room; we talked over home matters, and then set about devising ways and means for my welfare. Col. A. J Brown, 8th Tennessee Cavalry, who was a Union citizen when I had command of the Post of Jonesboro, in May, 1862, was employed as counsel, and my uncle, after arranging matters as we all thought most prudent, left for home.

Mrs. Boyd brought me a nice plate of delicious blackberries, and some young lady sent me a good novel to read on the 28th. The next evening Dr. Joe Clark, of this county, took lodgings with me, being charged with arson: he had just come from a two months' term in the Knoxville jail, charged with *treason*. (Why didn't they have *the whole Confederacy* in the calaboose on the same charge?) He was released from there on $10,000 bail, and from here by giving $2,500 security for his appearance.

Sergeant Mathias Garber, 60th Tennessee, C. S. A., was, on the 1st day of July, admitted to my sanctum to answer to the charge of a murder during the war, which it was well known that he *simply witnessed*. The judge admitted him to $5,000 bail, and he has been confidently expecting a release for the past week.

For ten days the weather has been oppressively warm, but we have stood it well, considering. Several ladies have been to *peep in* at us, and throw us apples, like little boys to the caged wild beasts. It was fun to us, but their faces indicated sorrowful and sympathizing hearts, and sometimes, as they would bid us good-bye and turn to go away, tear-drops would trickle down their cheeks. God bless all such dear women! Mrs. Boyd has fed us well all the time, and furnished us one of her best beds to sleep on, and we have danced, sung, talked at discretion, and, I might almost say, had a good time generally.

Reader, I have given you the bright side of prison life; I would perpetuate all the pleasing memories of the past, but the sad ones I would fain obliterate. It is now late in the evening, and the midnight hour will not find me here. In the meantime I shall bid adieu to prison walls—I hope forever.

CONCLUSION.

At Home, Anderson County, Kentucky, }
July 25, 1865. }

I left Jonesboro jail at eleven o'clock on the night of the 15th, and was conducted by Jailor Boyd, through the dark and rain, to the residence of Colonel A. J. Brown, with whom my uncle had bargained for a horse, and who had promised to escort me, or have me escorted, beyond danger. He had engaged Mr. Billie Patterson, a disloyal citizen, to perform the service. I mounted Col. Brown's war steed, and at the dead hour of night we rode through the main street of Jonesboro, wending our way in the direction of Bull's Gap, forty miles distant.

We encountered no more serious difficulty than getting lost several times in the dark, and at daylight were at Mr. Jacob Naff's, twelve miles on the way, where we stopped an hour to give our horses a bite and ourselves a nap in his barn. After riding all day through an incessant rain we passed through Bull's Gap an hour by sun. Mr.

Patterson's contract being complete, he turned back, and I went on to Mr. Taylor's, in the edge of Jefferson county, where I met with my old neighbors, Scott, Green and James McCoun.

The thought may occur to the reader, was that meeting accidental? No; they had come all the way from Central Kentucky to meet and escort me home through the mountains. During most of the year 1862 I occupied so prominent a position before the people of East Tennessee that I was known everywhere from Bristol to Chattanooga, a distance of two hundred miles, and the news of my arrest and imprisonment had been spread abroad. I had intended to go through on the cars, and keep rather secluded, to avoid being recognized; not that I felt that I had any reason to be ashamed or afraid of recognition, but because, as I have said a little way back, Confederate soldiers were every day being assaulted and insulted as they passed over the railroads, and I did not wish to subject myself to a similar indignity. Now, it would not do to think of going that way, for my life would have been in jeopardy, and I would have run a great risk in going alone through the mountains just then, consequently matters were arranged as already indicated.

And then again comes the question, How about the bail? It will be remembered that his august Majesty, 'Squire Somebody, fixed it at $2,000.

When court came on the judge reduced it one-half, and laid the case over till next term.

[February, 1870.—It may well be imagined that, under the then existing circumstances, I did not report at Jonesboro at the appointed time. The consequence was I lost my $1,000, as well as $700 more in defraying expenses. That draining of my purse seems to have been ample atonement for my sins against the laws of Tennessee, for, at about the second sitting of the court, the prosecuting attorney ordered a *nolle prosequi* to be set opposite my case. Such a thing as legal justice to a rebel in that country was then unheard of, and, besides, there was absolute danger of personal insult and injury, as I could have proved by the most loyal men in that region.

In September, 1865, I went to Brig.-Gen. Harlan and Maj.-Gen. Rousseau, U. S. A., both prominent Kentucky lawyers, and laid the facts before them as now laid before the world, whereupon each of them pronounced it a gross outrage, from beginning to end, but said I would have to run the risk of getting justice before the Tennessee authorities. I did go to Nashville to see the Governor (*it must be remembered that Billy Brownlow was now at the helm of State*); he was absent, but, after some talk with the Secretary of State and several other knowing ones, I found that *I was barking up the wrong tree*, and concluded to do as the boys advised the Yankee soldiers that we passed between Sandusky and Mansfield, *en route* South, nor have I bothered my brain over the matter since.]

Early in the morning of the 17th Messrs. McCoun, Green and myself were homeward bound, and at night put up at Tazewell, thirty-six miles on the way. The next day we passed through Cumberland Gap, and after riding thirty-eight miles stopped with the genial and hospitable lady of Mr. Joe Smith. The day following we passed through Barboursville and London, and at the end of forty-one miles took lodgings at Camper's. On the 20th of July we passed through Mount Vernon and Crab Orchard, and stayed over night at the Meyer's House in Stanford. July 21st we came through Danville, Harrodsburg and Lawrenceburg, and I reached home at dusk, after an absence of three years, eleven months and nineteen days, almost one-half of which time had been spent in prison.

Though our journey through the mountains of Tennessee and Kentucky was tiresome, there were many pleasant incidents connected with it, for my companions were jolly fellows, and knew every foot of the ground, having for years past driven stock South by that route and put up at all the stopping places. From Crab Orchard to Bull's Gap, 150 miles, the marks of devastation are everywhere plainly visible. One-half of the houses are burnt, most all the fencing is gone, and the wreck of war material is scattered along the whole distance. Cumberland Gap, which will hereafter be a historic name, looked like a thriving little city, and is now garrisoned by about 400 Ohio troops. Looking South from the peaks around the Gap, one can see fifty miles away, and the view is the most grand and picturesque that I ever witnessed.

Most of the rough country in East Tennessee has rich soil, and water is abundant and excellent; but from Cumberland Gap to Crab Orchard, Kentucky, there is little desirable land and the water is miserable in quality, nor is there an abundance of it. Several Northern companies are now boring for oil in the vicinity of Barboursville and London, Kentucky, and there are immense beds of coal and other valuable ores in the bowels of the earth all through that region.

The foregoing is but a meager sketch of what I have actually seen and experienced during the time consumed by the narrative, and I will not probably in all the balance of my life pass through as much as in the four years just gone by. All that I have risked and suffered has been for nothing; but almost every project in life is an uncertain experiment, and, not unfrequently, the most plausible and reasonable attempts prove abortive. I can not say that I now regret what I have done, but I will try to profit by the lessons of the past, and make the most of the future.

During my absence many, many changes have been wrought. Almost a generation of children seem to have sprung up, and I even do not recognize many that were my schoolmates. Some who went to the wars with me came not back; some have died at home and some have moved away. Most of the negro population have gone either to the grave, the army, or to live in filth and poverty in some hovel or camp whither they have repaired *in search of freedom (?)*

The war is at an end, but peace and prosperity are not yet returned, and, in many sections, long years must yet roll by ere the people get over the terrible scourge of civil war. My only hope and expectation have been to survive the struggle sound in limb and constitution, and a return to my home and friends, which has come to pass even so. Before the war I did not know what it was to provide for myself, but now my all has been swept away, and, if I would rise or prosper, it must be through my own merits and efforts. Nor have I been for an hour cast down, but conclude that it may be even for the best, since I have noticed that a majority of the best men in our land are those who have risen by their own exertions.

War life is not desirable, but altogether I can not say that my experience has been more unhappy than it might have been in civil life, and I can ever reflect back along my war path and find scenes and incidents upon which it will be pleasant to dwell. And, though most of them I will never see again, I can not, and would not, forget the many good, kind friends I found all over Dixieland.

Probably four-fifths of all the Confederate prisoners who have read this narrative through will exclaim that it is a brighter picture of prison life than their own experience would warrant. And it would be nothing less than the truth, for I have given it from my own stand-point, which was more favorable than that of the large majority. How and why it was more fortunate will have been gleaned by the careful reader.

And now, in conclusion, I would say to those who struggled with me in the Lost Cause: Let us no longer cherish an enmity against those who were our adversaries, simply because they did, and do yet, differ with us in opinion, but, with a generous spirit, give due honor, friendship and kindness to all who were honest, gallant and faithful. And, though our mutual desires and hopes have been disappointed and we scattered over the earth, let us remember that we should still be as a band of brothers, cherishing an affection for, and a remembrance of, each other. And last, but not least, will we, *can we*, forget that we owe a debt of fraternal and paternal sympathy to the helpless widows and orphans of our fallen comrades who sleep on a thousand battlefields and in almost every burial ground in the Southern land?

APPENDIX.

The following Medical History was not written for publication in this work, but, as its heading will show, was read before a society of medical men in Alabama. Its tone is so entirely in consonance with that of my book, and it contains so many interesting facts, that I regard it as a valuable addition to the merits of the work. And I am sure the medical profession will appreciate the statistics and practical comments concerning the diseases in prison and their treatment.

The author is now a member of the faculty of the College of Surgeons and Physicians in this city.

St. Louis, Mo., *March, 1870.*

[Read before Montgomery Medical Society, April 30th, 1866.]

A MEDICAL HISTORY

OF THE

United States Military Prison

ON JOHNSON'S ISLAND, LAKE ERIE.

MONTGOMERY, ALA., *April 25th, 1866.*

In writing this paper I would have it distinctly understood that I am actuated by no feelings of a political or sectional character. I do not desire to place on record any facts which may be used in adding to the embittered feelings and political agitation now so widespread in this great but politically unfortunate country. I do not desire that this record should be considered as an offset for the alleged brutalities to Northern prisoners at Andersonville, or as a Southern testimonial of the humane and generous treatment of Southern prisoners by the Federal government. I simply present it to my professional brethren as a medical record of prison life on Johnson's Island.

An explanation of the circumstances under which the succeeding observations were made is necessary before they can be properly appreciated.

I participated in the late war as Colonel of the 1st Regiment Ala. Vols., and was twice made a prisoner of war, and confined each time chiefly on Johnson's Island. The first time, in the summer of 1862, for two months only. The second time, from Oct., 1863, to March, 1865, eighteen months. During the last imprisonment, at the earnest solicitation of my fellow prisoners and with the approval of the Post Medical authorities, I accepted the position as one of the medical officers of the Prison Hospital. Associated with me at different times were Capt. L. E. Locke, of Selma, Alabama; Capt. Joseph F. Sessions, of Holmes county, Miss ; Col. Wm. S. Christian, of Urbana, on the Rappahannock, Virginia, and Col. G. Troup Maxwell, of Tallahassee, Florida—all gentlemen of medical education and ability, and now, as before the war, practicing physicians. The usual hospital records were kept under my supervision during my connection with the hospital, embracing a period of nearly eighteen months. I preserved a copy of this record, and it is from this document that I take the statistics used in this paper.

Johnson's Island is situated in the southwestern end of Lake Erie, at the entrance of Sandusky

Bay, and is three miles distant from Sandusky City, Ohio. It is very nearly in the same latitude as New York City. The island is small, containing about two hundred acres, more or less. It has been heavily timbered with oak, hickory and maple, but since the occupation as a military post this timber has been cut down, and the island is now bare. The surface of the island is generally elevated from four to fifteen feet above the surface of the lake, sloping from the center to the lake. The prison is situated on the northeastern part of the island, and is an enclosure of eight or ten acres, more or less. The surface of this enclosure is a gradual slope to the lake. The wall surrounding it is about twelve feet high. A stratum of limestone underlies the surface of the prison yard or enclosure at a depth varing from eighteen inches to six feet, rarely more. The drainage of the prison is of the simplest character, consisting of a large open ditch running around on the inside of the walls, with smaller ones, from twelve to eighteen inches deep, running through the yard at irregular intervals and emptying into the lake, which runs very nearly up to the eastern prison wall. All the drains are open ones and dependent upon washing rains for a thorough cleansing.

The prison barracks are white pine frame buildings, thirteen in number, built in two rows, with a wide street, perhaps fifty yards, running between. The thirteen buildings are of the same size; about 125 feet long by 30 feet wide; two stories high; the lower floor generally about 18 inches above the ground. Four of these barracks are well and comfortably constructed, and divided into small and comfortable ceiled rooms, each containing a stove. The remaining nine buildings are divided into two large rooms below and three above, with a small room attached to each end for cooking purposes. There was no means of ventilation, except a limited number of windows, which would have been sufficient for a small population. But, when crowded as these rooms were with from fifty to eighty men, this amount of ventilation was totally unsufficient. The result was, that each prisoner would cut a small hole in the walls near his head, through which to get air and light. This gave the buildings a grotesque, ragged appearance, especially during the winter when the many devices for windows were arranged to close these holes.

Some of these nine barracks were ceiled, some were not. A small ditch surrounded each building, emptying into one of the small cross drains.

Each building, during my residence in the prison, accommodated from two to three hundred prisoners, who slept on bunks, three stories high, arranged against the walls. The large rooms were heated by stoves, burning wood. But during the prevailing intense cold of that latitude in winter, the rooms were insufficiently warmed, and there was consequently great suffering; the supply of blankets and clothing being scant for men unaccustomed to cold winters. The supply of wood was not sufficient to keep up fires during the night.

The prison hospital is inside the prison walls, and is one of the thirteen barrack buildings. In construction it is the same as the barracks, except that the building is divided into four wards, two up stairs and two below, with small rooms at the ends for a dispensary, kitchen, surgeon's quarters. dining room and laundry. The building is plastered inside with one rough coat, and this whitewashed.

The supply of water for the prison was from a number of holes in the middle of the street, from six to eight feet deep; this water was highly impregnated with lime. In addition to these holes there were three pumps on the lower side of the prison, connecting by pipes with the lake. In the midst of winter, when the wells and pumps were frozen up or out of order, the prison gates were opened, morning and afternoon, and the prisoners permitted, in detachments, to go on the ice and get water in their buckets, barrels, tubs, jugs, tin cans and canteens, through the holes cut in the ice for that purpose.

The hospital had no appliance for water beyond the general arrangements for the prison. Hence the supply of pure water was insufficient, especially for hospital purposes.

The privies for the use of the prison and hospital were simple sinks dug in the rear of each building, at distances varying from thirty feet to thirty yards. Over each sink was a shed. There was no drainage from the privies. The substratum being a limestone rock, these sinks necessarily filled up very rapidly, and were constant sources of disease.

The prison hospital accommodated about sixty patients, but in emergency would hold seventy-five, by crowding the wards. The hospital was plainly furnished, so as to render patients as comfortable as the character of the building would permit. Each ward was warmed by a large stove, which was insufficient in much of the extreme cold weather of the winters there. The wards were ventilated by windows and a box or flue passing through each room out at the top of the house. But the arrangement for ventilation was exceedingly defective.

The physicians, nurses and attendants in all the departments were from among the prisoners, so that the sick received all the attention and kindness within the means of their comrades.

The medical supplies were issued to the hospital in accordance with the supply table of the Medical Department, U. S. Army, but were frequently insufficient, in consequence of the great prevalence of disease among the prisoners.

The supply of food to the sick was generally ample in quantity, but of too coarse a character for sick men. There was a systematic effort on the part of the surgeon of the post, Dr. Eversman, to supply the necessary diet suited to the sick, but, from the want of sufficient funds or proper authority, his efforts did not accomplish the good always intended by him. Here I would state that Dr. Eversman and Dr. T. Woodbridge, U S. A., who were the post surgeons during my connection with the prison, always evinced a desire to do all in their power for the relief of sick prisoners; yet, in consequence of the rigid orders from Washington regulating the treatment of prisoners of war, their good intentions availed but little in relieving the vast amount of suffering, which could at least have been greatly ameliorated by a generous supply of the wants of our sick.

I regret that I have not at command a record of the temperature of this locality, hence I can only speak from memory. The lowest point at which I saw the mercury during my two winters' residence was twelve degrees below zero. This was a rare occasion, but it was not unusual to see it approximate zero. From December 1st to March 1st it was rare that it was as high as thirty-two degrees, never remaining above this point but a short while. The bay generally freezes over in December and breaks up in the latter part of February. Navigation being closed during this time, the supplies for the prison and garrison were hauled over the ice in wagons. Snow was very frequent, covering the ground for weeks at a time. The ground in the prison yard rarely thawed during the middle of winter. The island having little timber, the prison was constantly exposed to the bleak winter winds blowing from the lake.

In estimating the effects of disease in this prison, the character of its inmates must be held in mind. This was a prison especially constructed and located for the confinement of officers, and, with a few exceptions, none others were ever kept here. These men were from the best classes of the Southern people; they were men of education and property; the great majority of them were young and in the prime of life. Hence, a better class of men, considered in every aspect, has never been, or never will be assembled again, in the same anomalous situation. It is to these favorable circumstances that I attribute the very light mortality in this prison, in comparison with the great amount of disease which prevailed there.

Below I give a condensed view of the total admissions into the hospital, with the mortality from each disease, during my connection with it; that is, from November, 1863, to April, 1865. The average number of prisoners confined upon Johnson's Island during this time was about twenty-five hundred. In the latter part of 1863 there were not more than two thousand; in 1865 there were three thousand.

TOTAL ADMISSIONS

Into the Prison Hospital, U. S. Military Prison, Johnson's Island, Lake Erie, from November 1st, 1863, to March 20th, 1865, with the mortality resulting from each disease.

Disease.	No. of Cases.	Deaths.	Disease.	No. of Cases.	Deaths.
Dysentery	258	6	Measles	4	...
Chronic Diarrhœa	125	10	Hæmoptysis	3	...
Intermittent Fever	89	...	Convulsions	3	...
Prison Fever	60	1	Diabetes	3	...
Scurvy	56	...	Stricture	3	...
Rheumatism	43	...	Secondary Syphilis	3	...
Remittent Fever	43	...	Colic	3	...
Wound	36	2	Abscess	2	...
Bronchitis	36	...	Fracture	2	...
Neuralgia	34	...	Nephritis	2	...
Catarrh	33	...	Orchitis	2	...
Pneumonia	26	9	Epistaxis	2	...
Erysipelas	19	1	Caries	1	...
Typhoid Fever	17	5	Dislocated Shoulder	1	...
General Debility	17	1	Ulcerated Leg	1	...
Small Pox	13	1	Ptyalism	1	...
Tonsilitis	13	...	Chorea	1	...
Dyspepsia	11	...	Inflammation of Brain	1	1
Spinal Irritation	9	...	Congestion of Brain	1	1
Congestive Fever	8	3	Itch	1	...
Angina	8	1	Hæmaturia	1	...
Gastritis	8	1	Ulceration f'm Vaccin'n	1	...
Jaundice	7	...	Paraplegia	1	...
Hepatitis	7	1	Hernia	1	...
Phthisis Pulmonalis	6	1	Gonorrhœa	1	...
Dropsy	6	...	Asthma	1	...
Pleuritis	5	...	Cholera Morbus	1	...
Conjunctivitis	4	...	Insanity	1	...
Cystitis	4	...	Total	1047	45

I now propose to make such practical remarks upon the principal diseases recorded in the above statistics as will give a general idea of the influence of prison circumstances upon these diseases. Hence I do not desire that medical men should regard these descriptions as complete histories of the diseases, but simply practical notes explanatory of the statistics of the hospital record.

Frequent reference appears in the succeeding portions of this paper to the diet of prisoners confined in this prison, and the best manner in which I can convey a correct idea on this subject is to insert here a copy of a statement written by the physicians of the prison hospital in the autumn of 1864.

Prison Hospital, Johnson's Island,
November 16, 1864.

Colonel: The undersigned officers of the Confederate States army (prisoners of war) are, in times of peace, practicing physicians. We are now acting as surgeons in our prison hospital.

We adopt this method of informing you (if you are not already aware of it) that the prisoners confined here are *suffering seriously* from want of food.

First. We make this painful announcement *from our personal experience* and observation among our comrades. Food is the constant theme of conversation among them, and we are *repeatedly* told, "We are hungry; we do not get enough to eat." Instances are not unfrequent of repulsive articles being greedily *devoured—rats*, spoiled meat, bones, bread from the *slops*, &c.

Secondly. We wish to demonstrate to you, from physiological data, that the ration *issued* is insufficient to maintain health.

Prof. Dalton says: "With coffee and water for drink, we have found that the entire quantity of food required during twenty-four hours by a man in full health and taking free exercise in the open air is as follows:

Meat (butcher's), ounces avoirdupois..................	16
Bread, ounces avoirdupois..................................	19
Butter or fat, ounces avoirdupois......................	3½
	38½ oz.

That is to say, rather less than two and a half pounds of solid food." (See Dalton's Physiology, page 115.)

Colonel Hoffman, Commissary-General of Prisons, in his published order regulating the ration of prisoners of war, establishes the following:

Pork or bacon (in lieu of fresh beef), ounces......	10
Fresh beef, ounces...	14
Flour or soft bread, ounces................................	16
Hard bread (in lieu of flour or soft bread), ounces....	14
Corn meal (in lieu of flour or soft bread), ounces....	16

to each ration.

APPENDIX.

Beans or peas, pounds	12½
Rice or hominy, pounds	3
Soap, pounds	4
Vinegar, quarts	3
Salt, pounds	4¾
Potatoes, pounds	15

to one hundred rations.

Accompanying this communication we inclose the abstracts of rations *actually received* during the month of October for the first and second divisions of the prison. The abstracts have been carefully prepared for this purpose by the chiefs of those divisions from their memoranda taken at the time of issue. By carefully estimating the average daily ration in ounces of solid food from these abstracts for October, you will find that each prisoner receives 28 1-2 ounces.

Colonel Hoffman's order allows him about 34 1-2 ounces; Professor Dalton would give him 38 1-2 ounces.

Your commissary, therefore, has given us *ten* ounces *less* than the physiological requirements of health, and *six* ounces less than Colonel Hoffman's order.

This deficit of six ounces is the result: First, of a short issue of bread of about 1 1-2 ounces; second, of a short issue of beans or peas, rice or hominy and potatoes (only one, instead of three, having been issued daily), 3 1-2 ounces;

third, no issue of meat at all for three days, 1 ounce—6 ounces.

As to the *quality* of the ration issued for October, the beef consisted almost entirely of *forequarters*, *neck* and *shank*, the large proportion of bone reducing the actual meat received nearly one-half, or to seven ounces (7 oz). *Salt beef and fish*, now issued about twice a week, are not included in Colonel Hoffman's published order as a part of the ration. Salt fish, with our want of facilities for properly preparing them, make a most unpalatable dish, and, from the testimony of our comrades, are only used from dire necessity, to satisfy the cravings of hunger. Moreover, salt beef and salt fish do not contain sufficient *oil* or fat to answer the requirements of health during winter in this latitude.

Though Colonel Hoffman's order falls short of the physiological requirements of a man in health by three and a half ounces, yet we believe that if his order be *faithfully executed* health can be maintained for a long while, considering the limited amount of exercise generally taken by prisoners.

But, Colonel, it is our solemn conviction that if the inmates of this prison are compelled to subsist for the winter upon this reduced ration of ten ounces less than health demands, and six ounces less than Colonel Hoffman's order allows, *all* must suffer the horrors of continual hunger, and many must die from the most loathesome diseases. As physicians, we *ask* you, for humanity's sake, to compel your commissary to do his duty faithfully and honestly by issuing the ration we are entitled to; as prisoners of war, we *demand* it.

Relying upon your early attention to this urgent and important subject, we are,

  Respectfully, yours, etc.,
    I. G. W. STEEDMAN, M. D.,
      Col. 1st Reg't Ala. Vols.
    L. E. LOCKE, M. D.,
      Capt. 53d Ala. Cavalry.
    G. TROUP MAXWELL, M. D.,
      Col. 1st Florida Cavalry.
    Acting Surgeons Prison Hospital.
To COLONEL PALMER, Commanding Post.

This article, it will be seen, was written under the pressure of the immediate circumstances surrounding us. But the facts as stated there will not apply to the period of time embraced in this report, between Nov., 1863, and July, 1864. The ration issued to prisoners was cut down by general orders from Washington, about July, 1864; up to that time the ration was sufficient in quantity.

DYSENTERY.

It will be seen that two hundred and fifty-eight (258) cases of dysentery were admitted into the prison hospital; the building being too small by one-third to accommodate the sick of the prison, a discrimination had to be made. The milder cases were always rejected when more serious ones demanded attention. Those failing to obtain admission were treated in quarters by physicians (prisoners) living in the barracks with the sick man. The prescriptions for all cases in quarters were filled at the hospital dispensary. No records of prisoners sick in quarters were kept; hence I have no means of estimating the frequency of disease in quarters except by the number of prescriptions presented at the dispensary. It was a common occurrence for from one hundred and fifty to two hundred prescriptions to be filled there daily, beside the regular hospital prescriptions, and four hundred on some days. These prescriptions, of course, were not all for dysentery, but the various diseases existing among the prisoners. No other prescriptions were filled in this dispensary except for prisoners, so that the 258 cases by no means include all the dysentery which occurred in this prison. The same can be said of many other diseases in the above record.

The dysentery prevailing in the prison was endemic, but could not be called technically epidemic dysentery or flux, as we see it ordinarily in civil practice. Few prisoners escaped an attack of it. From the numerous cases coming under my observation and treatment, I regarded it as the direct result of prison diet, bad water and the impure air of the crowded rooms. The remedies ordinarily in use in the treatment of dysentery were of little avail. The only successful plan of treatment was, to effect a total change in the diet and habits of the patient. Give him light, nutritious, well-cooked food, composed, as far as practicable, of vegetables and fresh meat; place him in a well ventilated, quiet ward, and give him pure water from the lake. The ordinary anodynes, astringents and other medicines used in the disease were useful, but effected nothing as long as the patient lived on prison diet, &c. When brought to hospital these cases would rapidly recover, but as soon as returned to quarters many would soon relapse. In this way began the numerous cases of chronic diarrhea and dysentery with which prisoners suffered so much.

CHRONIC DIARRHEA.

The records show one hundred and twenty-five cases of chronic diarrhea admitted into hospital. This number includes only the worst class of cases, the milder ones being treated in quarters. A limited number of cases of this disease were admitted into prison sick, having contracted the disease in the army; but the great mass of them originated in the prison, beginning as occasional attacks of acute dysentery or diarrhea.

Chronic diarrhea in prison was an incurable disease. I can not say that I ever saw a prisoner recover from it while in prison. It very soon became the great dread and fear of the prisoner. When the physician told him his case was one of confirmed chronic diarrhea, he regarded it as equivalent to the announcement of his death penalty, if he remained in prison. I can not say that medicine was not useful in the disease as a palliative, but as a curative it was of no avail.

All possible changes were wrought upon the many remedies recommended by our standard authors, but, regardless of everything, the disease maintained its hold upon its victim, slowly but surely emaciating and prostrating him, until he was but a living skeleton. The circumstances surrounding us in prison forbade post mortem examinations of our dead, hence I am unable to give any description of the pathological condition of the bowels in this disease. But, from close study of it in all its phases, I was convinced that the mesenteric glands were seriously diseased, perhaps the seat of tuberculous deposits; that is, the disease was really a consumption of the bowels. Physicians from the Southern States, familiar with the marasmus or tabes mesenterica which destroys so many children, especially negroes living in our prairie and limestone regions, could not fail to take this view of the chronic diarrhea as existing in prison.

Our great efforts were to change entirely the diet and habits of the patient, to give him fresh, digestible meat and vegetables instead of his salt food. The hospital ration did not permit us to carry out this idea as it should have been, the supply of vegetables only permitting a substantial vegetable soup to such cases as required it once a day. Much relief was given to this class of sick by boxes of suitable provisions and hospital supplies sent to prisoners by friends in the border States of Kentucky, Missouri and Maryland. But early in 1864 the Government forbade the reception of such supplies, except under such restrictions as practically closed this avenue of relief to our sick. Had the Government permitted it, our friends in these border States and elsewhere would have amply supplied the prison hospital with that class of food so sadly needed, viz.: fresh and dried fruits, pickles, jellies, onions, etc.

Luckily for many cases of chronic diarrhea in this and other prisons, the two Governments agreed in the summer of 1864 to exchange the chronic sick prisoners. Under this arrangement our hospital and prison were relieved of a very large number of unfortunates, who must otherwise have inevitably died. After their release I have heard of many recoveries, yet a great number died. The chronic diarrhea of prisoners was certainly the most fatal result of bad and insufficient food, bad water, crowded, badly ventilated rooms, and the many other depressing influences surrounding prisoners of war.

SCURVY.

In the period of time embraced in this report, fifty-six cases of scurvy were admitted and treated in the prison hospital. These were the severe cases of the prison; the milder cases were very numerous, but were not admitted into hospital, but treated in quarters. I place scurvy immediately after dysentery and chronic diarrhea, from the fact that I regard the causes of the three diseases as occurring in prison the same.

Before this time it had never been my misfortune to see scurvy except in its sporadic form, only a rare case occurring here and there. As seen in prison, it presented the usual softening, bleeding ulceration of the gums and loosening of the teeth; but the great prostration of muscular power, the swollen, bruised and painful condition of the legs and thighs, were the prominent features of the disease. The swelling generally began on the legs, in the bend of the knee, and extended down to the feet and up to the hip. At first a red, swollen and inflamed patch would present itself, extending frequently over the whole limb; in a few days the part first inflamed would turn dark, losing its redness and assuming a bruised, mottled appearance, as if the limb had been severely beaten. The swollen parts were very hard and firm, and presented none of the ordinary soft, elastic sensation of a sound part. This state of things was at first very painful. The muscles attacked about the knee were greatly contracted, flexing the leg back toward the thigh. In the slighter cases, the patient could walk by touching the tips of his toes to the ground and supporting himself on his stick or crutch, but the effort was very painful. The more serious cases were confined to bed, the leg so drawn up as to forbid any locomotion. There was rarely any febrile excitement. The worst cases presented an eruption of dark, livid spots, varying in size from a pin's head to a picayune, generally covering the whole body, but thicker on the swollen lower limbs. These were cases of purpura hæmorrhagica, yet I rarely saw any serious loss of blood from any of the mucous surfaces in these cases. Many of these cases were complicated with diarrhea; then bloody discharges occasionally occurred.

I have seen ulceration of the cornea in a small number of the worst cases, yet they were rare. I never saw a prisoner lose his sight from this cause; the ulcer would heal as the general health improved.

Scurvy was especially amenable to treatment. I have never been more gratified at the results of medicine than when I saw my prostrated, bruised, deformed and miserable companions and friends daily rapidly improving under the use of the muriated tincture of iron, tonic doses of quinine, and a free use of vinegar, and such fruits and vegetables as could be commanded in the hospital. We generally had a moderate supply of cabbage or turnips, Irish potatoes or onions, but not more than enough to make a good vegetable soup once a day for such cases requiring it. In addition to this, these cases were occasionally supplied with dried apples or pickles, sent them by friends or relatives in the border States, or purchased for them by some of the charitable associations organized among the prisoners; the chief of these were the Masonic and Young Men's Christian Associations, organizations which effected great good among the prisoners, especially in nursing the sick and supplying such delicacies as circumstances permitted. The commander of the post, Col. Charles Hill, frequently extended privileges to these associations which he could not to individuals.

Under the above plan of treatment, even the

worst cases of scurvy recovered moderate health in a month. A single case of scurvy did not die in prison.

At the time when scurvy was most prevalent in the prison, one of the medical inspectors who periodically visited the prison ordered an issue of fifteen pounds of onions or potatoes to the one hundred rations, three times a week. This issue would give each prisoner one very large or two medium sized onions or potatoes at each issue. The result was almost magical. In two months scurvy disappeared from our midst. But very soon after the discontinuance of this ration the disease returned, to be again cured by another issue of onions or potatoes.

ERYSIPELAS.

The records show but nineteen cases of erysipelas treated in hospital. One ward of the hospital was set apart for the reception of this disease, and only in extreme emergencies were such cases admitted into the other wards; though it was not regarded by the physicians as contagious, yet the prisoners, especially the sick, were exceedingly loth to come in contact with it. Sometimes there was difficulty in securing sufficient nurses for such cases. From my own knowledge and correspondence with my fellow physicians who were associated with me in the medical service in this prison,

I estimate one hundred and fifty cases of erysipelas treated in the prison during the time embraced in this report.

The great majority of the cases were idiopathic erysipelas, yet there were many cases of traumatic origin. The disease prevailed more especially during the autumn and winter of 1864 and 1865; indeed, during this time the disease was endemic in the prison. So much was this the case that we never dared to use the knife for surgical purposes, except in cases of absolute necessity to save life or the great destruction of tissue; the smallest cuts were followed by erysipelas. Even blistered surfaces took on erysipelatous inflammation. Many of the old suppurating wounds were attacked.

Nine-tenths of the idiopathic erysipelas which came under my observation began on the face; most frequently in the inner angle of the eye, on the prominence of one of the cheek bones, or the tip of the nose; sometimes on the ear. When not on the face, a hand, arm or the leg was its most frequent site. From a slight blush confined to a spot, the swelling and redness would gradually but surely extend until, in the great majority of the cases, the whole face was implicated, and very often the whole head and scalp, sometimes the neck down to the shoulders. I can not say that I ever saw idiopathic erysipelatous inflammation, originating on the face extend beyond the neck and shoulders. The disease would require generally about three, sometimes four, days to reach its limits; so that when the last parts were at the hight of inflammation, the first part attacked was growing better. In the acute stage of the disease, the skin is very red and tender to the touch, the swelling is great, extending into the subcutaneous structures. When the whole or a great part of the face is implicated the patient's most intimate friend would not recognize him; the eyes are closed, and instead you see a great swollen mass protruding over each one, the flaccid tissues covering the eyelids suffering especially from the inflammation. The nose is very large, intensely red and shining; the ears lose all due proportion to the healthy organ, the external orifice being frequently closed by the thickened tissues. When the scalp is implicated, the head is as large as two ordinary heads. After a considerable portion of surface is implicated, the febrile excitement is very considerable; pulse full and frequent, but compressible; skin hot and dry; tongue coated, with thirst and loss of appetite. The chief complaint of the patient is from the hot, burning and painfully inflamed surface, the inconvenience occasioned by the closure of the eyes and ears and the pain resulting from the pressure of the back of the head on the pillow. In the severe cases there was great headache, followed by severe cerebral disorder. But these brain symptoms did not generally appear until the subsidence of the superficial inflammation. After the headache came delirium, of a low, muttering character, sometimes coma; such cases were very grave, the delirium persisting four and five days. In these cases the asthenic character of the disease was especially marked, the patient exhibiting all the evidences of what we style a "typhoid condition." In some of the severer cases I have seen the inflammation extend into the fauces, resulting in great destruction of tissue, and always in death. Nearly every case involving much tissue resulted in suppuration, the tissues around the eyes suffering especially, large abscesses forming and continuing to discharge for days, and upon healing leaving a permanent scar under the eye where it had been opened. I have seen the whole scalp undermined by one abscess; by opening it at one point the most remote part could be discharged. This disposition of erysipelas to result in suppuration was almost universal, and had to be considered in the treatment of the early stages of the disease.

After the first few cases, the following plan of treatment was universally adopted as the most successful: Twenty drops of the muriated tincture of iron and two grains of quinine every two hours until the patient complained of a fulness or pain in the head, showing that he was under the influence of the remedies; then the size and frequency of the dose was diminished so as to maintain the constant influence of the remedies. Toward the close of the disease (about the end of a week) the dose was quite small, and repeated about three times a day. At first we attempted to arrest the spread of the inflammation by circumscribing the inflamed spot by cauterizing a narrow strip of the skin with the nitrate of silver. This was useless, and only caused additional pain and soreness; the disease spread over these lines as if they had not been made. After the first few cases were tortured in this way, we abandoned it and substituted painting the whole inflamed surface with a diluted tincture of iodine—at first three times a day until the skin grew tender from it, and then once or twice a day, as needed. Contrary to what we would expect on theoretical grounds, this painting gave great relief to the local distress, the patients begging for it before the regular "painting hour" arrived. Its tonic, stimulating influence on the skin seemed to prevent suppuration and hasten the arrest of the disease, the iodine always being applied an inch in advance of the inflamed edge.

This plan was eminently successful; I saw but two cases of erysipelas die, and these were where the brain and fauces were attacked. I am aware that idiopathic erysipelas has never proved very fatal, but the great number of cases treated under such adverse circumstances by the above plan not only convince me of its great value, but of the asthenic character of the disease. I regard it as a blood disease and asthenic in type.

The traumatic erysipelas, or those cases starting in wounds, were generally far more grave than the idiopathic; the cases were of longer duration and much less amenable to treatment. The wound, as soon as attacked, ceased all curative process, and, on the contrary, sometimes sloughed. The cases starting in blistered surfaces generally resulted fatally, as the blister had been applied for pneumonia or other fatal disease.

PRISON FEVER.

Sixty cases of a fever called by the physicians who treated it prison fever, were admitted into hospital. It was not typhoid fever, presenting none of the enteric symptoms of this fever, or any other of its distinguishing marks except a continued fever. Its duration was generally from two to four weeks. There was no evidence of any special organic lesion, no eruption, no diarrhea, some prostration, but not so marked as we see it in typhoid fever or severe typhus; rare if any delirium or other evidence of cerebral disorder. It was simply a mild, continued fever, and I cannot classify it otherwise than as a very mild form of typhus fever. This fact was very early remarked by me: When a case of this form of continued fever was admitted into my wards, I invariably asked him if he lived in a crowded room, and if he slept in an upper bunk. These questions were almost invariably answered in the affirmative. Some of these rooms contained eighty men. The heated air and the human exhalations rising to the higher parts of the room were breathed by the occupants of these bunks, who became the subjects of prison fever. A case rarely occurred on a lower bunk.

I would remark here, in connection with this and other continued fevers of the prison, also as to erysipelas, that the applications for admission into hospital were much more numerous during very cold, raw and disagreeable weather, when prisoners could not exercise in the open air. As soon as a few days of clear and pleasant weather occurred a marked diminution of this class of disease was at once apparent. The prison fever was a blood poison, resulting from rebreathing a confined, impure air, and the other depressing circumstances surrounding a prison. Had these prisoners been confined for a long time to these barracks, without the privilege of exercise in the open air, we should certainly have had the genuine typhus fever of a grave type.

MALARIAL FEVER.

Eighty-nine cases of intermittent fever, forty-three of remittent and eight of congestive fever were admitted into the prison hospital. Some of these cases were undoubtedly relapses of old attacks of malarial fever contracted in the army before admission into prison; but the great majority was contracted in prison. I arrived at this conclusion against preconceived ideas. I was a prisoner on this island for two months, in the summer of 1862, and I did not see a case of malarial fever among the twelve hundred prisoners confined there. I could see no local cause for malaria; there are no marshes, ponds or other sources of malaria on the island or vicinity within my knowledge. The lake is a body of pure, fresh water, never stagnant or unhealthy from any cause, so far as I could see or learn.

During the winter few cases occurred, but as soon as spring weather came malarial fevers were frequent, the months of May and June presenting the greatest number. I have not seen the effect of malaria more apparent in Alabama during August and September than on Johnson's Island in May and June. I can only account for it in this way: During winter everything of a fluid character freezes in that latitude; thus the ditches, drains, &c., were filled with the accumulations of animal and vegetable matter. The whole surface of the prison yard, especially privies, also collected filth, which, in consequence of ice and snow, was not removed until spring. When the the thaws of spring came on this mass began rapid decomposition, filling the air with malaria. By the month of June the prison was thoroughly cleansed and malarial fevers nearly ceased, yet occasional cases occurred during the summer. These fevers, though, were by no means so severe as we see them in Alabama. They were more amenable to treatment and less likely to relapse.

RESPIRATORY ORGANS.

Of this class of disease there were treated in this hospital: Of catarrh, 3; pneumonia, 26; tonsillitis, 13; angina, 8; phthisis pulmonalis, 6; pleuritis, 5. Of catarrh, angina and tonsillitis many hundred occurred in the prison, but not of sufficient gravity to require hospital treatment.

But the amount of disease of the respiratory organs was far less than I had anticipated. All my preconceived ideas of the effects of extreme cold upon men entirely unaccustomed to it had led me to expect a vast amount of lung disease among our prisoners. I can not say that I saw a case of phthisis which had its origin in the prison. There was certainly little disposition to the development of tubercles in the lungs, and hence I infer no great exciting cause.

Much could be said by the mental philosopher upon the effects of imprisonment upon the mind. I saw in this prison many cases of decided mental aberration, but they were generally so slight as not to be detected, except under favorable circumstances. They were monomaniacs upon some subjects, yet I can not say that these were cases of insanity, though for the time the reason was unbalanced. But one case of positive insanity was admitted in hospital. He was exchanged soon after the development of the disease, and I have not learned the result.

In conclusion, I would say that I do not consider that any local cause of disease exists on Johnson's Island. On the contrary, where persons are well protected, in substantial houses, suited to the climate, well fed and clothed, it is a healthy locality. I say this because I know that there was an almost universal idea among the Southern people that the locality, independent of the treatment of prisoners, was the cause of disease among them. This idea had its foundation in the fact of the intense cold on this island, but I did not find the cold productive of disease where ample protection was provided against it.

I. G. W. STEEDMAN, M.D.

www.ingramcontent.com/pod-product-compliance
Lightning Source LLC
Chambersburg PA
CBHW030350230426
43664CB00007BB/594